CRITIC'S CHOICE

AND OTHER COMEDIES

WORKS BY IRA LEVIN

NOVELS

Son of Rosemary

Sliver

The Boys from Brazil

The Stepford Wives

This Perfect Day

Rosemary's Baby

A Kiss Before Dying

PLAYS

Footsteps

Cantorial

Break A Leg

Deathtrap

Veronica's Room

Dr. Cook's Garden

General Seeger

Critic's Choice

Interlock

No Time For Sergeants

(from the novel by Mac Hyman)

MUSICALS

Drat! The Cat!

(music by Milton Schafer)

CRITIC'S CHOICE

AND OTHER COMEDIES BY

IRA LEVIN

CRITIC'S CHOICE, BREAK A LEG, AND CANTORIAL

BLACK STONE PUBLISHING

CONTENTS

STAGE DIRECTION REFERENCE

"One word of advice to those not accustomed to reading plays: Don't worry too much about the chairs and tables. It rarely matters whether they're at stage right or stage left, or whether the doors are upstage or down. What does matter is the dialogue. Try to hear it, and try to hear the pauses too, that's where the shivers are."

—Ira Levin, Introduction to
"The Mousetrap" and Other Plays

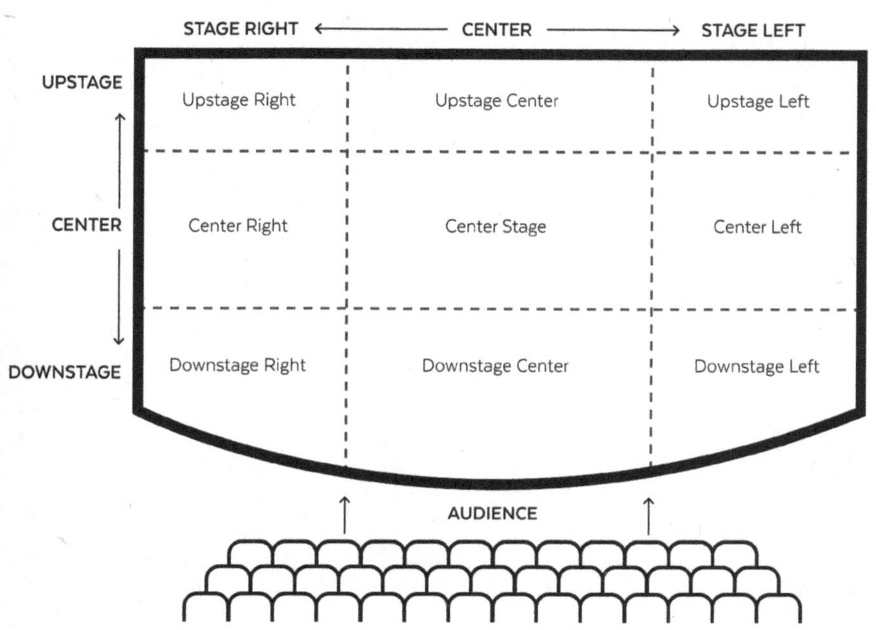

CRITIC'S CHOICE

CRITIC'S CHOICE

INTRODUCTION

(CRITIC'S CHOICE)

It's somewhat staggering that the creator of *Rosemary's Baby* also wrote flat-out *comedies.* But *Critic's Choice*—the *"laugh laden"* (*The American*) study of a critic handicapped by his sense of ethics, bristling with *"sparkling venom"* (*Boston Globe*)—is hilarious proof of that fact. The play is one of no less than six comedies (or comedy-hybrids) that Levin produced during his career.

Despite its *"sly and sophisticated . . . belly laughs"* (*Delaware Morning News*), undergirding *Critic's Choice's* frothy veneer is an earnest quandary facing reviewer *Parker Ballantine*: to remain true to his convictions, and in so doing, risk all—or to compromise them, and live with the burden of having done so. So many of Levin's works concern characters wrestling with, shall we say, devil's bargains.

As the epigraph notes, Levin based the play on a challenge from Pulitzer-winning critic and dramaturgical multi-hyphenate Walter Kerr. Levin and his wife Gabrielle (to whom the play is dedicated) were visitors to the Kerr household, and Levin held Kerr in high regard (ditto his wife Jean, a well-known humorist); *Critic's Choice* is, notably, a tale of *critic-as-paragon.* . . .

It's interesting that *Critic's Choice* and Levin's later *Break A Leg* both involve behind-the-scenes peeks at the world of the theater, and specifically the thorny relationship between writers and critics. And Levin's 1978 *Deathtrap* itself features a romantic partner writing a play the other wishes they weren't (to put it mildly). A hint of *Deathtrap*'s later masterclass in *metatheatricality* can be seen in the knowingly comic, self-referential way the Ballantine's maid's single brief appearance delivers squarely on the overly-facile writing technique Parker carps about in act one.

Parker was played on Broadway by Henry Fonda—Levin had written the part with him in mind, and so could not have been happier when the revered actor agreed to star. Parker's not the only critic on stage, though—his and Ivy's precocious son *John* was played on Broadway by thirteen-year-old Eddie Hodges (fresh from the original run of *The Music Man*.) His would be the only child's part Levin would ever write (for the stage, that is—as *The Boys from Brazil* attests). Though Hodges himself was equal to the task, after seeing the grown-up demands made by Broadway on a youngster (the arduous rehearsals, the eleven p.m. worknights), he vowed never to subject another to it.

Angela was played by veteran Georgann Johnson—though Gena Rowlands was originally cast in her part. (Rowlands was reported to have left the show over issues with its producer/director Otto Preminger; Levin would shortly after write the initial screen adaptation for Preminger's film *Bunny Lake Is Missing*—a story unto itself.)

The Broadway production of *Critic's Choice* had a noteworthy visitor; per *The New York Times*, on January 8, 1961, then President-Elect John F. Kennedy attended the play, twelve days before his inauguration. (He arrived late, but the curtain was held for him; when he exited the theater—prior to the audience, for security reasons—he received a standing ovation from the crowd.)

The costumes for *Critic's Choice* were designed by no less than Oleg Cassini, and its poster was created by noted designer Saul Bass (*Psycho*, *Anatomy of a Murder*).

In 1963, a film adaptation of *Critic's Choice* was released by Warner Brothers starring comedy royalty Bob Hope and Lucille Ball—another fortunate turn of casting. Yet, as with *Deathtrap*'s (1982) screen adaptation, the play's humor was blanched in the transfer—and the whole affair was reduced to the level of broad slapstick.

It's helpful to recall in reading *Critic's Choice* that while it's indeed reflective of its time's rigid gender roles, Levin would follow it with two feminist-leaning works of note: *Rosemary's Baby* and *The Stepford Wives*. But, at the time he was writing *Critic's Choice*, *Father Knows Best* was still in production, broadcast in literal (if not figurative) black-and-white. Despite that, Levin's characters still transcend the day's provincial views.

As to Parker's dilemma, the clearest indication of where Levin stood on the matter is likely found in Charlotte's counsel to Parker: *"I've got news for you: honesty is* not *the most precious thing on earth; adding machines have honesty. Love is the precious thing, and if you want it you have to give something for it, just as you have to give for anything else worth having."*

We now give *you . . . Critic's Choice.*

Nicholas Levin
New York City
January, 2025

CRITIC'S CHOICE

To GABRIELLE

"I sometimes have visions of a gag conference in which that slick character who is traditionally known as Manny bounces in, eyes ablaze, and bubbles over with: 'Listen. This guy's a dramatic critic, see? So his wife writes a play. He's *got* to review the play. Take it from there.'"

—WALTER KERR
"How Not to Write a Play"

CRITIC'S CHOICE was presented by Otto Preminger at the
Ethel Barrymore Theatre, New York City, December 14, 1960,
with the following cast:

IN ORDER OF APPEARANCE

PARKER BALLANTINE . . . . Henry Fonda

ANGELA BALLANTINE . . . . Georgann Johnson

JOHN BALLANTINE . . . . Eddie Hodges

DION KAPAKOS . . . . Murray Hamilton

ESSIE . . . . Billie Allen

CHARLOTTE ORR . . . . Mildred Natwick

IVY LONDON . . . . Virginia Gilmore

Directed by OTTO PREMINGER
Production Designed by GEORGE JENKINS
Clothes by OLEG CASSINI

The action takes place in the Ballantine apartment, near Washington Square. The time is last season. There are three acts.

CRITIC'S CHOICE

ACT ONE

*The Ballantines—*PARKER, ANGELA, *and* JOHN*—are a healthy, happy, comfortable family, and their apartment looks it. It's a duplex near Washington Square, in an elegant old house that will probably be torn down any day to make way for an NYU College of Dentistry, and more's the pity. What we see onstage is the living room, with the entrance foyer* UPSTAGE CENTER, *and the door to the kitchen at stage* LEFT; *the staircase,* UPSTAGE CENTER RIGHT, *leading up to* PARKER *and* ANGELA*'s bedroom door, and a hallway going offstage* RIGHT (*to* JOHN*'s bedroom and the guest room); and* DOWNSTAGE RIGHT *a portion of* PARKER*'s study, which is something like the inside of a filing cabinet. The dining area is* DOWNSTAGE LEFT; *a round table near a tall, sheerly draped window.*

The furniture in the apartment is mostly antique, good pieces picked up at auction and tossed together with a casual disregard for period and style; a couch, the usual chairs and tables, liquor cabinet near door to study. A TV set is someplace, and so is the hand loom on which ANGELA *started weaving a scatter rug last summer. Desk, typewriter, and many, many books in the study, some of the latter beginning to leak out and absorb the living room, like the blob in a horror movie. Lots of pictures are sprinkled around the living room walls; some of them sketches by Matisse and Dufy, some of them enlarged snapshots of various people and places. A telephone is near the couch. The entrance door and a closet are in the foyer.*

The total effect is pleasant, busy, interesting, and comfortable.

AT RISE: Ballantines are discovered at breakfast, all three reading sections of the morning paper. They read in silence for a moment.

PARKER, sitting at CENTER, is in his late thirties or early forties. He is wearing gray flannels, a white shirt open at the collar, and a very old and favorite cardigan.

ANGELA, in sweater and skirt, is sitting at PARKER's RIGHT. She is twenty-seven or twenty-eight, a bright and delectable blonde.

JOHN, sitting opposite ANGELA and at PARKER's LEFT, is twelve. He is wearing slacks and a flannel shirt and isn't eating his cereal.

PARKER
(An item from the paper.)

Here's a fellow swimming the English Channel, and he's got himself all greased up—you know—and he gets cramps, and he's so slippery, they can't pull him into the boat . . .

(ANGELA and JOHN smile, JOHN goes back to his paper.)

ANGELA

Come on now, John, just eat *some* of your cereal. Don't you want to have *energy?*

JOHN

What do I need energy on Saturday for?

ANGELA
(To PARKER.)

Explain to him why he needs energy.

PARKER

(*Pointing to* JOHN's *plate.*)
Eat.

JOHN

All right, all right . . .
(*He eats and reads.* PARKER *and* ANGELA *exchange a
smile.*)

PARKER

You're a fine one to talk; one cup of black coffee.

ANGELA

I am *five pounds overweight.*

PARKER

You're a skinny, scrawny wretch and I'm not letting another
fashion magazine inside that door. Women are *not* supposed to
have square corners.

ANGELA

I won't have *square corners.*

JOHN

Boy, this is the best review you've written all season.

PARKER

It was a wonderful play.

JOHN

Do I get to see it, or is it another dirty one?

PARKER

Well, parts of it may be a bit over your head . . .
          (*To* ANGELA.)
If we're lucky . . .

ANGELA

Oh, take him, Parker! It's so—*warm and bright* . . . !

PARKER

          (*To* JOHN, *smiling.*)
Next Saturday afternoon.

JOHN

Good deal. Hey, this is one of mine! This one! "As much fun as
your first circus!" That's mine! Remember!

PARKER

Are you sure? It was typed.

JOHN

I type them sometimes! It was in my first big batch; about a
dozen for the white box and twenty or thirty for the black box.
A year ago. You paid me only ten cents for this.

PARKER

You were a child. I didn't want to spoil you.

JOHN

Boy, ten cents and you build half a review around it . . .
          (*He puts aside the paper.*)

ANGELA

Here's a woman named Triplet who had quadruplets.

PARKER

They make those things up, so the columns come out even.

ANGELA

No, here's a picture.
(*Shows him. Hands* PARKER *the paper.*)
Aren't they cute?

PARKER

(*Smiling. Passes paper to* JOHN.)
Mmm . . .

JOHN

(*As he puts the paper down.*)
According to Godfrey Von Hagedorn it's all psychosomatic, your not being able to get pregnant.

ANGELA

Oh, it is, is it?

PARKER

In thirty seconds we're going to have "Spank-the-Precocious-Children Hour."

ANGELA

No, I want to hear this. Go ahead. According to Godfrey Von Hagedorn . . .

JOHN

Well, he says Dad had me with Ivy, so *he's* all right, and you have a wide pelvis so *you* ought to be all right, so the trouble must be psychosomatic.

PARKER

Would someone mind identifying Godfrey Von Hagedorn? Just for us laymen?

JOHN

Godfrey, you know. *Godfrey.* The kid from downstairs.

PARKER

That *peanut* who sits here and watches Wyatt Earp with you?

JOHN

Mm-hmm.

ANGELA

During the commercials they talk about my pelvis.

PARKER

We should be honored, Angela! Think of it; right here in our own living room; Godfrey Von Hagedorn, the famous twelve-year-old gynecologist!

JOHN

Godfrey *knows* all this psychosomatic stuff. His father's an analyst. Godfrey puts a glass up against the wall and listens. He says you probably feel inferior to Ivy, because she's a glamorous actress and you're just from Random House. You're afraid that your baby won't turn out as good as hers did. Me, I mean.

    (*He eats.*)

PARKER

You'd better watch TV down in their apartment for a while.

JOHN

We can't. I'm not allowed in.

PARKER

Why not?

JOHN

Oh, Dr. Von Hagedorn's writing a play, and he showed me the first act, and then he asked me my opinion of it . . .

(ANGELA *rises, takes* PARKER*'s bowl and casserole to tray on TV,* UPSTAGE LEFT.)

ANGELA

Godfrey does psychoanalysis for your family and you do drama criticism for his.

JOHN

Oh, sort of . . .

PARKER

I wonder if kids ever play mumblety-peg any more.

JOHN

Play *what?*

PARKER

Never mind.

(*A beat.*)

ANGELA

You know, *I've* been toying with an idea for a play . . .
       (*Crosses* DOWNSTAGE *to table with coffee pot.*)

PARKER

You have?

ANGELA

Mm-hmm . . .
       (PARKER *and* JOHN *exchange a glance.*)
That comedy last week, about the boarding house; it reminded
me of an uncle of mine. The family character. *He* took in roomers, odd-ball types; a broken-down juggler, an old woman who
kept *pigeons* in her closet . . .
       (ANGELA *takes coffee pot to* UPSTAGE *of table, pours coffee*
       for PARKER *and herself. Takes* JOHN's *bowl to tray on TV,*
       UPSTAGE LEFT.)
I ran away from home once, when I was fifteen; Mom and Sally
and Marge had gotten to be too much for me. Uncle Ben took
me in, and the four days I spent in that rooming house could
make a *wonderful* play; funny, and tender, and moving too, in
a wistful kind of way . . .

PARKER

I think I know the sort of play you mean . . . . Youth learns from
old age, and vice versa.

ANGELA

Mm-hmm . . .
       (ANGELA *takes cup, drinks coffee, holds cup.*)

PARKER

The girl goes home to Mother and her sisters, willingly, and the roomers go out one by one into the no-longer-so-terrifying world; the juggler juggling again, the old woman setting free her captive pigeons . . .

(ANGELA *has turned to* PARKER, *surprised and encouraged, nodding.*)

The final curtain would be Uncle Ben, all alone in the gathering twilight, dusting off the old placard and propping it up in the window. "Rooms For Rent."

ANGELA

Yes! Yes, sort of . . .. Something like that. Do you think it would go?

PARKER

In Boston tryouts alone it's already folded twelve times.

(PARKER *and* JOHN *laugh.* ANGELA *glares.*)

ANGELA

I suppose you think you're terribly funny.

PARKER

(*Touching the cheek which she averts angrily.*)
I think *you're* funny. *And* tender. And moving too, in a wistful kind of way.

(*Kisses the averted cheek.*)
I love you.

ANGELA

Well, I'm just liable to try it. It isn't new stories the theater needs; it's new insights into the old ones! You said that yourself in one of your Sunday pieces!

PARKER

Did I?

JOHN

Back in September.

PARKER

I was dead wrong.

ANGELA

I've made up my mind. I'm going to do it.

PARKER

And with those words, flung bravely in the face of a hostile
mocking world, there began the career of Angela Ballantine, or
as we know her today, Lillian Hellman. Author of *Kindly Old
Uncle Ben* and twice winner of the Clare Boothe Luce Award
for America's Cutest Playwright.
      (ANGELA *turns away angrily*.)
Ah, come off it, Angie. You're the most wonderful girl in the
world, but you're not a writer. It's all you can do to compose a
letter to your mother once a week.

JOHN

Dr. Von Hagedorn's play is about this noble analyst who goes
around *saving* people.

PARKER

Amateur night, huh?

JOHN

And how.

ANGELA
(*Rises, takes her cup and glass up to TV set.*)
Are you typing today or pacing and dictating?

PARKER
Pacing. I want to make a start on that *Harper's* thing.

ANGELA
Then may I use the typewriter?

PARKER
(*A beat.*)
What's mine is yours.

ANGELA
Thank you.
(*She takes dishes and exits into the kitchen. A pause.*)

JOHN
I don't think you handled it right.

PARKER
Don't worry.
(PARKER *reaches across table, gets paper. A wave of the hand.*)
Nothing.
(*Crosses* RIGHT. *Sits sofa.*)

JOHN
Will she really do it?

PARKER
Oh, she'll—

(ANGELA *re-enters, takes the remaining dishes, and exits again.*)
She'll begin it, all right; the way she began that scatter rug last
summer. She won't stay with it, though. A week at the most.
She has all the bulldog endurance of a snowflake.

JOHN

(*Rises and crosses* DOWNSTAGE *of table to ottoman, sits*
DOWNSTAGE RIGHT *side of ottoman.*)
Boy, if she *does* finish it, it's going to be like Ivy all over again.
She'll be having tryouts in New Haven and Philadelphia, and
we'll be here, eating those *TV dinners.*

PARKER

(*Smiles at* JOHN's *depression.*)
Hey, you know what Angie's done?

JOHN

What?

PARKER

Given me an idea for that *Harper's* article . . . . Everybody's
always encouraging amateur playwrights: "Write That Play!"
"Earn Those Royalties!" Somebody ought to discourage them;
point out the ridiculous odds, winnow the ranks a little. "Don't
Write That Play!" How's that for an article?

JOHN

I don't know . . . it sounds kind of . . . precious.

PARKER

(*Mock outrage.*)
I'll give you—!

JOHN
(*Rising and going to the stairs.*)
Well, you asked for my opinion, didn't you?
(PARKER, *smiling, rises and goes into the study.* JOHN *mutters on as he climbs the stairs.*)
Boy, everybody asks for an opinion, and you give it to them, and then they get sore at you . . .

(JOHN *exits. In the study,* PARKER *sits at the desk and takes up a portable tape recorder. He fiddles with its switches.* ANGELA *comes out of the kitchen and crosses into the study. She picks up a small beat-up portable which stands in its carrying case against* UPSTAGE RIGHT *wall.*)

PARKER
Dishes all done?

ANGELA
It's Saturday; Essie does them.
(*Resting the portable on the desk.*)
May I have some paper, please?

PARKER
(*Opening a drawer.*)
What do you want: white, yellow, onionskin . . . ?

ANGELA
Um . . . A little of each.

PARKER
(*Collects the paper, smiling, gives it to her.*)
The rent on the typewriter is a kiss an hour.

(ANGELA *gives him a peck.*)
You just bought four seconds.

ANGELA

(*Puts the portable on the floor as* PARKER *draws her into his lap.*)
Oh, Park, why do you have to be such a damn tease? Maybe I can accomplish something. . . . Uncle Ben wasn't as much of a cliché as he sounds.

PARKER

(*Still teasing.*)
He wasn't?

ANGELA

No he wasn't.
(*She kisses* PARKER *soundly.*)

PARKER

Whew. You are now the proud owner of a secondhand Underwood.
(ANGELA *rises, takes the portable again.*)
I wish you luck, honey. I wish you *The Glass Menagerie* and *The Time of Your Life* and *Come Back, Little Sheba.*

ANGELA

Now you've gone and scared me.

(*She goes out and up the stairs, and exits* RIGHT. PARKER, *smiling after her, takes up his recorder.*)

PARKER

Saturday, November seventh. Notes for essay: "Don't Write That Play." Opening paragraph:

(*Gets up, walks around the desk.*)

All over the nation housewives, psychiatrists, butchers, barbers, sitting down to . . . defenseless typewriters. A million plays in progress, all beginning with the maid answering the telephone and subtly feeding information. Sample dialogue: "Good afternoon. Snodgrass residence. This is the maid. Mr. Snodgrass?

(*Sits on* DOWNSTAGE *edge of desk.*)

He's in his office and can't be disturbed. Mrs. Snodgrass? She's at the hairdresser's, prettying herself up for the big party tonight. Junior Snodgrass? Oh, he's in jail on a narcotic rap."

(JOHN *enters on the balcony and comes down the stairs.*)

Most beginners conk out early in the game because they try to base play on personal reminiscence. This is *not* a good idea unless you are Lucrezia Borgia or All Capone.

(JOHN *knocks on study door and opens it.*)

JOHN

Hey, Dad?

PARKER

Yo?

JOHN

(*Entering study.*)

I've got one for the white box and one for the black.

PARKER

Let's hear them.

JOHN

(*A beat.*)
She's in the guest room, and the typewriter's going like a machine gun.

PARKER

Don't *worry!* Believe me, one week and she'll toss in the sponge. We've *had* our career woman; Angie is *not* Ivy.
(*Sits in the desk chair.*)
Come on, let's hear.

JOHN

This is the white one. It's only fifteen cents. It's for a really wonderful play.
(*Reads from a slip of paper.*)
"The stage took wing last night, and carried a fortunate audience closer, much closer, to the stars." It's just fifteen cents . . .

PARKER

All right, I'll take it . . .
(*He takes the slip of paper, reaches into his pocket for change, and pays* JOHN.)

JOHN

And one black one. This is a dollar.

PARKER

A dollar! You've gone mad in that room up there.

JOHN

This is for a play that's absolutely awful in every department.
(*Reading from a second slip.*)

"The actors were wooden and rigid, and so was the script. In fact *everything* last night was wooden and rigid, with one exception, and that, unfortunately, was the scenery."

(PARKER *gives* JOHN *a dollar and seizes the slip.* JOHN *runs out, closes the door, and goes happily up the stairs, while* PARKER *gets the white and black file boxes out of the desk compartment and files the two slips. The lights fade quickly and come up again as* ANGELA, *in a smock, comes out of the kitchen, thoughtfully peeling a banana.*)

ANGELA
(*Reciting to herself as she crosses toward the stairs.*)
Yes, Uncle Ben, I have run away from home. They don't need me there. Mother and Sally and Marge are so efficient and well organized that—that I am just the fifth wheel.
(*Stopping halfway up the stairs, counting on her fingers.*)
Mother, Sally, Marge . . . I am the *fourth* wheel?
(*Continues up. On the landing, the solution hits her.*)
I am the *spare tire!*

(*She hurries offstage* RIGHT. *The telephone rings.* PARKER *opens the study door, and takes the phone.*)

PARKER
Hello?
(JOHN *enters through the front door, key in hand, carrying a briefcase and* Variety.)
Yes. Just a minute, please.
(*Calling upward.*)
Angie!

JOHN

Hi.

PARKER

Hi. Go call Angie, will you?

JOHN
(*Right where he is, bellowing.*)
ANGIE!

PARKER

Thanks a lot.

ANGELA
(*Offstage* RIGHT, *upstairs.*)
What is it?

(JOHN *puts the briefcase and* Variety *on the couch, and takes off his coat.*)

PARKER

Telephone!

ANGELA
(*Offstage.*)
Who is it?

PARKER
(*Into phone.*)
Who's calling, please?
(*Aloud.*)
S. P. Champlain!

JOHN

The producer?

ANGELA

(*Appearing on upstairs landing, pencil in hand, wide-eyed.*)

The producer?

(*A beat.*)

PARKER

(*Into phone.*)

The producer?

ANGELA

Park!

(*She flees into the bedroom, shutting the door.*)

PARKER

Just a second. Here she is.

(*Listens, then hangs up.*)

I suppose it *could* have been S. P. Champlain the laundry-man.

JOHN

Is he going to be *Angie's* producer?

PARKER

Of what? Act One?

JOHN

She's halfway through Act Two now.

(JOHN *sits* LEFT *end of sofa, starts reading* Variety.)

PARKER

S. P. Champlain is not about to concern himself with an unfinished play by an amateur playwright. Although . . . last season he *did* put on that musical version of *Anthony Adverse.* . . .
    (*His hand glances the phone.*)
Would it hurt you very much to find out that your father listens on extensions?

JOHN

Heck, no! Go ahead!
    (*A beat.*)

PARKER

    (*Moves* DOWNSTAGE RIGHT *toward sofa.*)
No, no . . . . It would hurt *me* to *have* you find out.
    (*He ruffles* JOHN'*s hair.*)

JOHN

    (*Deeply disappointed.*)
Ohh . . .

PARKER

We'll wait. Angie'll tell us.
    (*Sits on the couch, takes* Variety *from* JOHN.)
What's in *Variety?*

JOHN

Ivy's doing a musical in the spring.
    (*He takes his coat* UPSTAGE.)

PARKER

I know. She called me for advice. And ignored it, of course.

JOHN

(*Hanging his coat in the closet.*)
I don't remember Ivy ever singing.

PARKER

You're a lucky boy . . . .

JOHN

Say, how did he find out about Angie? S. P. Champlain.

PARKER

I don't know. . . . She talked about the play last week, at a party
we went to.
(*A pause.*)

ANGELA

(*Entering from the bedroom, on the landing.*)
Guess what!

(PARKER *and* JOHN *look up.*)

PARKER

(*Putting aside* Variety.)
I give up.

JOHN

(*Matter of fact.*)
S. P. Champlain is going to produce your play.

ANGELA

No, don't be silly. But he wants to read it as soon as I'm done.
I told him what it's about and he thinks it's a great idea!

PARKER

(*Rising, singing and doing a buck and wing.*)
"Hello, I'm Anthony Adverse,
And tho' this may be a bad verse,
   I'm mighty glad that I'm he-ere!"
   Doodily, doodily . . .

ANGELA

(*Icily.*)
Every producer makes his mistakes, and S. P. Champlain has made fewer than most.

PARKER

But it's the *quality* of his mistakes, not the quantity!
(ANGELA *glares.*)
Ah, forgive me for teasing. Congratulations, darling.

ANGELA

There's nothing to congratulate me for—yet. And what's more, I know he only called because I'm your wife. But he wouldn't *still* be interested after I told him about it, would he, just because of that?

PARKER

No, he wouldn't, Angie.

ANGELA

Well then . . . !

PARKER

(*With a grin.*)
Just watch out if he invites you to have lunch with him. I hear the "S. P." stands for Sneaky Pincher.

(*He exits into the study, leaving* ANGELA *on the landing, uncertain whether or not to be angry.*)

JOHN

Congratulations.

ANGELA

Thank you. It's premature. He isn't still working on that nasty little article, is he?

JOHN

(*Sitting on couch, taking up* Variety.)
He's making it into a book now.

ANGELA

Hmm!

(*She exits* RIGHT. *The light irises down to spot on* JOHN *as he sits reading.*)

JOHN

(*Singing softly.*)
"And now we'll sing you a sad verse,
Good-bye old Anthony Adverse."
Doo-doo-doo-doo-doo-deedily-doo . . .

(*The spot fades on* JOHN *and comes up on* PARKER *at the desk in the study, dictating.*)

PARKER

Tuesday, January nineteenth. Notes for book: "Don't Write That Play"; Chapter Twelve. Recapitulation of difficulties. Each scene tougher to write than scene before, demanding greater craftsmanship, stronger discipline, and larger waste basket.

> (ANGELA *enters and comes down the stairs, reverently bearing a thick manuscript. She is nervous, but her cheeks are glowing with a serene pride—rather like a new mother.*)

If a third act were no harder to write than a first act, the fees of the copyright office would support the entire government. The number of unfinished plays is in direct proportion to the number of—

> (ANGELA *knocks on the study door.*)

Come in. The number of unfinished plays is in direct proportion . . . to the . . . number . . .

(*He trails off, gazing at* ANGELA, *who stands at the door holding script.*)

ANGELA

I'm done.

PARKER

With Act Two?

ANGELA

With Act Three. Done. Finished. Complete.

> (*Puts script on desk. A pause.*)

PARKER

> (*Into recorder.*)

To be continued.

> (*He puts aside the recorder.*)

ANGELA

Of course I'll have to do some rewriting, but I think it's—
optionable.

PARKER

(*Takes up script.*)
The Gingerbread World . . .

ANGELA

There were all kinds of Victorian trimming around the house,
and it seemed sort of like a retreat from reality . . .

PARKER

It's a nice title, I like it . . . *The Gingerbread World* . . .
(*A beat.*)

ANGELA

Read it.
(*A pause.*)

PARKER

Are you sure you want me to?

ANGELA

You're the best critic in the whole apartment.
(*A smile between them, and then a pause.*)

PARKER

I won't lie, Angie. This isn't a cake or a hair-do or a slip
cover.

ANGELA

I don't want you to lie. And I don't think you'll have to. I think
you're in for a surprise.

PARKER

I hope so. I do.

(*He holds up crossed fingers.* ANGELA *backs out of the study.*)

ANGELA

I'll be very quiet . . .
> (*She closes door as the light irises down to spot on* PARKER.
> *He lights a cigarette, draws on it, his eyes never leaving
> the waiting manuscript. After a moment he turns the title
> page, leans forward on one elbow and begins to read. The
> spot fades out and comes up on* ANGELA *in the living room,
> at the telephone.*)

Person-to-person to Washington, D.C. The number is District
7-4855, and I'd like to speak to Mrs. Charlotte Orr, O-R-R . . .
Gramercy 7-3935 . . . Hello, Mom? Angela. How are you? . . .
Fine, Mom. I finally finished it! Just this morning! . . . Thank
you!! . . . Well, *thank you, darling!* Listen, I'm counting chickens
before they're hatched, but could you possibly come take care
of Park and John for three weeks or so, in the spring or maybe
the fall? Essie can give us two extra days a week, but Park just
gets *sick* over her cooking. He says she makes everything taste
like dentists' fingers . . . Well, I may have to go out of town. S.
P. Champlain is interested and if he decides to put it on . . . S.
P. Champlain . . . Yes, the producer . . . Well, they *always* take
them out of town first, to try them out and see how—to try
them out— Oh, for Pete's sake. Mom, it's the *play* that I finished, not the scatter rug!!!

(*Blackout. The spot comes up on* PARKER. *He reads the last few lines of the manuscript, closes it, and sits with his face in his hands. After a moment he emits a long, low, miserable moan. He opens the manuscript gingerly, peeks at one line, then quickly closes the manuscript, as though contagion might escape. Another moan. The lights come up in the living room.* ANGELA *is sitting as close to the study door as she can get.* JOHN*'s coat and briefcase are on the couch.* JOHN *enters from the kitchen, eating a cookie.*)

JOHN

I'm going—

ANGELA

Shh!

JOHN
(*Whispering, as he takes his coat.*)
I'm going out. I'll be back in a few minutes.

ANGELA
(*Whispering.*)
All right.

  (JOHN *quietly exits.* PARKER *rubs his eyes, sighing. He rises, picks up the manuscript, faces the door, draws a deep breath, and opens the door.* ANGELA *leaps to her feet and backs away, almost upsetting her chair. They smile, an awkward pause.*)
I was—just sitting here—

  (PARKER *moves* DOWNSTAGE CENTER *to* LEFT, *avoiding* ANGELA*'s anxious eyes.*)
Well?

PARKER

(PARKER *crosses to sofa and sits.*)

Angie . . . darling . . .

(*Pats sofa for her to sit.*)

I'm looking for an affirmative beginning . . . I keep coming back to the title.

(*Facing her now.*)

It's a *good* title, Angie.

ANGELA

But the play . . . ?

PARKER

(*Shaking his head.*)

No, dear . . . No . . . I'm sorry.

(*Clenches his fists and continues.*)

The characters are . . . sugar and spice and everything nice, but that's not what people are made of, not even little girls. These are . . . Kewpie dolls, all of them. And the dialogue is . . . clumsy, Angie. That's the only word. Except "pretentious" where I think you were trying to be poetic. The structure . . . ? There's none. This isn't a play at all, honey; it's a—a fuzzy, inexact memory; it hasn't been shaped or focused or organized or—or anything.

(*A pause.* ANGELA *is white-faced, as though slapped.*)

ANGELA

How's the typing?

(PARKER *extends the manuscript toward her.*)

PARKER

I'm sorry, Angie. I wish I could have said something else.

(ANGELA *takes the manuscript. A beat.*)

ANGELA

Do you? Is that what you wish?

PARKER

(*Tenderly taking her shoulders.*)
Angie baby, believe me, I wouldn't—

ANGELA

(*On "believe," ruefully.*)
Suddenly I'm "Angie baby." For two and a half months you've been sticking pins in a little statue of me and now I'm "Angie baby."

PARKER

Ah, don't, Angie . . .

ANGELA

(*Drawing away, rises, crosses* RIGHT *to* UPSTAGE *of sofa.*)
It's true, isn't it? I've heard you wandering around, crooning your *voodoo* into that recorder . . .

PARKER

(*Rigid.*)
The play is no good, Angie. You asked me to read it and I warned you, no lies.

ANGELA

(*Crossing to* UPSTAGE CENTER.)
Did you read it? *I* don't think you read my play.

PARKER

What does that mean?

ANGELA

I think you read the play you were *hoping* I'd write, not the
one I *did* write. I think I could have put—*Hamlet* in front of
you, and all *you* would have seen would have been—one more
mixed-up teen-ager with family problems!

PARKER

(*Tight-jawed.*)
I read the play objectively, Angela.

ANGELA

(*Sits ottoman.*)
Objectively?

PARKER

Yes, *objectively!* That happens to be my business! And I happen
to be considered pretty good at it!

ANGELA

No; not this time! No! This is a—a tender, simple, touching drama!
It has *heart*, and it has *warmth*, and it has—it has *sweetness*—

PARKER

Oh, it has sweetness, all right! Put that on a stage and you'll
decay every tooth for ten miles around!

ANGELA

Well, that is one man's opinion!

> (*Rises, crosses* DOWNSTAGE *of sofa to phone, takes a slip of
> note paper from her pocket, puts down the manuscript.*)

One man's biased, partial, prejudiced, one-sided opinion!

> (*Reading number, dialing phone.*)

Let's just see what S. P. Champlain will say! *He* isn't a self-satisfied
male chauvinist who thinks a woman's place is in the broom
closet! Nor does he tend to confuse himself with God and
George Jean Nathan rolled into one!

> (*She completes dialing, waits.*)

PARKER

If Anthony Adverse answers, hang up.

ANGELA

Mr. Champlain, please. Angela Ballantine.

> (*Hand over phone.*)

It just infuriates you, doesn't it, that I actually *finished* the play.
The *Kitty Hawk* is up in the air now, and you're standing on
the ground shouting, "It won't fly, it won't fly!"

PARKER

The *Kitty Hawk?* Up in the air?

> (*Pointing at manuscript.*)

That—that HUPMOBILE?

ANGELA

> (*Step to* LEFT *of phone table.*)

Mr. Champlain? How are you? . . . Just fine. Just wonderful.
I'm finished, Mr. Champlain, and I couldn't be more pleased!

> (*Eyes on* PARKER.)

The characters, the dialogue, the structure; they're all *exactly* as I wanted them to be! I even like the typing!

(*She laughs, then listens.* JOHN *enters.*)

PARKER

Go outside for a while, John.

JOHN

I've just *been* outside!
> (*Stays* UPSTAGE CENTER, *listening, removing his coat, hangs coat in closet, comes* DOWNSTAGE CENTER *to sit on ottoman.*)

ANGELA

Wonderful! . . . Yes . . . The fourth floor . . . And then you'll call? Wonderful, Mr. Champlain.
> (*Hangs up, picks up manuscript. With hauteur.*)
A messenger is coming for the script in fifteen minutes.
> (*She ascends the stairs and exits* RIGHT.)

PARKER

He'd better have cab fare because they'll never let him inside a bus with that thing.
> (*To* JOHN.)
Did you read it?

JOHN

She kept it locked in the closet. And she hid the key.

PARKER

I said "Did you read it."

JOHN

Well, just the first act.

PARKER

What did you think?

JOHN

It was better than Dr. Von Hagedorn's first act.
(*Shrugs.*)
. . . Like a broken arm is better than a broken back . . .

PARKER

(*Muttering.*)
God and George Jean Nathan rolled into one . . .

JOHN

(*Gesturing at phone.*)
Do you think he'll produce it?

PARKER

Don't be ridiculous.

(PARKER *rises and exits into the study.* ANGELA *enters* RIGHT, *descends the stairs, fastening the manila envelope containing her manuscript.* JOHN *hangs his coat in the closet.* ANGELA *puts the envelope on side table in foyer and continues* DOWNSTAGE LEFT *toward the kitchen.* JOHN *rises and crosses to* ANGELA.)

JOHN

Angie . . .
(ANGELA *stops.* JOHN *comes* DOWNSTAGE *to her.*)
Don't be angry with Dad. Please.

(*A beat.* ANGELA *touches* JOHN*'s arm, draws herself up coolly.*)

ANGELA

I'm not angry with him. If he chooses to despise my play, that's his privilege. Anger is an immature emotion, and I like to think I've outgrown it. I'm not angry; not angry in the least.

(*She is holding him tight.*)

JOHN

You're hurting my arm . . .

(ANGELA *breathes a quick "I'm sorry," kisses* JOHN*'s arm, and exits into the kitchen as the lights fade out. The spot comes up in study.* PARKER *is at the desk, dictating irritably into recorder.*)

PARKER

Monday, February—oh, twenty-second, twenty-third; *I* don't know! Notes for book: "Don't Write That Play"; Chapter Fourteen. So your play is optioned. So the announcements have been published,

(*Crosses* LEFT.)

and the phone has been ringing, and there hasn't been a moment's peace in a whole damn month!

(*Crosses* RIGHT *to desk.*)

Cut "damn."

(*Crosses to* CENTER.)

And now, gentle reader, you think your troubles are over? Ha-ha! They *begin*, my friend, they *begin!* A producer was *easy* to find; anyone with a dime and a phone booth and the telephone number of a man with money is a producer!

(*Crosses* RIGHT *to* DOWNSTAGE *of desk.*)

But now you need a *director*. Without a skillful, energetic director to tear your play apart and punch it back together again, to tear a dozen *actors* apart and punch *them* back
(*Crosses to* CENTER LEFT.)
together again, without such a man you are lost, my neophyte; and the skillful, energetic directors, you will soon learn, are both busy.
(*Sits at desk. The lights come up in the living room.*)
What you will find available instead of energy will be sterility; the tired mechanic who has directed seven thousand plays—

(*During this,* ANGELA *enters through the front door, wearing a coat and holding a bound manuscript. With excitedly flushed cheeks, she ushers in* DION KAPAKOS, *a hatless, hot-eyed wunderkind of twenty-nine or thirty, very skillful and energetic-looking, and wearing heavy black-rimmed tortoise-shell glasses. He strides* DOWNSTAGE CENTER, *checking over the room as though he has just bought it.*)

DION

Nice, nice, nice. Nice. Nice.

(*He opens his woodsman's coat and rubs his hands with restless vitality. Under the coat he wears a heavy knitted turtleneck sweater, dungarees, heavy wool knit socks, and what were once white sneakers.* ANGELA *goes to the study door.*)

PARKER
(*Continuing over the above without a break.*)
—and lost somewhere along the way whatever vibrant enthusiasm he may have possessed in his greener years. Instead of skill there will be available only the automatic hack work of Hollywood has-beens, or the lifeless, checkerboard staging of men

so complacent in their established authority, so gross with the
gross receipts of their past successes, that any new and dynamic
attack is as far beyond their powers as—

(ANGELA *knocks on "far."*)

                          ANGELA

Parker!

                          PARKER

Yo?

                          ANGELA

There's someone here I'd like you to meet.

(PARKER *puts down the recorder, rises, and opens the door.*)

                          PARKER

Hi.

                          ANGELA

Park, this is Dion Kapakos.

(*A beat, then* PARKER *goes enthusiastically* UPSTAGE *of sofa to* DION.)

                          PARKER

Well . . . hello!

                          DION

How are you, sir!

(*They shake hands warmly, while* ANGELA *beams.*)

PARKER

I've been hoping we'd run into each other!

DION

Same here, sir, same here!

PARKER

Someone told me you had a beard!

DION

I did! But it was just insecurity. One hit show and out came
the old razor.

(*All laugh.* DION *sits on ottoman.* PARKER *sits on* DOWNSTAGE
LEFT *end of sofa.*)

ANGELA

(*Sweetly.*)
Dion is going to direct *Gingerbread*.
(ANGELA *sits on arm of sofa.* PARKER *gapes.*)
He was my first choice; I remembered all those wonderful things
you said about him last season.
(PARKER *still gapes.* ANGELA *smiles complacently on* DION.)
"The drive and thrust of a jet-engine . . ."

DION

You know, I wrote you a three-page letter, sir, after that review
of *Oh, Doctor!*

PARKER

I don't remember—

DION

I tore it up. It was—too damn slushy. You're kind of like a father image for me. It's true; I'm an arrogant little snot and you're just about the only man alive whose opinion I really respect. I mean that. The other critics? Hell, you throw a serious drama at them, it's like—throwing a medicine ball at a baby. And comedies? Ha! Half of them don't know their *farce* from a hole in the ground!

(DION *grins,* ANGELA *laughs,* PARKER *can't quite make it.*)

PARKER

You're going to direct—
(*A gesture at the manuscript in* ANGELA'S *hand.*)

DION

(*Leaning back.*)
Love at first sight. The minute I finished reading it I called my agent and burned my bridges. I was all set to do the musical version of *David Copperfield,* you know.

PARKER

I heard . . .

DION

(*Rising. Striding around.*)
But I've *had* musicals. *Oh, Doctor!* was just a way to get off the summer circuit. *Drama* is my meat. I'm Greek, you know. Kapakos? That is, my grandfather was Greek. From Epidaurus, where the amphitheater is. I went back there last summer, sat on those stone steps in the moonlight . . . I found *roots* there, I really did.
(*A beat.*)

ANGELA

(*Looks at* DION— *then* PARKER.)

You two talk; I'll get the notes.

(*She goes up the stairs and into bedroom.*)

PARKER

Notes?

DION

(*Sits on ottoman.*)

On *Gingerbread.* I want to go over all the stuff Angela discarded.
We're going to do a full rewrite, from the ground up.

(*Leans forward confidentially.*)

Hey, would you mind telling me where you find a girl like that?
Beauty, sensitivity, modesty . . .

PARKER

Random House, but they're out of stock.

DION

(*Gets up, walks* LEFT. *Takes cigarette out of shirt pocket.*)

Yessir, she and I have *work* ahead of us! And rehearsals in just
four weeks! That's March twenty-second, then New Haven,
April thirteenth; Boston, April nineteenth;

(*Lights cigarette.*)

New York, May third.

PARKER

Champlain moves fast . . .

DION

(*Walks over to table* LEFT *and drops match in ashtray.*)

He's a producer. A real one. You know, some of them have no talent at all; just a dime and the phone number of a money-man.

PARKER

(*Looking toward study.*)

Mmm . . .

DION

(*Walks back to* PARKER.)

Benson Hedgeman is pretty well set for Uncle Ben. Perfect casting, isn't it? His arm is clean as a whistle; hasn't been *near* the stuff in over a year.

PARKER

Say, do you . . . *really think* Angie has—Greek drama there?

DION

(*Sits* LEFT *arm of sofa.*)

Not now, but wait till I'm finished with it. Between you and me, that script of her is carrying fifty pounds of fat in all the wrong places, and it's wrapped up in tinsel and ribbons up to its eyeballs. Inside, though, it has bones; fine, lean bones. It's like a big fat overdressed woman. Me, I'm Slenderella.

(*Leans back and laughs.*)

PARKER

Personally, I think it's a job for Mandrake the Magician.

DION

(*Smiling.*)

Oh, I know; Angela told me how *you* feel. *You* I would *love* to make a monkey out of!

PARKER

Overthrow the father image?

DION

(*Grinning.*)

Sort of.

PARKER

Well, you *did* pull off one miracle with *Oh, Doctor!* . . . If ever I walked into a theater thinking I was stepping aboard the *Titanic*, that was the night.

DION

Now wait, don't give *me* all the credit. *Oh, Doctor!* was built on the best foundation of any musical in the past five years. There aren't many novels around that can top *Arrowsmith*, you know.

(ANGELA *enters from bedroom with manila folder, descends the stairs.*)

ANGELA

I got together whatever I could find, but it doesn't add up to very much.

DION

(*Rising, going to her.*)

It'll all help. We have to go right back to the *roots* of the play.

(*He takes the folder, looks in it.*)

PARKER

Where are you working?

DION

(*Throwing it away.*)

My place. I have a hole in the wall over on Bleecker Street. In the phone book, if you're the nervous type.

(*A sly grin.*)

PARKER

I'm not. Opening tonight, Angie. Early dinner.

ANGELA

I know.

DION

(*Over her.*)

Oh, she'll be early. Today we just shake hands and promise no fouls; tomorrow is round one.

(*Closes the folder, crosses to* PARKER.)

It's been a pleasure meeting you, sir. It really has.

(*They shake hands.*)

PARKER

You can drop the "sir" if you'd like; I missed the Civil War by a good five years.

DION

Sorry; I guess it's the father-image bit. Parker—

(*He offers his hand again.*)

PARKER

(*Shaking it.*)

Dion.

(DION *joins* ANGELA *at foyer. She holds the manuscript clasped to her bosom.*)

DION

(*Turning to* ANGELA.)
Ready for the fray?
(ANGELA *nods solemnly.* DION *taps the manuscript.*)
This is just the *beginning* of a play, girlie, but—
(*Turning to* PARKER, *grinning.*)
you know what *I* always say?

PARKER

I'll bite; *what* do you always say?

DION

"A playwright's reach should exceed his grasp, or what's New Haven for?" Ha, ha, ha, ha . . .

(*All laugh.* DION *takes* ANGELA*'s arm, they exit.* PARKER *watches them off. He turns, looking puzzled, as the lights fade. The lights come up in the living room.* JOHN *enters through the front door, wearing a coat, suit, and necktie. He looks terribly sad.*)

JOHN

Dad?
(*Morosely hangs away the coat. Louder.*)
Dad?

(*The study door opens.* PARKER *looks out.*)

PARKER

How was it?

JOHN

(*Coming* DOWNSTAGE.)

Awful. I should never have asked Angie to let me in. I should have kept my mouth shut and gone to a movie.

PARKER

Lots of first run-throughs are pretty bad. It's practically a tradition.

JOHN

Not like this; it *couldn't* be.

PARKER

(*Coming into the living room.*)

What has Kapakos done to the script?

JOHN

It's worse than it was before. The roomers in the boarding house, they're like a Greek chorus now. They stand at the side of the stage and *chant* things.

PARKER

Oh, God . . .

JOHN

At the end, when everybody leaves, Uncle Ben shoots himself.

PARKER

No . . .

JOHN

And they changed the title; it's not *The Gingerbread World* any more, it's *A Houseful of Silence*.

PARKER

Oh, Lord . . .
> (*Paces, then strikes his palm angrily.*)

The fool! The damn fool! That man had the makings of a first-rate director! First-rate! And then he had to go sit on the steps of an amphitheater in the moonlight! Are you *sure* it's that bad? Who else was there?

JOHN

There was a cleaning woman sitting near me.

PARKER

Did she listen?

JOHN

For five minutes. Then she said, "Why should I be sitting here when I can be doing the men's room," and she went out.

PARKER

Oh, Lord . . . how's Angie taking it?

JOHN

> (*Sitting on the couch.*)

She looks worried. They *all* look worried, except Mr. Kapakos.
> (PARKER *paces.*)

Angie asked me what I thought about it. I said, "I'm a kid; what do *I* know?"

PARKER

In June, when the season's dead, we're going to take her to Paris. That's the one thing she's always wanted. I'll switch around my vacation. If I can't, I'll take a leave-of-absence.

JOHN

Dad . . .

PARKER

What?

JOHN

Are you going to review it? When it opens in New York?
A Houseful of Silence?

PARKER

If it opens, you mean. I think so. I'm not sure.

JOHN

Would you tell the truth?

PARKER

No, I would lie, the way I always do.

JOHN

All right, don't get sore . . .

PARKER

Well, what kind of question is that; would I tell the truth . . .

JOHN
(*Worried.*)
It's going to be like Ivy all over again . . .

PARKER

Now, look—

JOHN
(*A sudden frightened anger.*)
Well, you told the truth about Ivy, didn't you?

(*A beat.* PARKER *sits beside* JOHN.)

PARKER
Now, look. There is nothing for you to get—scared about. There are good marriages and there are bad marriages. Ivy and I had a bad one. For nine years we piled up unhappiness between us, and it was all those tons of *unhappiness* that caused our divorce, *not my review of her Helen of Troy.* The review may have been the spark, but the nine years of unhappiness were the gunpowder. Are you with me?
(JOHN *is listening very intently, but he doesn't nod yet.*)
Angie and I have a *good* marriage. If I say bad things about *Gingerbread* she may—

JOHN
A Houseful of Silence.

PARKER
If I say bad things about *A Houseful of Silence,* Angie may be hurt, and angry with me. But there *ain't no gunpowder* in this apartment. A good marriage doesn't break up like a ten-cent glider; you got that?
(JOHN *nods.*)
Okay . . .
(*Rises, patting* JOHN's *hand.*)
Now go eat a cookie.
(*He starts toward the study.*)

JOHN

I still don't see why you can't let someone *else* write the review . . .

(PARKER *stops, turns, takes a deep exasperated breath.*)

PARKER

Who? Harvey Rittenhouse?

JOHN

He's not *that* bad . . .

PARKER

Harvey Rittenhouse is a blithering idiot who sits in those off-Broadway theaters and sees nothing but *me* walking into an open manhole! Not while I'm breathing will I hand him the reins, and especially not for *A Houseful of Moonlit Greek Amphitheaters!* He's just ass enough to be polite about it.

JOHN

What if he is? What difference does it make?
(*A beat.*)

PARKER

A spade ought to be called a spade . . .

JOHN

And you don't *care* if you hurt Angie and make her angry . . .

PARKER

Sure I care! What do you think I am; Bluebeard?
(*Crouches down beside couch.*)
John, listen . . . Sometimes you *have* to hurt people. Even

people you love. . . . If I lie about Angie's play, or if I get off the hook by letting Harvey Rittenhouse cover it—I'm going to lose a good-size piece of my self-respect. Maybe a piece of my self-respect sounds tiny compared to hurting Angie, but if I start disliking myself a little, I'm going to start disliking the *whole world* a little, Angie included. And you. You're both sharp; you'll sense that, and *you'll* start disliking *me* a little. And I'll sense *that* and bingo!—there we are, in the worst kind of vicious circle there ever was. I know it from experience. And you do too. Remember the—old crank I was four or five years ago? And the little crumb that *you* were?

> (JOHN *nods soberly.* PARKER *rises from his crouching position.*)

Never sell off a piece of yourself just to avoid hurting someone. The people who matter will understand and forgive, and the people who *can't* understand and forgive—well, they don't matter.

(*A pause.*)

JOHN
(*Looking up at him.*)
Boy, that's the biggest thing you ever told me, isn't it?

PARKER
Bet your life it is.

JOHN
Except about sex, maybe.

(PARKER *laughs.*)

PARKER

Hey, you know what? I'll bet you five bucks *A Houseful of
Silence* never even gets on the train.

JOHN

You really think so?

PARKER

If the run-through was as bad as you say, Champlain isn't going
to pour away *more* money, is he?

JOHN

Is it *his* own money?

(*The lights slowly iris down to a spot on* PARKER *and* JOHN.)

PARKER

It's *money*, never mind whose. He isn't going to pour it away, is he?

JOHN

I guess not . . .

PARKER

I'll *bet* not! Never! It's going to be rough on Angie, though . . .

JOHN

No New Haven . . .

PARKER

We're going to have to treat her like a princess.

JOHN

Help her get over the disappointment.

PARKER

She's worked so—darn hard . . .

(*The spot fades out as a second spot comes up on the bedroom door.* ANGELA, *in a traveling suit, plants a large, heavy suitcase on the landing and steps back into the bedroom. After a moment she reappears, with a smaller suitcase and a hatbox, and puts them down.*)

ANGELA

(*Calling offstage* RIGHT.)

And if your father takes you to any of the openings you do your homework first, you hear?

JOHN

(*Offstage.*)

I hear!

(ANGELA *takes her coat and purse from a chair within the bedroom door.*)

ANGELA

And if you happen not to like whatever play it is, you just sit there quietly. None of that *groaning* business!

(*She picks up the hatbox, and comes downstairs. As she descends, late afternoon light comes up in the living room.* PARKER *is lying on the couch, the Dictet is before him on the coffee table.*)

PARKER

(*Holding recorder as a microphone.*)

All ashore that's going ashore. Whoooooo . . .

(ANGELA, *paying him no attention, puts down the hatbox*

*and coat, opens her purse, takes out a pencil and a slip of
paper, crosses out something.*)
When is train time?

ANGELA

We're not taking the train; we're driving. Dion has an MG.

PARKER

He would . . .

ANGELA
(*Next item on her list.*)
Now remember, Mom's train gets in at Penn Station, not Grand
Central. Ten fifty-five Monday morning.

PARKER

I'll have the band there at ten-thirty, just to be safe.

ANGELA

Tell her I'll call Monday night.

PARKER

Check.

ANGELA

There's food inside for tonight, and you can take John out tomorrow night. I left a list of stores for Mom. On the refrigerator.

PARKER

Check.
(*A beat.*)

ANGELA

She'll spoil you, you'll see. She runs a home ten times better than I *ever* will.

PARKER

That I doubt.
(*A beat.*)

ANGELA

Tell her to watch out for the short butcher, the one who has to lean on the scale.
(*She pantomimes, craning up to read an imaginary dial while pressing where the tray would be.*)

PARKER

(*Into recorder, à la Dick Tracy.*)
Watch out for short butcher. That is all.
(*A beat. They smile.* PARKER *sits up.*)

ANGELA

(*Putting purse on hatbox.*)
Well, I'd better . . .

(*She goes up the stairs.* PARKER *puts the recorder on the table, and rises.*)

PARKER

Wait, I'll get the big one.
(ANGELA *is coming downstairs with the smaller suitcase as* PARKER *ascends. He puts his hand across to the banister, blocking her. They look at each other, then kiss twice, husband-wife kisses, nothing orgasmic.*)
I was beginning to forget little off-the-cuff kisses . . .

ANGELA
(*Touching him.*)
Park . . .
(*The doorbell rings.*)
It's Dion.
(*They kiss again, then* PARKER *goes up and* ANGELA *down. The doorbell rings again—impatiently.*)
Coming!

(ANGELA *puts down the suitcase and goes to the front door, as* PARKER *picks up the large suitcase and starts down.* ANGELA *opens the door.* DION *enters, picks up* ANGELA *by the waist, whirls her around and carries her* DOWNSTAGE, *singing over her cries of "Dion! Put me down! Dion!"*)

DION.
"Off we go, into the wild blue yonder,
Climbing high, into the sun
Into the sun, hey!"

(*He puts* ANGELA *down and thrusts a hand at* PARKER, *who has just put down the large suitcase and is looking somewhat undelighted.*)

DION
Hiya! Don't mind me!
(*Shakes* PARKER's *hand.*)
I get this way at this stage of the game! All front; underneath it I'm scared silly! Knees like water!

ANGELA
(*Straightening herself, muttering.*)
We haven't even left yet and I'm worn out . . .

(JOHN *appears on the landing, watching.*)

DION

Don't worry; I've got a glove compartment full of Benzedrine and caffein pills.
(*Sees* JOHN.)
Hey, there's that Johnny-boy who was at the run-through! How ya doin', Johnny-boy?
(*Waves at* JOHN.)

JOHN

(*Coming down a few steps.*)
Fine . . .

DION

(*To* PARKER.)
Wonderful kid! I love kids! We *communicate!*

PARKER

With two tin cans and a long string?
(PARKER *crosses to sofa, sits.*)

DION

Ha, ha, ha, ha! Hey, Angie, did you ask him?

ANGELA

No. I thought I would wait until you—

DION

(*Crosses to sofa.*)
Park—

PARKER

Yes, Di?

(*A beat.* DION *smiles uncertainly.* ANGELA *moves* UPSTAGE RIGHT *above sofa.*)

DION

(*Sits* RIGHT *of* PARKER.)

We're having a bit of trouble, Angie and I. Champlain has got producer-itis. He's trying to bully us into using a new third act that he's dreamed up with some cretin of a script reader. I think it's the third act of *Bertha, the Sewing-Machine Girl*. On top of that we have to break in a new Uncle Ben. Turns out Benson Hedgeman has been junked all along and now he's *really* flying.

PARKER

I thought you said his arm was clean as a whistle.

DION

It is. He's been shooting the stuff into his *leg*, the damn sneak.

ANGELA

Dion and I would like you to come up to New Haven for a couple of days next week. There are no openings after Wednesday night.

(DION *looks at her and leans back on sofa.*)

DION

And Boston too, if you've got a few days around the twenty-fifth. Just to look at things and drop a suggestion here and there.

(*A beat.*)

PARKER

I'm sorry; I can't do that.

ANGELA

Why not?

PARKER

(*Gets up, moves* LEFT *of* CENTER.)

If I contribute something to the play, how can I review it? It's going to be hard enough to be objective as it is.

ANGELA

How can you re—?

DION

You're going to *review* it?

PARKER

(*At chair,* RIGHT *of table* LEFT.)

Yes, I am. I've talked it over with my editor, and myself, and I'm going to.

DION

We assumed you would—disqualify yourself.

PARKER

(*Crossing* RIGHT *to ottoman, sits.*)

Sorry, I'm a vampire; nothing disqualifies *me* but a stake through the heart.

JOHN

Or being caught outside the coffin in direct sunlight.

PARKER

(*To* DION, *pointing back over his shoulder at* JOHN.)
The world's leading authority on vampires.

ANGELA

But—but that's not *fair!* You *read* the play! You *hated* it!

PARKER

I'd review it if I loved it. I'll do my best to be objective.

DION

But damn it, she's your *wife!*

PARKER

No, she isn't, not on opening night.
(*To* ANGELA.)
You're a playwright, I'm a critic; let's both do our jobs as well as
we can, and shake hands before and after.

ANGELA

Surgeons don't *operate* on their wives!

PARKER

I'm not going to *operate*, Angie; I'm going to look at a play and
write an opinion on it.

DION

Can't you forget you're a critic for a couple of weeks and give
us a hand?

PARKER

No, I can't.

ANGELA

Oh no, not he! He *never* forgets he's a critic! Not even on his wedding night!

PARKER

(*Self-conscious, puts hands to eyes.*)
Angie, if you're going to dig up that old—

ANGELA

Do you know what he did? Do you know what this witty, perceptive—

PARKER

It was a *joke*, Angie!

ANGELA

Oh sure, a joke! The morning after our wedding! Do you know what he did?

PARKER

(*Rises. Strides away to* LEFT, DOWNSTAGE *of table* LEFT.)
Holy mackerel . . . !

ANGELA

The morning after our wedding. I woke up. He was in the shower. There was a note on the pillow next to me. Do you know what it said?
(DION *shakes his head.* ANGELA *sets each word up on an imaginary billboard.*)
"A memorable evening'—Parker Ballantine"!

PARKER

(*Sits* DOWNSTAGE *of table* LEFT.)
It was a joke. You laughed for five minutes.

ANGELA

(*Crosses* LEFT *to chair* RIGHT *of table* LEFT.)
Sure I laughed! Even in the Chinese water torture the first few drops tickle a little! Not once have you forgot you're a critic! You've been sitting in judgment on me day and night for nineteen months! Criticizing me for not being a good enough housekeeper, criticizing me for—

PARKER

(*On latter "criticizing."*)
When have I ever criticized you? I've never criticized!

ANGELA

Always! Criticizing me for not finishing that damn scatter rug,
(*Points to loom on balcony.*)
criticizing me for not having a baby . . .
(*A beat.*)

PARKER

I have never criticized you, Angie. *You* are your critic, not I.

ANGELA

And now you're going to step on my play . . . . One thing I've done, one thing I've accomplished, and *you're* going to grind it under that witty, perceptive heel of yours!

PARKER

I'll call as I see it. It's my work. I have to do it.

DION

(*Gets up. Comes above sofa to* ANGELA. *Taking up* ANGE-
LA's *coat, holding it up behind her.*)
Come on, Angie. He doesn't want to help, we'll do it without him.
(*Goes* UPSTAGE.)

ANGELA

(*Moving away from* DION, *toward* PARKER.)
How noble you make it sound! "It's my work. I have to do it."
And is that your work too?
(*Pointing at the recorder on the table.*)
All that phony-baloney "Don't Write That Play"? That snide,
oily sarcasm? I've heard you! "You'll never finish Act One, you'll
never get a producer, you'll never get a director . . ."

DION

(*Coming up again with the coat.*)
Come on, Angie. Don't let him get you. That's the girl . . .

ANGELA

(*Allowing* DION *to put the coat on her.*)
A critic is supposed to point *up*, not *down*, you—you
hatchet-man! "You'll never get into rehearsal, you'll never get
out of town . . ."

DION

(*Putting purse and hatbox into* ANGELA's *hands.*)
Let's go, honey . . .

ANGELA

You know, Shakespeare's first play was an amateur's work too,
Mr. Ballantine!

(*A pause.* PARKER *is silent.*)

DION

Let's go . . . Please . . . Angie, damn it, I'm *double*-parked. . . .

PARKER

I'm sorry, Angie, but I've got to review your play, and review it truthfully. I've lied and evaded before. Six times. For Ivy. I can't do it again. It's a question of . . . keeping my self-respect . . .

ANGELA

Keep your self-respect! I don't want it! Just—just *quit hijacking mine!*

(*On the edge of tears, she runs out.* DION *picks up her two suitcases, goes to the door, turns and faces* PARKER.)

DION

She and I are coming back into town with the best damn play you've ever seen.

    (*Starts out.*)

PARKER

Who's in the suitcase; Tennessee Williams?

(DION *exits.* PARKER *moves* DOWNSTAGE. JOHN *comes down a few steps.*)

JOHN

    (*After a pause.*)

Are you *sure* there's no gunpowder in this apartment?

PARKER

Go eat a cookie.

JOHN

I never saw Angie like that . . .
> (*Coming down the remaining steps.*)

I don't like that Dion Kapakos . . . I don't like the way he called
me "Johnny-boy," and the way he helped Angie on with her
coat. He made it look as if he were helping her on with . . .
I don't know, some kind of a *bathrobe* . . .

PARKER

In thirty seconds we're going to have "Spank-the-Precocious-
Children Hour."

JOHN

What did I say? Didn't you see the way he sort of rubbed—

PARKER

> (*On "sort."*)

Go eat a cookie! Go on!

(*A beat.* JOHN *crosses quickly to the kitchen door, glances at* PARK-
ER'*s back, exits.* PARKER *strikes his palm, takes a breath, swallows
a portion of his anger. Crossing to coffee table he snaps up the recorder, holds it as though he might throw it, then weighs it on
his palm, his lips clenched. He calms, his eyes cloud. He turns
a knob on the recorder and flips a switch. There is a continu-
ous low buzzing sound. With the recorder on his palm,* PARKER
sits in a low chair. He watches the humming instrument dourly.
JOHN *enters from the kitchen, eating a cookie. He stands
near* PARKER.)

JOHN

Erasing?

PARKER

Yeah, I'm going to erase the whole business. She hit it on the nose. Snide, oily sarcasm, pointing down, not up. Precious, as you said in the very beginning.
(*A beat.*)

JOHN

But gee . . . it's a few months' work . . .

PARKER

Big deal . . .

(JOHN *sits on the ottoman. A pause. The recorder buzzes on.* JOHN *and* PARKER *watch it.*)

JOHN
(*Takes bite of cookie.*)
You know what's in the refrigerator?

PARKER

What?

JOHN

TV dinners.

(PARKER *sinks lower in his chair with a miserable "Oh, boy" as—*)

THE CURTAIN FALLS

ACT TWO

AT RISE: *The living room is bright with afternoon light. At the desk in the study,* PARKER *sits reading by dim lamplight. The study door is closed.*

The telephone rings, once, then again, then a third time. PARKER *is deaf to the ringing.* ESSIE *enters from the kitchen. She is in a hat, coat, and dress, her work finished. She carries an old canvas satchel, which she puts down near the foyer before answering the phone on the fourth or fifth ring.*

ESSIE

Good afternoon, Ballantine residence. This is the maid . . . Yes, Mr. Ballantine's here, but he's got himself locked up in his study and don't want to be disturbed . . . Mrs. Ballantine? *She's* up at the theater on Forty-fourth Street. They're having one last rehearsal before the big opening of her play tonight . . . Well, Mrs. Orr is here. That's Mrs. Ballantine's mother that's been here three or four weeks now. She's upstairs in the guest room, resting . . . John is still at school . . . Do you want me to get Mrs. Orr? . . . Oh. Well, who should I say called? Hello? Ma'am? Hello?

(*Looks at receiver, shrugs, hangs it up, and mutters.*)
Crazy phone calls in this apartment . . .

(*She picks up her satchel and goes out the front door, and that's
the last we see of* ESSIE *until the curtain calls. After a moment*
CHARLOTTE ORR *comes down the stairs. She is an attractive and
smartly dressed woman who looks as though she could improve the
management of Lord & Taylor and still have her afternoons free.*)

CHARLOTTE
(*Knocking on study door.*)
Parker, may I speak with you for a minute or two, please?

PARKER
I'm working, Charlie.

CHARLOTTE
No, you're not, dear, you're reading Agatha Christie.
(PARKER's *resigned shrug confirms this. She picks dust cloth
off floor* DOWNSTAGE *of sofa. Crosses* LEFT *to mirror.*)
Now come on, don't be stubborn; come out of your filing
cabinet.
(CHARLOTTE *moves away and adjusts the level of a few
pictures.* PARKER *rises, unlocks and opens the door.*)
I'll say this for that girl Essie; she's not much trouble to straighten
up after. Come on, take a breather. Once you've read fifty Agatha
Christies you've read them all.
(CHARLOTTE *exits into kitchen with dust cloth.*)

PARKER
(*Coming into the living room.*)
Ahh, I'm just looking for a foolproof way to bump off Lillian
Hellman and Clare Boothe Luce.
(*He sits disconsolately on the sofa.*)

CHARLOTTE
(*At kitchen door.*)
And if it works on them you use it on Angela, right?

PARKER
Right.

CHARLOTTE
Poor Parker . . .

PARKER
It ought to be part of the unwritten law; any man who catches
his wife alone with a typewriter—pow!
(*He fires his forefinger, then blows the smoke from its
muzzle and holsters it.*)

CHARLOTTE
(*Crosses* DOWNSTAGE *to chair* RIGHT *of table.*)
I had hoped that when she got back from Boston a truce would
be negotiated.
(*Indicating the bedroom.*)
Up in—headquarters.

PARKER
(*Shaking his head.*)
No, the barbed wire is still strung clear across the room. And
you can guess which piece of furniture it cuts right through
the middle of.

CHARLOTTE
(*Sitting.*)
Parker, have I put my nose into this business *once* during the

weeks I've been here? Have I lectured you or pushed you or given you even a *pinch* of advice?

PARKER

No, you haven't.

CHARLOTTE

I may have been a lousy mother but I am the best damn mother-in-law in existence.

PARKER

I don't imagine you were such a lousy mother, Charlie.

CHARLOTTE

Believe me, Parker, I was. The proof is in the puddingheads. In my fever to be mother *and* father to those poor girls I stifled all three of them, not just Angela. My deadly efficiency;
(*Rises. Crosses* CENTER STAGE *to* UPSTAGE *of ottoman.*)
I didn't even let them lick their own stamps! And look at them today. Angela in New York; married, but scared stiff she can't fulfill a woman's role. Sally in Paris; *she's* fulfilling a woman's role, all right, even by *French* standards, only she's not married. And Marge in *Kyoto* . . . the first non-Japanese ever to take the full twenty-year course in flower arranging . . . Now that I've got you smiling, Parker, I'm going to give you some advice.

PARKER

Charlie . . .

CHARLOTTE

I am, and you're going to listen! Being the ideal mother-in-law is all well and good,

(*Crosses* RIGHT *to sofa.*)

but ten minutes ago, up in my room, it suddenly dawned upon me just *why* mothers-in-law are always lecturing and pushing and giving advice to their sons-in-law. It's because we *know more,*

(*Sits sofa.*)

that's why!

PARKER

(*Yielding with amusement.*)

I give up. What's the advice?

CHARLOTTE

This evening, when we leave for the theater, you take that

(*Points to study.*)

little white box of yours and put some of the slips in your right-hand pocket and the rest of the slips in your left-hand pocket. That's all.

(*A beat.* PARKER *shakes his head.*)

PARKER

No. Mm-mnn. One pocket white, one pocket black; the same as always.

CHARLOTTE

You're a fool.

PARKER

Charlie, I saw your face when you came back from that preview last night! You looked as though you'd swallowed a dish of raw sweetbreads!

CHARLOTTE

All right, it's *not* the best play that's ever been written . . .
(PARKER *fixes her with a juryman's gaze. She shifts.*)
I'll even allow it isn't a very *good* play . . . . That critic in Boston,
how did he put it? "Fair-to-maudlin."

PARKER

That critic in Boston is one of my closest friends and a gen-
tleman of the old school, the one Sir Walter Raleigh attended.

CHARLOTTE

Oh, Lord, you're going to make me come right out and say it,
aren't you? All right, the play stinks. I sat there in that audience
and I wanted to *apologize to* all those poor people. Even the ones
who were there on passes.

PARKER

(*Rising.*)
One pocket white, one pocket black.

CHARLOTTE

(*Pause.*)
Lie a little! No one will execute you! Women will admire you,
men will feel compassion! And maybe Angela will understand
once and for all how much you love her. That wouldn't hurt,
you know.

PARKER

(*Crosses behind sofa.*)
Charlie, I'm a nut, I know I am, but I still have *nightmares* once
in a while about those fake reviews I wrote to keep Ivy happy.
And when I say nightmares, Charlie, I mean pajama-soakers!

I'm in a plane, a passenger plane, flying over mountains. The stewardess comes around with cocktails, and those six reviews are printed on the little napkins. Suddenly everybody is ugly-drunk and coming at me with their knives and forks. "Look, folks, look, I told the truth about *Helen of Troy!*" And then the pilot comes out, played by my high-school English teacher, and he taps me on the shoulder and informs me that we're overweight and one passenger has to jump . . .

CHARLOTTE

Good grief, I can imagine what *your* upbringing must have been . . . !

PARKER

(*Smiling.*)

A montage of hairbrushes and whistling belts. It gave me standards of right and wrong, though.

CHARLOTTE

Fine. Now, where are you going to look for your *third* wife, at Simon and Schuster?

PARKER

Charlie . . .

CHARLOTTE

(*Urgently.*)

Angela ran away from home once before, don't forget!

PARKER

She isn't running anywhere. Believe me, you know the girl, I know the woman. She's going to stay right *here*.

CHARLOTTE

Parker, please, listen to—
(*The doorbell rings.*)
Ohh . . .
(CHARLOTTE *rises and starts for the door.* PARKER *heads
for the study.*)
You stay away from that study; I'm not through with you yet!
(CHARLOTTE *opens the door.*)

IVY

(*In hall.*)
How do you do. I'd like to see Mr. Bal—

PARKER

Ivy! For God's sake—!

IVY

(*Sweeping in, crossing* DOWNSTAGE RIGHT *to* PARKER.)
Parker-Love! How *are* you!

(*She kisses* PARKER *exuberantly on his reddening cheek, while* CHAR-
LOTTE *stares, still holding the door open.* IVY LONDON *is glossy,
electric, glamorous, and admits to thirty-four years. She is carrying
an alligator handbag and wearing a slack suit under her swirling
coat of horizontal-stripe mink.*)

PARKER

What on earth are you—

IVY

(*Crosses* DOWNSTAGE *of sofa to* UPSTAGE CENTER LEFT.
Looking around apartment. Whirling away.)

Visiting, love, just visiting! What a *heaven* apartment! You must be taking *bribes*, darling! And look!

(*Looks up at gallery.*)

A loom! Angela weaves!

(*To* PARKER.)

How clever of her!

(*Now* CHARLOTTE *slams the door.*)

PARKER

Ivy—Charlie, this is Ivy London. Ivy; Charlotte Orr, Angela's mother.

IVY

(*Pointing at* CHARLOTTE. *Crosses* RIGHT *to* CHARLOTTE.)

Charlotte Orr? A decorator? Washington?

CHARLOTTE

Yes.

(*At* CENTER stage.)

IVY

(*Seizing* CHARLOTTE'S *hand.*)

But I *love* you! You did Lissy Ramarandhi's apartment! Where oh where did you get those marvelous ivory masks? I've been searching everywhere for them! Here, Washington, Dallas—

(*Looks at* CHARLOTTE.)

CHARLOTTE

There's a little shop in Johannesburg . . .

(*This creates a small breech, into which* PARKER *manfully jumps.*)

PARKER

I thought your show was in Boston, Ivy.

IVY

(*At ottoman.*)

Oh it was, darling, but we folded—we died. A horrible death.
They all but threw the usherettes at us.

(*Drops the alligator bag, shucks off her coat.*)

God, I'm exhausted! I just came from the train. May I sit?

(*Sits on sofa as she asks.*)

Oh, you were right, Parker! You were right! When oh when
will I learn to listen to you? There are some books that simply
cannot be made into musical comedies and *Twenty Thousand
Leagues Under the Sea* is one of them!

CHARLOTTE

You came visiting directly from the train?

IVY

(*A smile.*)

Yes. Well, there *is* something I have to discuss with Parker . . .

(*A beat.*)

CHARLOTTE

If you'll excuse me, I think I'll take a little nap.

(*She goes to the stairs.*)

PARKER

You don't have to, Charlie.

CHARLOTTE

(*Ascending.*)

It's been a pleasure meeting you, Miss London.

IVY

My pleasure, Mrs. Orr.

CHARLOTTE
(*On the landing.*)
I admired you when I first saw you in *Kiss Me Good-bye,* and since then I haven't missed one of your Washington engagements. It's heartwarming to see that your vivacity isn't only stagecraft and that your beauty is more than makeup and amber lights.
(*She exits* RIGHT.)

IVY

She hates me.

PARKER
(*A step to sofa.*)
What are you talking about? That was the nicest speech anyone ever made to you.

IVY

It was in code; you pick out every other word and you get the real message.

PARKER

Well, it was damn thoughtless of you to come bursting in this way, today of all days. Angie might have been here, and seeing you would hardly have helped her opening-night nerves.

IVY

Don't growl, Parker-Love. I made sure the coast was clear before I came.

PARKER

Made sure?

IVY

Yes, I did. And by the way, you have without a doubt the most
talkative maid this side of the New Dramatists League.

PARKER

(*Sitting on sofa.*)
All right, what do we have to discuss that rates a personal appearance?

IVY

(*Leaning back.*)
Please, let me catch my breath. I still have Boston in my lungs.
How's John?

PARKER

Dynamite.

IVY

I saw Angela in Boston; did she tell you?

PARKER

No.

IVY

We overlapped. My company came in a week before hers left.
We were all at the same hotel; her company, my company, and
one other company that was in town too. It was a madhouse.
There's no people like show people, all right; depraved, las-
civious, corrupt. . . . The goings-on! I tell you, that place was

simply a hotbed of—hot beds. Angela, though, looked wonderfully radiant.

PARKER

She always does.

IVY

And dear Dion Kapakos, the scourge of the summer theaters. The barns that faun has chased me through! I'm not bragging, darling; you know young genius types; it's either one little boy or every woman in sight. Of course the girls in our company found him rather preoccupied last week, what with all sorts of conferences, and long meetings in the wee small hours . . .

PARKER

Ivy . . . I can't thank you enough for this vivid picture of life on the road . . . but if there's something you want to discuss, get to it. I happen to be in the middle of some extremely important work.

(*He gestures toward the study.*)

IVY

My, you *are* inhospitable. It's been at least six months since we've seen each other, and all you can think of is—John! Johnny-Love!

(JOHN *has entered by the front door during the above line, in a zipper jacket, carrying a briefcase. A beat.*)

JOHN

(*At door.*)

Hello.

PARKER

Ivy's come to pay us a little visit.

IVY

Come here! Let me look at you!

      (JOHN *puts down the brief case, comes* DOWNSTAGE.)

My God, you're enormous! You're a giant!

      (*Taking* JOHN*'s hands.*)

How old are you now? No, no! Never mind! Never mind! Give
me a kiss.

      (JOHN *still loves* IVY *a little, despite the casual way he*
      can speak of her. It shows in the shyness with which he
      kisses her and receives her kiss. She holds him off at arm's
      length.)

My, oh my, oh my! At least we achieved one good thing between
us, didn't we, Parker?

PARKER

Oh, he's all right, I guess.

JOHN

How are you?

IVY

Wonderful, darling.

JOHN

Is your show coming in?

IVY

No, lamb, it's gone out, way out.

JOHN

I'm sorry.

IVY

Of course you are, sweet. Everybody is sorry, except Jules Verne.

(*She releases* JOHN's *hands. He unzips his jacket and removes it.*)

Do you have some cottage cheese around by any chance? I'm ravenous. Couldn't get a thing on the train; the dining car was all full of Egyptians or Shriners or something. Do you have some? Cottage cheese?

(*A beat.*)

PARKER

Probably . . .

IVY

Johnny-Love, do you think I could have a dab of it? Just about enough to put under a microscope?

(JOHN *looks to* PARKER.)

PARKER

Sure . . .

JOHN

Sure.

(*He goes* LEFT *to the kitchen.*)

IVY

With a dash of pepper, darling.

JOHN

Okay.

(*He exits.*)

IVY

What are you *feeding* him? He's grown three full inches!

PARKER

(*Smiling.*)

We don't feed him anything. Angie grabs one end; I grab the other; and we pull.

(*A smile between them.*)

IVY

(*Touches his shoulder.*)

I miss you so much . . .

PARKER

I miss you too, on my masochistic days.

(*Rises, and crosses* RIGHT, DOWNSTAGE *of sofa, to* RIGHT *of it.*)

IVY

(*A protest.*)

Parker . . .

PARKER

Come on, don't get sentimental just because you've had a flop. What did you come here to talk about?

(*A beat.*)

IVY

Something that isn't easy to say . . .

PARKER

Try a simple declarative sentence; a subject, a verb, an object.

IVY

All right . . . Well, Dion is the subject, and Angela's the object.
The verb, I'm afraid, is rather Anglo-Saxon.
            (PARKER *doesn't blink, he just stands looking at* IVY.)
It's true, my darling. It was all over the hotel. Bring me a Bible
and I'll swear on it.

(*Still no reaction from* PARKER. JOHN *enters from the kitchen* LEFT
with a plate of cottage cheese and a fork. PARKER *and* IVY, *eyes
locked, seem not to notice.*)

JOHN
            (*Standing at sofa.*)
Here's the cottage cheese.

PARKER

Hold the plate over her head and tilt it forward.

(JOHN *stares at him.*)

IVY

Daddy's joking, darling.
            (*Takes the plate from* JOHN'*s hand.*)
Thank you.
            (*She eats a nibble of cheese. Puts plate on coffee table.*)

PARKER

John, are you still *persona non grata* down at the Von Hagedorns'?

JOHN

Does that mean I can get in or I can't get in? I haven't got that straight yet.

PARKER

Can you get in?

JOHN

Yeah, I told Dr. Von Hagedorn I can get house seats for any show on Broadway.

PARKER

Go down there for a while, will you? Play with Godfrey? I want to tell Ivy how well you're doing in school and your head is swollen enough as it is.
>(*A beat.*)

JOHN

Okay.
>(*He takes up his jacket.*)

PARKER

Say good-bye. Ivy can't stay long.

JOHN

Good-bye . . .

(*He kisses* IVY*'s cheek, she kisses his.*)

IVY

Good-bye, my darling. It's been wonderful seeing you. This summer we're *definitely* going to spend a week at—Lake Whatever-it-is.

(JOHN *starts* UPSTAGE.)

PARKER

Come back in time to dress.

JOHN

Right.

IVY
(*Takes plate from coffee table.*)
You're obliging, John; I like that.

JOHN
(*At door.*)
He beats me.

(*Smiles at* PARKER. JOHN *exits.* IVY *absorbs herself in her cottage cheese. She wrinkles her nose.*)

IVY

Ich! Whose cottage does this cheese come from; the Ancient Mariner's?
(*She inspects it closely.*)

PARKER
(*Rising.*)
There's a soda fountain on the corner that's famous for cottage cheese. Tell them I sent you.

IVY

(*Puts plate on coffee table.*)

Parker, please, hear me out. I don't pretend I've come here with unselfish motives. I'm lonely. I've made a life for myself and I'm sick of it. I want you back. I want you back more than I've ever wanted *anything*, and that includes to be an actress at age eight. It's true about Angela and Dion. Long after they were done with their rewriting they were spending whole nights together, in her room. They were overheard, not saying anything. You don't deserve that kind of dirty deal. I did a thousand rotten things to you, and I lash myself with each of them every day and every night, but I never did *that* rotten thing, and you know it.

PARKER

(*Crossing* DOWNSTAGE *of sofa to ottoman. Picking up her coat.*)

You'd better go now, Ivy. You'll feel better when you have a show set for next season.

IVY

I'm telling the truth, Parker.

PARKER

(*Holding the coat open.*)

Angie will be here soon and I don't want her to see you.

(*A pause.*)

IVY

Okay, I'll go quietly.

(*Rises, slips her arms into the coat. Over her shoulder to* PARKER *as he helps her on with mink.*)

You haven't said one word about my new coat.

PARKER

I thought it was the old one turned sideways.

IVY

(*Goes* UPSTAGE, *kisses her finger tips.*)
I still love you. I will always love you. Ancestors of mine have died in institutions.

(IVY *exits.* PARKER *closes the door, stays facing it.* CHARLOTTE *appears on the landing.*)

CHARLOTTE

(*At railing.*)
How much do you believe?

(PARKER *turns, stares.*)

PARKER

(*Deeply shocked and offended.*)
Charlie . . . !

CHARLOTTE

(*Coming down the stairs.*)
Well, you didn't think I *wouldn't* eavesdrop, did you? In my book any woman who looks *that* good in slacks is a bitch, period.

PARKER

(*Coming* DOWNSTAGE, *shaking his head.*)
Boy . . .

CHARLOTTE

(*At* UPSTAGE CENTER RIGHT *back of sofa.*)
Well, how much do you believe?

PARKER

Only the last part, about the ancestors dying in institutions.
(*He crosses to sofa, sits.*)

CHARLOTTE

And the first part? Virtue dying in Boston?

PARKER

Do you even have to ask, Charlie?

CHARLOTTE

Yes, I do.

PARKER

(*Rises, crosses* DOWNSTAGE *of sofa* LEFT *to table.*)
I don't believe a word of it. Not one syllable. You can relax.

CHARLOTTE

That's what I expected. I, personally, think it's probably
true.

PARKER

(*Turns around.*)
What?

CHARLOTTE

I do!

PARKER

(*Steps* RIGHT *to* CENTER LEFT.)
Charlie, you're—you're her mother!

CHARLOTTE

Does that mean I have to be as naive as her husband?

PARKER

Naive? I'm— I'm—
(*A step closer to ottoman.*)

CHARLOTTE

You're *naive!* I *met* that Dion Kapakos last night; he's the young-est dirty old man I've ever seen!
(PARKER *sits on ottoman.*)
You leave Angela in his hands for three and a half of the most trying weeks in her life, you're free to visit her, but no, you sit right here on your fat integrity—how did you *think* they were going to wind up; bird-watching?
(*She sits on sofa.*)

PARKER

(*Leans to her.*)
You're—you're accusing your own daughter of infidelity!

CHARLOTTE

I'm accusing her of nothing but being frightened and vulnera-ble and insecure and having a fool for a husband.

PARKER

(*Rising.*)
I just don't understand you . . .

CHARLOTTE

I told you before; I'm a lousy mother.

(PARKER *paces, stops.*)

PARKER

Ivy London, as a source of information, is about as reliable as
a fortune cookie.

(*He paces again.*)

CHARLOTTE

(*Reminiscently.*)

I had a fortune cookie once that said, "A good name is better
than precious oil." Next day, Esso dropped seven points.

(*Picks up the plate of cottage cheese, sniffs it, grimaces.*)

You know, I could swear this stuff was absolutely fresh until
she touched it.

(*She puts down the plate.*)

PARKER

(*Sitting on ottoman.*)

No . . . I—I don't believe it. Not Angie. No.

CHARLOTTE

Only an egotist could have such faith in his wife. Parker,
last night at that theater I saw Angela hanging on to Kapakos's hand as if he were the traffic cop at the school crossing.
Pan that play tonight and it's ten to one you wake up tomorrow morning with more integrity and less wife than any man
in town.

(*Rises, steps to* PARKER, *pats his shoulder.*)

Please don't risk it, Parker. You two are all I've got to brag about,
now that I'm losing my figure.

PARKER

(*Looks up at her.*)

God! Is there a woman somewhere who doesn't demand dishonesty of a man?

CHARLOTTE

I've got news for you: honesty is *not* the most precious thing on earth; adding machines have honesty. *Love* is the precious thing, and if you want it you have to give something for it, just as you have to give for anything else worth having. You've barricaded yourself with rules of what's right and wrong, what's honest and dishonest, and you're saying to Angela, "Obey all my rules; I'm not interested in any of yours." Well, that's not a husband talking, it's a tyrant; and the trouble with being a tyrant is that sooner or later comes the—Boston Tea Party.

(*A pause.*)

PARKER

(*Rises, crosses* DOWNSTAGE LEFT.)

I do not believe that Angie slept with Dion, and I do not believe that she'll run off with him if I review her play truthfully.

CHARLOTTE

(*A long sigh, sits sofa.*)

All right, we'll change the subject. Let's talk about—geography. Tell me, Parker, how do you *know* the world is flat?

(ANGELA *enters through the front door, tired and subdued.*)

ANGELA

(PARKER *is facing front*—DOWNSTAGE LEFT.)

Hello.

CHARLOTTE

Angela! We'd forgotten all about you! We've been sitting here talking about Agatha Christie. Parker is positive she has no staying power.

ANGELA

(*In the foyer, removing her coat.*)

Hm?

PARKER

(*Turns to her, still* DOWNSTAGE LEFT.)

Joke. How was the rehearsal?

ANGELA

All right. Dion just wanted to keep everybody from sitting at home and worrying.

(*She hangs her coat in the closet.*)

CHARLOTTE

(*Sotto.*)

Well, he didn't quite succeed.

PARKER

I made a dinner reservation for the four of us, at six-thirty.

ANGELA

(*Coming* DOWNSTAGE.)

I'm sorry . . . I won't be able to make it . . . Dion's coming by at six; he's getting some gifts for the company; we want to give them out, and there are some other things he has to do at the theater.

> (*Going to stairs and going up.*)

Besides, I couldn't eat anyway. I'm going to lie down for a while.

PARKER

Butterflies in your stomach?

ANGELA

Butterflies, bats, birds, bees . . .

CHARLOTTE

There's a lifetime supply of telegrams on the dressing table.

ANGELA

You ought to see the pile at the theater. Sally sent a cable from Paris.

CHARLOTTE

> (*With unconcealed disgust.*)

I suppose *Marge* will send *flowers*.

PARKER

> (*Two steps to* CENTER STAGE.)

Angie—

> (ANGELA, *about to exit into the bedroom, stops and turns back.*)

Angie, I—I've decided to break down and wear my dinner jacket for once.

> (*A beat.*)

ANGELA

(*On gallery.*)
For me? For little old worthless me? You're going to put on your great big painful dinner jacket, with the heavy lead collar and all those steel spikes in the lining? Why, Ah declare, Mister Parker, you keep on this way, you're just goin' to spoil me rotten!

(*A beat.* JOHN *enters through front door, jacket slung over his shoulder.*)

JOHN

Hi.

(JOHN *crosses* DOWNSTAGE *to* CENTER STAGE. *A beat.*)

ANGELA, PARKER *AND* CHARLOTTE

Hello.

(*Another beat.* PARKER *exits into the study.* ANGELA *exits into the bedroom.* CHARLOTTE *rises, takes the plate of cottage cheese, exits into the kitchen.* JOHN *looks around at the suddenly empty room.*)

JOHN

Oh boy.

(*The lights fade to darkness. The telephone rings. A spot comes up on the telephone.* CHARLOTTE *answers it.*)

CHARLOTTE

Hello . . . Yes, she is, but I'd rather not disturb her unless it's urgent. Is there any message I could take? I'm her mother . . . Just a second.

(*Finds pencil and paper, writes.*)

Francine Huskey . . . Is that H-U-S-K-E-Y? Oh, I-E. Right. And you're calling in reference to?

(*Puts down pencil.*)

Passes for the show . . . Are you a friend of Angela's? Oh, I see. When was that? *Last* January? Oh, a *year ago* last January . . . And tell me, Miss Huskie, did you sit next to Angela for the *entire* train ride? . . . Just as far as Philadelphia . . . Well, Miss Huskie, I'm sure Angela will be delighted to send you free tickets. Any particular night? Saturday; of course . . . Are you sure one pair will be enough? Fine. Now just give me your address and we'll put the tickets right in the mail. Slowly now; I'm writing . . .

> (*With the phone tucked against her shoulder, she begins methodically tearing to shreds the piece of paper on which she wrote the name.*)

Mm-hmm . . . Mm-hmm . . . Is there any apartment number? Mm-hmm. Oh, thank *you*, Miss Huskie.

> (*Drops scraps of paper in basket* DOWNSTAGE *of phone.*)

And look, dear, for pity's sake don't be *selfish* about this; I mean, if you should happen to run into any of the *other* people who were on the train that day . . .

(*The spot fades out. The doorbell rings. The lights come up. It is six o'clock and the spring sunlight is beginning to wane. The stage is empty. The doorbell rings again.*)

PARKER

(*Offstage, in bedroom.*)

John, will you get it?

JOHN

(*Offstage* RIGHT, *upstairs.*)

Okay!

(JOHN *enters, dressed as before, he starts downstairs.*)

ANGELA

(*Offstage, in bedroom.*)

If it's Dion tell him I'll be down in two minutes!

(JOHN *goes* UPSTAGE *and opens the door. Sure enough, it is* DION, *in dinner clothes.*)

DION

(*Coming in as briskly as ever.*)

Hiya, Johnny-boy! How ya doin'?

(*Musses* JOHN*'s hair.*)

JOHN

(*Sarcastic. Closing the door.*)

Just great.

DION

(*Crossing* DOWNSTAGE CENTER.)

Isn't Angie ready yet?

JOHN

She said she'll be down in two minutes.

(*Crosses to mirror—fixes hair.*)

DION

(*At the foot of the stairs, calling up.*)

Hey, Angie! I'm double-parked!

(JOHN *idles* LEFT *toward the window.*)

ANGELA
(*Offstage, in bedroom.*)
I'll be as quick as I can!

JOHN
(*Peering out through the curtains.*)
Oh boy, there's a cop . . .

DION
(*Dashing* LEFT.)
Where? Where?
(JOHN *steps aside,* DION *looks anxiously through the window.*)
Where? Where?

JOHN
At the police station.

(DION *turns, stares at* JOHN. JOHN *smiles, then crosses toward the stairs.*)

DION
You're a real funny kid, aren't you?

JOHN
I get a yock once in a while.

(JOHN *starts up the stairs, then stops, as the bedroom door opens and* PARKER *emerges in dinner clothes.*)

PARKER
(*Into bedroom.*)
It's a *lovely* gown; I just said it's an unusual *color*, that's all.

(*He closes the door, and turns. He is facing toward* DION. *A beat.*)

DION

Hello.

PARKER

Hello.

(JOHN *resumes climbing the stairs as* PARKER *starts down.*)

You'd better get a move on; it's after six.

JOHN

I know.

(JOHN *exits* RIGHT. PARKER *comes down, goes to the liquor cabinet near the study door, and takes out a glass.*)

DION

(*Moving to* CENTER STAGE.)

That's a clever little fellow you've got there. How did you get him away from the Philip Morris people?

(PARKER *throws him a glare, then pours whisky.*)

Thanks, I will. Straight Scotch.

(PARKER *gets out another glass.*)

Do you always drink before an opening?

PARKER

(*Pouring.*)

Only when I'm expecting a snake bite.

(PARKER *holds out the drink,* DION *takes it.*)

DION

Thanks.
(*Toasting.*)
Cheers.

PARKER

(*Clearly, succinctly, and meaningfully.*)
Mud in your eye.
(*They drink.* PARKER *crosses to* RIGHT *end of sofa and sits.*)

DION

You know, you're an interesting guy, Parker. I've been doing some thinking about you.
(*Crosses to* LEFT *end of sofa.*)

PARKER

Have you, now.

DION

Ya. . . . Have you ever been analyzed?
(DION *drinks.*)

PARKER

Not all of me; little specimens once or twice . . .

DION

(*Smiling, crosses* RIGHT, UPSTAGE *of sofa, to* RIGHT *of it.*)
Not bad. But seriously, old man, look at the facts; you slammed Ivy London with a brutal review, didn't you?—and now you're all set to give Angie the very same treatment; it seems to me that you've got a pretty deep *hostility* toward the women you marry.
(*Long pause.*)

PARKER

Do I get to look at some ink blots, or is that it?

DION

Oh, come on now, don't get defensive. I'm in analysis myself, and it's done me a hell of a lot of good. Man, I was aggressive, destructive, a compulsive braggart, self, self, self, that's all I ever thought about.

PARKER

That was *before* analysis?
> (ANGELA *enters from the bedroom, looking smashingly beautiful even if her gown is an unusual color. She carries a purse and a fur stole.* DION *moves to the foot of stairs.* PARKER *drifts to* CENTER STAGE.)

Well, she's *prettier* than Tennessee Williams anyway.

DION

> (*To* ANGELA, *as she descends the stairs.*)

Prettier than anyone on earth.

ANGELA

> (*Crosses* DOWNSTAGE TO LEFT *of ottoman.*)

Thank you. Did you get the gifts?

DION

They're in the car. I got cuff links for the men, earrings for the women, and one of each for the rest of the cast.

(DION *smiles,* ANGELA *smiles,* PARKER *ignores them, sips his drink.* DION *takes* ANGELA's *stole, holds it for her.*)

ANGELA

(*Refusing it, eyes on* PARKER.)

No, not yet, Dion.

DION

Angie, I'm—

ANGELA

You're double-parked; I know. But we'll have to stay for another minute or two. I have to speak to Parker.

(PARKER *turns to face* ANGELA. *A beat.* DION *puts the stole on a chair.* ANGELA'*s eyes are still on* PARKER.)

What time is it?

DION

(*Glancing at his watch.*)

Ten after six.

ANGELA

All right . . .

(ANGELA *crosses to* LEFT *end of sofa.* DION *crosses to table* LEFT *and puts drink on it—stands at* RIGHT *of table.*)

Are you still planning to cover the show?

(*A beat.*)

PARKER

You know I am.

ANGELA

I don't want you to. I want you to call the paper and let Harvey Rittenhouse cover it.

PARKER

Harvey Rittenhouse is a blob.
   (*A beat.*)

ANGELA

   (*Great tension.*)
I don't want you to review my play.

PARKER

I'm sorry, Angie. I'm going to.
   (*A beat.*)

ANGELA

All right . . . I have a list here . . .
   (*Opening her purse, showing a folded sheet of paper.*)
A list of some of the things you've said about the play . . . Things
like—calling it a Hupmobile, and saying it would decay teeth. . . .
When you sit down in that aisle seat tonight, I'm handing this list
to Sid Champlain. I've spoken to him about this situation, and
he feels that a critic has no right coming into a theater as prejudiced as you are about *A Houseful of Silence.* If you review it, no
matter what kind of review you write, he's going to complain—
and complain *loudly*—to the League of New York Theatres, and
the paper, and whoever else will be interested in hearing him. He's
going to make trouble for you, all the trouble he can.
   (*Crosses* DOWNSTAGE *to* RIGHT *of ottoman.*)
You're not the most well-liked critic, you know.
   (*She pushes the list back into her purse, closes it. A pause.*)

PARKER

   (*Crossing to* ANGELA.)
Angie, you're under a terrific strain and you're saying things—
   (PARKER *tries to hold her arms.*)

ANGELA

(*On "and" as she pulls away.*)

Don't you make excuses for me! I know exactly what I'm doing!

PARKER

Then you ought to have your— I'm your *husband*, Angie.

ANGELA

(*Turns to him.*)

No, you're not! That's something else you said; on opening night you're a critic and I'm a playwright, and I'm not your wife. Then you're not my husband either.

(*Crosses* RIGHT, DOWNSTAGE *of coffee table.*)

DION

(*Moving closer to* ANGELA's *side.*)

You *did* say that, Parker. I was standing right here.

ANGELA

It's after six. It's opening night.

(*Crosses* RIGHT *to liquor cabinet, then* DOWNSTAGE *to* RIGHT *of sofa.*)

I'm a playwright and you're a critic; that's all. And I'm not going to let you come gunning for me with the kind of black-box review you've been dreaming up ever since I began the play! Well? Do I give the list to Champlain?

PARKER

Is that when you stopped being my wife; at six o'clock?

(*A beat.*)

ANGELA

When did you stop being my husband?
(*A beat.*)

PARKER

Ivy was here this afternoon. She says there was gossip in Boston
about you two.

(ANGELA *stays facing* PARKER, *motionless, angry.*)

DION
(*Turns and gets glass from table.*)
You know gossip, old man. Especially in Boston. I mean, what
the hell else is there to do *but* gossip?
(*He drinks, a pause.*)

PARKER

She said he was in your room, all night . . .

ANGELA

(*Coolly.*)
It's after six o'clock. Since when does a critic ask questions about
a playwright's personal affairs?

PARKER

Don't play games with me, Angie.

ANGELA

I'm not playing games.
(*Crosses to* DOWNSTAGE RIGHT.)
You think you can—throw away *one* half of me and still
cross-examine the other half? I am *one person* and you disowned

me and it's a little bit late to start wondering if anything happened in my room! *You should have been there!*

PARKER

You know why I stayed away.

ANGELA

(*Crosses to* DOWNSTAGE *corner of sofa. Her hurt showing again.*)

No I don't! I don't know anything! All I know is you lied for Ivy *six times*, and for me you won't even just keep quiet! Well, *Dion* feels differently about me! *Dion* was with me, believing in me and helping me, treating me as an equal, as an adult, not patronizing me and making fun of me!

(*Pointing at* DION.)

Dion happens to love me!

(PARKER *stares at* DION, *who would rather be anywhere else on earth.*)

DION

(*Squirms, crosses* DOWNSTAGE *a step.*)

Well, I *do* . . .

PARKER

(*Venomously.*)

You're double-parked.

ANGELA

Oh, no! No, he isn't! Not tonight.

(*Crosses* LEFT *to* DION.)

Tonight, I don't have a husband. You made the rules, not I. Now, tell me something, when does opening night end?

    (DION *helps her on with coat.*)
At midnight, at two, at six in the morning? When? Because
there's a party tonight after the show and Dion's taking me,
    (*She looks at* DION.)
and I'd like to know where I stand, and how much I should drink
and when I should leave and whose house I should go home to!
    (PARKER *stares at her, wordless.*)
Well?

    (*She waits another moment, then starts for the door.* DION *follows.*)

PARKER

Angie!
    (*She stops and turns.* PARKER *takes a ticket envelope from
his pocket, shows it, drops it on the table.*)
You win. Leave them at the box office in Harvey's name. I'll
call the paper.
    (*A beat.* ANGELA *is suddenly uncertain, dismayed. She
comes* DOWNSTAGE *and hesitantly takes the envelope.*)
One of those tickets was for John.

ANGELA

    (*Putting the envelope into her purse and taking out two
tickets.*)
I have *two* tickets, for you *and* for John. Next to the single that
Mom has.
    (*An uncomfortable beat.*)
Will you get the elevator, Dion?

DION

Right.
    (*He exits.*)

PARKER

Just leave one of them. I'm not going.
(*A beat.*)

ANGELA

All right.
(*Putting one ticket on the table, returning the other one
to her purse.*)
If that's the way you want it . . .
(*She starts* UPSTAGE.)

PARKER

It isn't. Nothing is the way I want it.

(ANGELA *stops at the door, and* turns.)

ANGELA

You should have loved me enough to *say* the play was good,
even if it isn't.

PARKER

No. No, that's not love.

ANGELA

Says who?

(*She exits.* PARKER *stands for a moment, then picks up his glass,
crosses to the liquor cabinet and pours another drink.*)

CHARLOTTE
(*Offstage* RIGHT, *upstairs.*)
Angela?

     (Enters on the landing, and goes to the bedroom door.)

Angela?

     (She opens the door.)

PARKER

She's gone.

CHARLOTTE

     (Turning.)

Why didn't she wait? I wanted to give her a speech about fortitude in the face of adversity.

     *(*PARKER *drinks.* CHARLOTTE *starts down the stairs. She is wearing an evening gown and a matching coat, and she carries a purse.)*

Don't just stand there; compliment me.

PARKER

You look swell.

CHARLOTTE

Thanks. I feel like Marie Antoinette, all dressed up for the guillotine.

PARKER

That ticket there is for John. Take it. I'm not going.

     (A beat.)

CHARLOTTE

     (Crossing DOWNSTAGE *to* CENTER STAGE.*)*

Not going at all?

PARKER

That's right.

CHARLOTTE

Well . . .
(*Going to the table, taking the ticket.*)
What finally got through that thick head of yours?
(*She puts the ticket into her purse.*)

PARKER

Just one of those steel balls they use to demolish buildings.

(*He drinks.* CHARLOTTE *looks at him with concern.*)

CHARLOTTE

Parker—

PARKER

Do you have money for dinner?

(JOHN *enters on the landing, wearing his best blue suit. He stops.*)

CHARLOTTE

No.

PARKER

(*Taking out his wallet.*)
I made a reservation at a place right across from the theater.
Chateau something . . .
(*He takes bills from the wallet.*)

JOHN

Aren't you having dinner with us?

(*A beat.* PARKER *doesn't turn.*)

PARKER

No, I'm not.
>   (*He gives the bills to* CHARLOTTE.)

CHARLOTTE

He isn't feeling well.

JOHN
>   (*Coming down a few steps.*)

You're going to meet us at the theater?
>   (*A beat.*)

PARKER

No. I'm not going to the theater. Charlie has a ticket for you.

JOHN
>   (*Coming farther down.*)

That's crazy . . . you went when you had the fractured hip, didn't you?

PARKER

I don't feel well and I'm not going, that's all.
>   (*He drinks.*)

JOHN

Who's going to cover the show?

PARKER

All the other critics. Don't worry; justice will be done.

JOHN
>   (*Stepping toward* PARKER.)

Who's going to cover it for *our* paper?

PARKER

I don't know . . .

JOHN

Harvey Rittenhouse?

PARKER

(*Busying himself with more whisky-pouring.*)
Probably . . .

CHARLOTTE

(*Moving to the foyer.*)
Come on, John; you're stuck with me; resign yourself.

JOHN

(*Not hearing her, facing* PARKER's *back.*)
Why aren't you going?

PARKER

(*Turning to him.*)
Because I'm not feeling well! Now go on with Charlie!

JOHN

(*Crossing close to* PARKER.)
You said as long as you were living you would never let Harvey
Rittenhouse—

PARKER

(*On "let."*)
*I'm not going because Angie doesn't want me to! Now will you get
out of here?* It's six-thirty, almost . . .

JOHN
(*A step to* UPSTAGE *of sofa.*)
You said sometimes you had to hurt people . . .

PARKER
Charlie—
(*He puts down the glass.*)

JOHN
You said you would hurt them more if you lost your self-respect!

PARKER
(*Over the above.*)
Charlie, will you get him out of here?

(CHARLOTTE *comes* DOWNSTAGE *and tries to pull* JOHN *away.*)

JOHN
(*Continuing without a break.*)
That was the most important thing you ever told me, all that
about self-respect!

PARKER
I was wrong! I changed my mind!

CHARLOTTE
(*Taking* JOHN'*s arm.*)
John—

JOHN
You said you would never sell a—

PARKER

(*On "would."*)

Will you stop telling me what I said? You're like that damn recording machine in there! Go on. It's late.

CHARLOTTE

(*Trying to draw* JOHN *away.*)

John . . .

(JOHN *won't move. A beat.*)

JOHN

Come on to the theater!

(*Reaches forward to take* PARKER'S *shoulders.*)

PARKER

Holy—!

(PARKER'S *hand comes up, then he ducks into the study, slams the door, leans against it.* JOHN *pulls away from* CHARLOTTE, *rushes to the study door and begins kicking it again and again.* PARKER *claps a hand over his eyes.* CHARLOTTE *pulls* JOHN *away from the door.*)

CHARLOTTE	JOHN
Stop it! John! John—now stop! Stop!	Let go of me! Let me go! I'll kick him! I'll kick that door! Let go of me!

(PARKER *opens the door. He musters his last vestige of authority.*)

PARKER

(*In doorway.*)

Now you listen to me, John. You go with Charlotte and you

go to dinner and you go to the theater, or so help me God I'll
give you a . . .

(*A pause.* CHARLOTTE *releases* JOHN. *He stands angrily.*)

Now do as I tell you.

(*A beat.*)

JOHN

(*Starts quietly.*)

I don't care if you *don't* go to the theater. I don't care if you
never go any place. I don't care if you get inside there and lock
the door and stay there until you're dead.

(*He turns, walks* UPSTAGE *and exits.*)

CHARLOTTE

(*Looks inquiringly at* PARKER.)

Parker . . .

PARKER

Stay with him . . .

(CHARLOTTE *hurries* UPSTAGE *and exits.* PARKER *wipes a
hand over his face. After a moment he takes his glass from
the liquor cabinet, and drinks. A pause. He looks at the
phone, goes to it. A beat. He puts down the glass, picks up
the receiver, dials a number, picks up the glass, drinks.
The sun is gone now, a dusky blueness has infiltrated the
room, and grows deeper until curtain.*)

Extension eighty-three . . . Leonard? Parker. Is Lee there? . . .
Well, leave a note for him, will you? Tell him that I'm not cov-
ering the opening tonight. The tickets are at the box office in
Harvey's name . . . Personal reasons . . . Yes. Now look, don't
you start telling me what I said! . . . How should I know where
Harvey is? Try the Laffmovie on Forty-second Street!

(He hangs up, goes to the liquor cabinet, refuels, drinks. A pause. He goes to the sofa, takes the phone, sits on the sofa, pulling the phone down beside him. One-handed, he lifts the receiver and dials the operator.)

Western Union, please . . . Gramercy 7-3935.

(Drinks.)

I'd like to send a telegram, please . . . Angela Ballantine . . . *Ballantine.* B as in beer, A as in ale, L as in lager—that's right; Ballantine. Forty-fourth Street Theater, East of Broadway, New York. This is to be delivered immediately.

(During this he stretches out full-length on the couch, with the phone sitting on his chest.)

"Congratulations . . . on the opening . . . of your first play. Certain it will be . . . a huge success . . . bringing you fame . . . fortune . . . and deep and enduring personal happiness." That's signed "Lillian Hellman and Clare Boothe Luce" . . . Gramercy 7-3935; Parker Ballantine.

(He hangs up, drinks, thinks, puts down the glass, looks at the phone, lifts the receiver, hesitates, slowly dials a number. A pause.)

Ivy? . . . You're a rat. And a louse. And several other small animals . . . *Sure* she denied it! Sort of . . . You're a rat; I just wanted to get it on the record . . . I *am* miserable. I'm kindly old Uncle Ben, all alone in the gathering twilight, hanging out the old placard, "Rooms For Rent." In the Greek version I shoot myself . . . No, it's just a joke. . . . Hey, Ivy, what are you doing? . . . Come on over, will you? Say funny things and rub my back for me? . . . Oh, Florence Nightingale is smiling down upon you . . . Run, do not walk . . . Hey, Ivy, Ivy-Rat, hey . . . I've been thinking it over about your Helen of Troy . . . It was a *beautiful* performance, Ivy, just *beautiful* . . .

THE CURTAIN FALLS

ACT THREE

The blinds have been drawn beneath the window curtains, and several lamps have been lighted. PARKER *is still supine on the couch, his back against its arm and his feet up. His shoes are on the floor, his dinner jacket is draped over a nearby chair, the telephone is back where it belongs, and the Scotch bottle is near at hand.* PARKER *takes it up and refills his glass.*

PARKER

I want to drink; I don't want to eat!

(IVY *enters from the kitchen with a tablecloth.*)

IVY

Just come drink at the table for a while; it *looks* nicer.

PARKER

No. Appearances count for nothing with us alcoholics.

(*During the following,* IVY *removes whatever is on the dining table and spreads the cloth. She is wearing another slack suit, or maybe these are lounging pajamas. Anyway, they're bright red and interesting to watch. She has on a postage stamp apron as well.*)

IVY

To think I would see the day when my old Parker would refuse a dish of Beef Stroganoff.

PARKER

(*Raising himself.*)

Beef Stroganoff?

IVY

Mm-hmm.

PARKER

You're kidding.

IVY

Scout's honor.

PARKER

(*Dropping back.*)

Ah, you can't even boil an egg; where did you learn to make Beef Stroganoff?

IVY

(*Sets flowers on table.*)

In the cab, on the way over here. "Place container in four-hundred-and-fifty degree oven for thirty minutes. Remove cover and serve." God bless America.

(*She exits into the kitchen.*)

PARKER

(*Calling after her.*)

All right, if it's Beef Stroganoff I'll eat. We'll just put a little Scotch in it, that's all.

(*Looks at his watch, listens to it.*)
What time is it?

IVY

(*Offstage.*)
Twenty-five of eight.

PARKER

(*Removing the watch.*)
What?

IVY

(*Entering with plates and napkins.*)
Twenty-five of eight.

(*During the following,* IVY *sets the table for two.*)

PARKER

(*Setting the watch, then winding it.*)
Eight o'clock the curtain goes up . . .

IVY

Revealing onstage an egg the size of a zeppelin.
(IVY *crosses* LEFT *into kitchen.*)

PARKER

(*Drinks.*)
At this moment, backstage at the Forty-fourth Street Theatre,
Dion Kapakos, boy louse, is feeding pep and optimism to his
hardy band of tomorrow's unemployed . . . while Angie flits from
dressing room to dressing room, distributing earrings and cuff
links; pennies on the eyelids of a corpse. And down the street
comes the rat-like figure of Harvey Rittenhouse,

(IVY *enters and crosses to table with silver and salt and
pepper shakers.*)
his tiny nose twitching with uncontrollable glee. What joy for
Harvey to enter a theater that is neither church basement nor
converted bordello!
(*He winds his watch some more.*)

IVY

(*Standing* UPSTAGE *of table, holding silver.*)
Does the knife go on the right or the left?

PARKER

In my back, baby, in my back.

IVY

(*Trying to decide where knife goes.*)
One-potato, two-potato, three-potato, four; five-potato,
six-potato, seven-potato, more.
(*She places the knife.*)

PARKER

(*Shakes the watch, listens.*)
I broke the spring . . .
(*Looks at* IVY, *she looks at him.*)
Symbolism . . . I cannot stand symbolism!
(*He hurls the watch across the room.*)

IVY

Parker!

PARKER

Don't worry, it's just the old watch my father gave me on his
deathbed . . .

(IVY *retrieves the watch, inspects it, puts it someplace.*
PARKER *sits up.*)
That worm Kapakos . . . I was supposed to be his father. "You're
a *father image* for me," he said.

IVY

(*Returning to the table.*)
Well, he *is* Greek, you know. Oedipus, and all that.

PARKER

Now I'm nobody's father image. John despises me.
(PARKER *lies on sofa—head at* RIGHT *end.*)

IVY

(*Finished with table setting, crossing* UPSTAGE LEFT.)
He'll get over it. What do you want on your salad?

PARKER

(*Sitting up.*)
Scotch.
(IVY *exits into kitchen.* PARKER *leans back, slips to floor
between coffee table and sofa.* PARKER *lies there for a
moment, then addresses an unseen inquisitor.*)
You ask me, sir, how I, a man of evident breeding and intellect,
come to be lying here in this Bowery doorway.
(PARKER *on floor,* LEFT *arm on coffee table,* RIGHT *arm
on floor.*)
. . . I shall tell you. When I was a youth in the small town of
Innocence, Nebraska, there chanced to fall into my hands a
volume, bound in green buckram; the critical essays of Max
Beerbohm. I read the volume once, twice, three times; ambi-
tion flamed in my bosom; I, too, would be a drama critic! Tying

together all my belongings in a polka-dot kerchief, I bade adieu to my kindly old parents and set forth on foot for New York City. When at last I reached the sprawling metropolis, I sought employment at the offices of its leading journal, and there, in the humble capacity of copy boy, I won the friendship of the kindly old drama critic, Sage Arbiter.

(*Sits up, both arms on coffee table.*)

He taught me all he knew, and then some. One day Destiny pointed its finger; my kindly old mentor fell victim to a tainted halibut. "Catastrophe!" cried the editor. "Who shall cover tonight's opening of the revival of Henrik Ibsen's immortal *The Wild Duck?*" Ah, you have guessed it! Yes, it was I who ran with heart thumping to the glittering theater and sat on the edge of the critic's aisle seat. The production was a disaster. I returned to the paper and wrote my first review. "If this is *The Wild Duck,*" I said, "then I'll just have the vegetable plate." Sixteen years later I was at the top of my profession. No symposium on the state of the theater was complete without my expressions of asinine optimism. I had a son who worshiped me, and a wife who adored me. The world was my oyster, and each day a pearl. And then, one morning, my wife turned to me, and smiled, and said, "Darling, I have an idea . . ."

(*Reaching out.*)

Please, sir, thirty cents for a bottle of muscatel . . .

(PARKER *gets back on sofa, head at* RIGHT *end.* IVY *enters with two bowls of salad. She places them on the table, steps back and surveys her handiwork.*)

IVY

That looks right, doesn't it?

PARKER

What time is it?

IVY

(UPSTAGE *of table—looks at watch.*)

Now look, this is a woman's wrist watch; if I have to read it more than once in an hour I go blind. It's seventeen minutes of eight, and that's the last report you get.

(*Draws out a chair* RIGHT *of the table, sits.*)

Whew! I'm exhausted.

(*She fans herself.*)

PARKER

(*Patting couch beside him.*)

Come here.

(*A beat.* IVY *rises, removes apron, puts it over the* CENTER STAGE *chair, goes to the couch and sits where* PARKER *patted. He draws her down. They kiss, lengthily and thoroughly.*)

IVY

(*As she sits up.*)

I tell you, they don't kiss like that any more . . .

PARKER

You say we've got thirty whole minutes before that Stroganoff is done?

(*He draws her down, they kiss again. Then they look at each other.*)

IVY

(*Sitting up.*)

No, we're going to eat. *Then* we'll pour some black coffee into you, and *then* we'll go over to my place. And we'll leave the dishes for Angela.

PARKER

Your place?

IVY

Mm-hmm.
(*She takes* PARKER'S *glass, sips.*)

PARKER

No . . . you don't want me now . . .

IVY

Oh, don't I! Ha! I'm not letting you out of my sight from here on in. That's a blood oath.
(*She sips.*)

PARKER

I'm just a husk of a man . . .

IVY

(*Leans forward, puts* RIGHT *hand under his head.*)
Ah, my poor baby, she really hurt you, didn't she . . .
(PARKER *nods,* IVY *feeds him some Scotch.*)
It never fails; the girls who wear those flouncy little dirndls are bitches, every one of them.

(PARKER *coughs.*)

PARKER

(*Pushes glass away and sits up.*)
No, no, not Angie. No, she isn't . . .

IVY

(*Picks up empty bottle from floor and crosses* UPSTAGE *of
sofa to liquor cabinet.*)

Taking your tickets from you? Locking you out of the theater?
Who does she think she is, the *Shuberts* or something?

(*Takes fresh bottle and pours drink. Crosses to* UPSTAGE
of sofa, leans over back of it. To PARKER.)

Oh, Parker, you were right to pan my Helen of Troy! You were!
I can face that now! It *was* Troy, New York! It was!

(*They kiss passionately.*)

I love you with all my heart!

PARKER

(*Kisses* IVY *lightly, pats her cheek.*)
You said you would rub my back for me . . .

IVY

(*She takes his arm and helps him over.*)
Oh, yes! Yes! Turn over, darling!

PARKER

(*Turning over.*)
Easy now; I'm a wounded veteran. . . .

(IVY *begins massaging his back. He reaches out.*)

Buy a poppy, sir?

(IVY, RIGHT *knee on sofa, soothingly rubbing the small of his back.*)

IVY

(*Soothingly rubbing.*)
Aaaaaahhhhhhh . . .

PARKER

Mmmmmmmmmmmmmm . . . She's not a *bitch*, but you know, she's not exactly a woolly lamb either.

IVY

I'll say she's not! Look what she's done to you. Pulverized you.

PARKER

Higher. Mmmmmmmm . . .

(*She massages his shoulder.*)

IVY

What kind of life can you have with her now? Can you ever stand up to her again, put her in her place?

PARKER

No, I can't . . . I guess I can't . . . Not after tonight.

IVY

She's trampled on you! I loathe her!
(*Rubbing him hard.*)

PARKER

Ow!

IVY

Oh, I'm sorry, darling, I'm sorry!
(*Kisses the back of* PARKER's *neck, rubs it tenderly.*)
Aaaahhhh . . .
(*A pause.*)

PARKER
(*Turns to look at her.*)
Those weren't my tickets I gave her . . . . They were something
infinitely more precious than my tickets!
(*He would rise, but* IVY's *massaging pushes him down.*)

IVY
That's right! And she took them from you!

PARKER
And now Harvey Rittenhouse has them!
(*Again he would rise, again* IVY *holds him down.*)

IVY
She's finished the marriage completely! It's done! Kaput!

PARKER
It is . . .
(*Interrupting massage, turning and sitting up—end
of sofa.*)
It's true . . . It is . . . kaput. Everything. Angie, John, me . . .
(*Rubs his forehead woozily.* IVY *turns, sits on legs on* RIGHT
end of sofa.)
I said I wouldn't sell out, and she scared me, and I *did* sell out,
and everything's . . . kaput . . . finished . . .

IVY
(*Throwing her arms around him.*)
I'm *glad* she's done it, my darling! I'll make things right for you!
And for John too! I'm a new Ivy, you'll see I am! Oh, Parker-Love—

(*She tries to kiss him, he fends her off clumsily.*)

PARKER

Ivy . . . Ivy . . . I've got to get to that theater . . .
(*Leans forward, tries to get up.*)

IVY

What?
(*Both arms around his neck.*)

PARKER

I've got to get to that theater, and see the show, and beat Harvey back to the office and *write my review!*

(*He tries to get to his feet,* IVY *pulls him down.*)

IVY

You can't go to the theater! It's too late! It's, it's—oh, damn this watch!

(*She turns away toward the light, and squints at her watch.* PARKER *rises unsteadily.*)

PARKER

Have to . . . Have to risk her leaving . . .

IVY

(*Catching his arm.*)
It's ten of eight! It's too late!

PARKER

Curtain won't go up till ten after. It never does; they announce it for eight, it goes up at ten after. They're liars, all of them . . .
(*Pulls his arm free and starts* LEFT *for his dinner jacket in gluey slow-motion.*)

Got twenty minutes . . . Cab up Eighth Avenue, cut across
Forty-fourth. Make it in plenty of time . . .

IVY

(*Still on sofa.*)
You're drunk, Parker!

PARKER

Ten more drinks and I'd still be a better critic than Harvey
Rittenhouse . . .
  (*Starts getting into his dinner jacket, it's not easy.*)
Have to risk her leaving . . . No chance for anything if I stay
here . . .

IVY

(*Rising, crossing to* LEFT *end of sofa.*)
You can't go to the theater in this condition! You're pie-eyed!

PARKER

(*Draws himself up, suddenly authoritative.*)
Actors can act when they're drunk, can't they? Playwrights can
playwrite when they're drunk. Well, damn it, I say a critic can
critic when he's drunk!
  (*Lapsing back into booziness. Looks down at his shoes.*)
Shoes . . . Must wear shoes . . . Never go to the theater without shoes . . .

(*He starts back toward the couch.* IVY *snatches up his shoes and
clutches them to her bosom.*)

IVY

I won't let you do this! I won't!

(PARKER *crosses to her between coffee table and sofa.*)
Come to *my* place, Parker! Let her have her little victory!
(*A beat.*)

PARKER

(*Pointing an icy finger.*)
Ivy . . . you give me those shoes . . . or I will dissect you, and put you in suitcases, and ship you to New Haven and Boston and Philadelphia and Washington.

(IVY *gives him the shoes. He sits on the couch, and laboriously puts them on.*)

IVY

You don't have a ticket! How will you get into the theater?

PARKER

Buy one from somebody. Ten dollars, twenty dollars; mezzanine, balcony . . .
(*Looks up, chuckles.*)
Ha, ha . . . Somebody's gonna get twenty dollars for a balcony seat for *Houseful of Silence!* Ha, ha . . .
(*He is back to the shoes.*)

IVY

I'm going with you! I'm not letting you out of my sight!
(*She runs* UPSTAGE, *gets her coat from the closet.*)

PARKER

(*Pulls lace out of* RIGHT *shoe and holds it up, then takes* LEFT *one and throws them* UPSTAGE.)
Shoelaces are unnecessary . . .

(*He rises and weaves toward the study.* IVY *comes* DOWNSTAGE, *putting on her coat.*)

IVY

(*At* CENTER LEFT.)

Review the play! Good! Go ahead! You'll blow the marriage into tiny pieces! Good! The sooner the better!

PARKER

(*Going* RIGHT *into study.*)

Cross that bridge when I come to it . . . Can't let everything be ruined without putting up a fight . . .

> (*He takes his black box from the desk, returns to the living room, puts the box on the coffee table and begins transferring its hundred slips of paper by fistfuls into his trouser pockets, side jacket pockets, breast pocket, every pocket.* IVY *watches fearfully, her hand over her mouth.* PARKER *mutters on as he arms himself.*)

Thinks because she's a playwright I have to stop being a critic. . . . Thinks she can scare me into giving my tickets to Harvey Rittenhouse. . . . Thinks I'm afraid of Dion Kapakos and Oedipus and S. P. Champlain and the League of New York Theatres . . .

> (*Turns emptied box upside down, shakes it, drops it on floor. Points to the door.*)

To Forty-fourth Street!

> (*He starts* UPSTAGE.)

IVY

(*Runs and grabs his arm at* UPSTAGE CENTER.)

Parker! For God's sake, stop! Look at yourself! *People will see you!*

(PARKER *stops, turns, stands undulating for a moment. He touches his rumpled hair, his undone tie, his pockets that are stuffed and brimming with bits of paper. He smiles innocently.* IVY *adjusts his collar.*)

PARKER

They won't believe it's me.

(*And out he goes, calling "Taxi! Taxi!" with* IVY *despairingly following and slamming the door as the lights fade. When the lights come up, everything is as before. The front door opens.* CHARLOTTE *enters, followed by* JOHN. CHARLOTTE *comes* DOWNSTAGE, *putting the keys in her purse and the purse on the table.* JOHN *stays sullenly in the doorway.*)

CHARLOTTE
(*Crossing* RIGHT *to study door.*)
Lordy! Never in my life have I attended a party where there was less to drink and more to get drunk about . . . Parker?
(*Looks into study, then glances around the room and up at the closed bedroom door.*)
Come in, John; nobody's going to bite you.
(JOHN *steps forward, closes the door, stays* UPSTAGE. CHARLOTTE *removes her gloves. Crossing* LEFT *to* UPSTAGE *of sofa.*)
You were my savior, darling. An older escort, and I would have had to stick it out until the reviews came in. I'd have wound up like S. P. Champlain. Did you see him, sitting there eating his handkerchief?

JOHN
The review on television wasn't so bad.

CHARLOTTE

"Periods of tedium" is not a complimentary phrase, John. Not
even in television.
(*Removing coat.*)
"Periods of tedium"; ha! If you ask me, the only period of
un-tedium was two minutes after the curtain went up, when
that old woman in the balcony started shouting about people
coming in late and drunk and stepping on her toes.
(*Puts her coat on a chair.*)
Now you can't stand there all night. Go up and apologize to
your father. Tell him you're sorry you said those unkind things.

JOHN

Something smells.

CHARLOTTE

(*Fluffing sofa cushions.*)
Don't be nasty.

JOHN

I'm not being nasty; something *smells*. In there.
(*He indicates the kitchen.*)

CHARLOTTE

(*Sniffs.*)
You're right . . .
(*She crosses quickly* LEFT *and exits into kitchen. A beat.*
JOHN *comes* DOWNSTAGE, *stands before the opened study
door, closes it. A beat.* CHARLOTTE *comes out of the
kitchen, bearing, on a pot holder, an aluminum container.
Within it is a hardened black residue which she prods with
a spoon.* JOHN *looks at her.*)

Your father doesn't resole his own galoshes, does he?
(*She crosses* UPSTAGE CENTER LEFT.)

JOHN

(*Crosses to table.*)
The table is set for two people . . .

CHARLOTTE

(*Putting the pot holder and container on dining table.*)
Yes . . . And somebody's been wearing Angela's party apron . . .
(*She fingers it.*)

JOHN

(*Looking at his chair* LEFT *of table.*)
And somebody's been sitting in my chair.

(*A beat.* CHARLOTTE *looks up at the bedroom door, puts a hand
on* JOHN*'s shoulder.*)

CHARLOTTE

You stay here . . .
(*Crosses, goes quickly upstairs, taps softly at the bedroom
door.* JOHN *crosses* DOWNSTAGE LEFT *looking at her.*)
Parker?
(*Taps again, then opens the door.*)
Parker?
(*She peers in, opens the door wide, steps back.*)

JOHN

(*Looking up at gallery.*)
Isn't he there?

CHARLOTTE
(*Looks offstage* RIGHT, *cranes her neck, shrugs.*)
No Papa Bear, no Goldilocks, no nobody.
(*She starts downstairs.*)

JOHN
(*Crossing* RIGHT *to* DOWNSTAGE *of coffee table.*)
The black box . . .
(*Goes to it, picks it up and opens it.*)
It's empty. Do you think someone broke in?

CHARLOTTE
(*Crossing* DOWNSTAGE *to coffee table.*)
Who; a band of daring young playwrights?
(*She goes to the sofa, picks up a whisky glass, rubs its edge.*)

JOHN
(*Putting down the box.*)
Lipstick?

CHARLOTTE
(*A hand on* JOHN'*s shoulder.*)
All right, you can go to sleep, Doctor Watson; I'll handle this case myself.

JOHN
Angie said I can play hooky tomorrow.

CHARLOTTE
(*Puts glass down on coffee table.*)
You still need some sleep. It's nearly one o'clock.

(ANGELA, *armed with a folded newspaper, flings open the front door like Carry Nation raiding a saloon.* DION *is behind her, several other newspapers under his arm.*)

ANGELA

(*Crossing* DOWNSTAGE CENTER *to* LEFT *of ottoman.* DION *crosses* DOWNSTAGE CENTER *to front of table.*)

Where is he?

CHARLOTTE

Parker?

JOHN

(*Crossing to* ANGELA DOWNSTAGE *of coffee table.*)

Are those the reviews?

ANGELA

(*Looking around.*)

Where is he? Hiding away in the bedroom?

CHARLOTTE

He's not here, darling. He's out. I don't know where.

JOHN

(*Standing* RIGHT *of* ANGELA.)

Are those the reviews?

ANGELA

(*Brandishing the newspaper.*)

He reviewed the play!

(*A beat.*)

CHARLOTTE

(*Softly.*)

What . . . ?

DION

He slashed it.

(*A beat.*)

JOHN

Dad . . . reviewed the play . . . ?

CHARLOTTE

But we saw that—that what's-his-name—Rittenhouse, sitting
there, smiling, nodding . . .

ANGELA

(*Showing* CHARLOTTE, *pointing.*)

Parker wrote the review!

JOHN

(*A look at* CHARLOTTE.)

He was . . . at the theater . . . ?

ANGELA

(*Looking at* LEFT.)

Yes, he was at the theater! Somewhere, somehow . . .

(*She hurls the folded paper to the sofa.*)

DION

(*Puts papers on table.*)

The other reviews aren't very good, but his is the crusher. We'll
be lucky if we last till Saturday.

JOHN
(*Takes up the newspaper, slowly, with both hands, reverently.*)
"'Opening Night Report,' by Parker Ballantine" . . . !
(*A beat.*)

DION
How does it feel, being the Son of Dracula?

(ANGELA *puts a restraining hand on* DION*'s arm.* JOHN, *reading raptly, moves* LEFT.)

ANGELA
They're in the closet, Dion. On the shelf. Just the small one.

DION
Right.

(DION *goes* UPSTAGE *to the foyer closet.* ANGELA *slips off her stole.*)

CHARLOTTE
Just the small what?

ANGELA
The small suitcase.
(*She puts down the stole.*)

JOHN
(*As he reads, with delectation.*)
Ooohhh . . . !

CHARLOTTE
Angela . . .

ANGELA

(*Crossing* DOWNSTAGE *a step. Keeping herself forcibly under control.*)
I'll only take a few things tonight. Tomorrow I want you to pack everything else. I'll tell you where to send it.

CHARLOTTE

Angela—

ANGELA

Don't advise me, Mother! Please. He *knew* how I felt. I told him! And he gave me his tickets!
(*To* DION.)
Upstairs . . .

(DION *crosses with the suitcase, and starts upstairs.* ANGELA *would follow, but* CHARLOTTE *catches her arm.*)

CHARLOTTE

Listen to me, Angela!

ANGELA

No! No, Mother, I'm not listening to anyone! Not any more! I'm listening to *me* for a change. This is *my* life and I'm taking charge of it! I'm going to do what I want to do, and be what I want to be, and I don't care if I never—

CHARLOTTE

(*On "care."*)
This is no time to recite "Invictus"!

(ANGELA *pulls free and starts upstairs as* DION *exits into the bedroom.* CHARLOTTE *looks around helplessly.*)

JOHN

(*With greater delectation.*)
Ooooooooohhhhh . . . !

CHARLOTTE

Oh, Lord . . .
(*She starts up the stairs after* ANGELA.)

ANGELA

(*Nearing the bedroom door.*)
There's a gray suit in the closet, Dion, and those shoes under the dressing table, and—

CHARLOTTE

(*Catching* ANGELA *in the doorway, pulling her back.*)
You stay out here for a minute!
(CHARLOTTE *closes bedroom door.*)

ANGELA

Mother—!

CHARLOTTE

(*A desperate whisper.*)
You're crazy! Insane! You can't go flying off to Never-Neverland with that Peter Pan in there!

ANGELA

(LEFT *of* CHARLOTTE.)
I don't know! I don't know *where* I'm going or with whom! But I can't stay here, Mama! I can't! Read that review! He's a bully and a sadist and an egomaniac and—and—

CHARLOTTE

And he's pompous and self-righteous and he takes his work too seriously and you love him!

ANGELA

No! I hate him! I never want to see him again, not if I live to be five thousand!

(*She exits into the bedroom, slams the door.*)

CHARLOTTE

(*Turning.*)

Oh, dear God, there goes my last daughter!

(*She leans wearily against the landing rail. A pause.* JOHN, *finished reading, looks up.*)

JOHN

You want to hear it?

(*A beat.*)

CHARLOTTE

All right . . . Give it to me slowly. One barrel at a time . . .

(*As* JOHN *reads the review,* CHARLOTTE *comes down the stairs, weakly, holding the banister.*)

JOHN

(*Taking* CENTER STAGE *and reading with pride.*)

"'Opening Night Report,' by Parker Ballantine. I think it's time for all us Transylvanian peasants to pick up our torches and march menacingly up to that castle on the hill, because Dr. Frankenstein is making monsters again.

(JOHN *looks smilingly at* CHARLOTTE. CHARLOTTE *groans. She sits on the sofa and does quite a bit of groaning throughout the following.*)
This time he's attached the arms and legs of Agamemnon to the torso of Rebecca of Sunnybrook Farm.

(*Another look at* CHARLOTTE.)
S. P. Champlain has led the creature over to the Forty-fourth Street Theatre, where last night it stumbled around for a few minutes, grunted, and fell over dead.

(ANGELA *and* DION *emerge from the bedroom,* ANGELA *with a light coat over her shoulders and carrying a small cosmetics case,* DION *carrying the suitcase. They start downstairs.*)
Just for the record, *A Houseful of Silence* was written by Angela Ballantine, directed by Dion Kapakos, and produced by mistake.

(*The front door opens.* PARKER *enters, rumpled but sober.* IVY *is with him.* ANGELA *has just reached the foot of the stairs,* DION *behind her.* ANGELA *and* PARKER *confront each other as* JOHN, *unaware of* PARKER's *entrance, continues reading.*)
Several actors were involved. The only thing they can do now is change their names and start over. Okay, men, light the torches! A cleaner Transylvania is up to us!"

PARKER

It's short, but I think it makes its point.

JOHN
(*Drops paper on coffee table, runs* UPSTAGE *to* PARKER.)
Dad! Boy! Boy—! Those were *all new* ones!

PARKER

(*Grins, takes* JOHN'*s shoulders, meets* ANGELA'*s eyes again.*)
I've already had my last meal. Do I get a cigarette before you shoot?
(*Crosses to between sofa and coffee table.*)

ANGELA

(UPSTAGE CENTER.)
I'm not shooting, Parker. I'm leaving.

DION

With me.

ANGELA

I've decided not to give Sid Champlain that list of your prejudiced witticisms. I'm not interested in taking petty revenge on
you; I'm interested only in getting out.
(*She turns to go.*)

JOHN

(*To* ANGELA.)
Don't go, Angie . . .

ANGELA

(*Stops and crosses* DOWNSTAGE *to* JOHN, *hand on his shoulder.*)
I'm sorry, John. When you're older you'll know more about
the man-woman relationship and you'll understand why I'm
doing this.

PARKER

You'll know *less* about the man-woman relationship; believe
me, you'll know less.

ANGELA

(*Looks at* IVY.)

I see *you* don't have any qualms about changing horses in midstream.

IVY

(*Crossing to* PARKER. *On* PARKER'*s arm again.*)

Smile when you say that, darling.

PARKER

Ivy came here to bandage the wounds that *you* inflicted on me.

(*Freeing his arm and taking* IVY'*s hand.*)

You've done a fine job, Ivy. Good nurse. Bless you.

IVY

I'm not going.

DION

"Dracula Meets the Spider Lady."

IVY

Dion . . . *dear* Dion . . . isn't it time you returned that tuxedo?

(*She slips off her coat, sits* DOWNSTAGE *of table.*)

ANGELA

(*Taking up the cosmetics case.*)

Let's go, Dion.

PARKER

Hold on a minute.

ANGELA

(*Turns to* PARKER.)

For what? A lecture?

(DION *moves up beside* ANGELA, *with the suitcase.*)

                        PARKER

A small speech.

                        ANGELA

No, thanks.

                        PARKER

You keep asking to be treated like an adult; then act like one.
Stop running. You're not fifteen any more.
          (*A beat.* ANGELA *stands frozen.* CHARLOTTE, *behind*
          DION, *gently detaches the suitcase from his hand, sets it*
          on floor, smiles sweetly at him. PARKER *crouches down*
          before JOHN.)
John, I'd like you to do a favor for me.

                        JOHN

What?

                        PARKER

I'd like you to go upstairs and get into your pajamas and get
into bed. Everything's going to be all right.

                        ANGELA

Huh!

                        JOHN
          (*Looks at* ANGELA, *then at* PARKER *again.*)
How can it be?

                        PARKER

It will be. Trust me.
          (*A beat.*)

JOHN

Okay.

PARKER

(*Stands straight.*)

I thank you, sir . . .

(JOHN *goes to the stairs.*)

JOHN

(*As he goes upstairs.*)

One of these days there's going to be a big scene and I'm not going to have to go offstage for it . . . .

(*He exits* RIGHT. PARKER *moves* DOWNSTAGE.)

CHARLOTTE

(*Sitting on the sofa.*)

I'm staying. *Somebody* has to represent the stockholders.

ANGELA

All right, let's have the speech.

PARKER

It would help if you would put down your luggage.

(*A beat.*)

ANGELA

(*Accepting the challenge.*)

All right.

(*She puts down stole and cosmetics case, comes* DOWNSTAGE. DION *touches her hand as she passes. She sits* LEFT *arm of sofa.*)

PARKER

(*Crosses to* ANGELA.)
First of all,
(*He looks at* DION. *A beat.*)
I have a couple of apologies to make to you.

IVY

Apologies? *You're* going to apologize to *her?*

PARKER

(*Over the "to her?"*)
Shut up, Ivy.
(*To* ANGELA.)
When you decided you were going to write a play, I poked fun at you, and heckled, and behaved in general like an all-round grade-A crumb. You said I hijacked your self-respect and you were right; that's exactly what I did. For that I most humbly beg your forgiveness.
(ANGELA *eyes him coldly.*)
You asked me to take a look at things in New Haven and Boston. I refused. Again I was wrong. I belong on your team. I think my objectivity could have survived the added strain . . .

DION

Boy oh boy . . .

CHARLOTTE

Shut up, Dion. Go on, Parker.

PARKER

I don't know what happened in Boston, but I do know this; if I'd been on your team, *nothing* would have happened. So if anything *did*, then for my share of the responsibility, Angie, again I most humbly beg your forgiveness.

DION

(*Crossing to* RIGHT *end of sofa.*)

Of all the presumptuous, conceited, egotistical . . .

IVY

What is this; Backwards Day??

CHARLOTTE

(*Rises.*)

If the *two* of you don't shut up, I'm going to bang your heads together!

(*Sits on coffee table.*)

ANGELA

Parker—

(*Rising.*)

PARKER

End of apologies. Now comes the unpleasantness.

CHARLOTTE

(*Gets up.*)

Parker, I don't think it's necessary to go into—

PARKER

Shut up, Charlie. Angie, I cannot and will not apologize for writing that review, nor for one syllable or semicolon in it. To my mind, which is the only measuring instrument I possess, *A Houseful of Silence* is exactly the monster I said it was.

(CHARLOTTE *crosses* RIGHT, *sits on phone table.*)

I've done my job, my readers have been warned.

(CHARLOTTE *sighs.*)

I know I take my work too seriously. Maybe it's because I feel that without their work people are vegetables.

(*He crosses* LEFT *to* UPSTAGE CENTER.)

I may have heckled you and discouraged you, because I assumed that you had chosen the wrong work to be doing, *but I never tried to lock you out of your workroom.*

(*Turns to* ANGELA.)

Tonight you tried to lock me out of mine.

(*Now* ANGELA'S *ice is cracking again.*)

I want you to stay, Angie. If you try another play I won't throw spitballs. If you ask for my help I'll give it, because helping you when you ask for help is also my work; that dawned on me somewhere in the course of this evening; about thirty seconds ago,

(*A look at* CHARLOTTE.)

to tell the truth. But if you ever hint that I should write a soft review for you, or ask me to quit my job for one evening because you've chosen a job that happens to conflict with it, if you ever again say, "Hand over those tickets," so help me Hannah, I will knock out your two front teeth.

(*Crosses* RIGHT *to* ANGELA.)

That is what the poet meant when he said, "I could not love thee, dear, so much, loved I not honor more."

(ANGELA *is liquefying rapidly.*)

Will you stay?

DION

(*Folding arms.*)

Tell me, would she retain the right to vote?

PARKER

Yes, she would retain the right to vote. She'd retain all her rights except the right to step on my rights. Nobody has that.

(*He sits ottoman.*)

Stay, Angie. I love you and I need you. And John loves you and needs you too. Don't you, John?

(*Louder.*)

I said "Don't you, John?"

(*A beat.* JOHN, *in pajamas, steps sheepishly onto the landing. They all look up at him.*)

JOHN

Yes. Please stay, Angie.

(ANGELA *is all but melted.*)

DION

When do you bring on the violins?

PARKER

(*Gets up. Smiling at* ANGELA.)

I would bring on the New York Philharmonic if I thought it would help.

IVY

Oh, Parker, damn you, why didn't you make that speech to *me,* four years ago?

(*An awkward pause.*)

CHARLOTTE

Because you would have stayed, that's why.

PARKER

Charlie . . .
        (*He looks with concern at* IVY.)

CHARLOTTE

I said it and I'm glad I said it . . .

(ANGELA *wipes a tear from her cheek.*)

PARKER

Angie . . . Please . . . ?

(ANGELA *looks at him for a long moment, then turns slowly to* DION.)

ANGELA

Dion . . . I—I . . .

(*A smiling gesture of helplessness.* PARKER *expels the breath he's been holding.*)

DION
        (*Going to* ANGELA.)
I'm not going to let you do this!
        (*Taking her shoulders.*)
You'll sit here and darn his socks and—and weave rugs and have a dozen babies— You'll *never* write another play!

ANGELA
        (*To* DION.)
I will if I want to . . . I can do anything if I want to.

(*Turning toward* PARKER.)

Anything . . . !

DION

(*Drawing her back.*)

Sure, he talks big about helping you, but wait till you get out that typewriter and then you'll see what kind of—

PARKER

(*On "you'll see", the voice of authority.*)

Dion.

(DION *stops, releases* ANGELA. PARKER *takes a step forward.*)

This is your father image speaking.

(*Points* UPSTAGE.)

Beat it. In thirty seconds we're going to have "Spank-the-Precocious-Children Hour."

DION

(*Moves closer to* ANGELA *and* PARKER.)

I'm not through yet, Ballantine; not by a long shot. She won't give Champlain *her* list, but I've got a list of my own to give him;

(*Pointing with* RIGHT *hand to liquor cabinet.*)

of the drinks I saw you take this evening, and the booze that's reeking from you now. You were *drunk* at that theater, chum, and a drunken critic is a dead critic.

(*A beat.*)

ANGELA

(*Turns to* DION.)

I'm the playwright. I was with him all evening and I didn't see him take a single drink.

CHARLOTTE

(RIGHT *of sofa*.)

Neither did I.

JOHN

Neither did I.

IVY

His breath is pure Lavoris.

(*Moving resignedly to* DION.)

Come on, Dion. You have to learn to lose gracefully, otherwise there's no applause on your final exit.

(DION *moves* UPSTAGE *surlily.* IVY *puts on her coat.*)

So long, Parker. It was nice sitting next to you again.

PARKER

So long, Ivy.

CHARLOTTE

Don't take any wooden musicals.

IVY

Johnny-Love . . .

(*She blows* JOHN *a kiss, he waves his hand minutely. Looking across* PARKER *at* ANGELA.)

I have two words of advice for you, Angela. Beef Stroganoff.

(*She takes* DION*'s arm and they exit.* JOHN *rushes downstairs and hugs* ANGELA. CHARLOTTE *rises and crosses to the dining table.*)

CHARLOTTE

Is *that* what that was? *Beef Stroganoff.*

(*She inspects the aluminum container incredulously.*)

PARKER

(*Pointing at* JOHN.)
You! Into bed.

JOHN

Yes, sir! Good night, Angie!

ANGELA

(*Kissing him.*)
Good night, darling!

JOHN

(*Going to the stairs.*)
See you in the morning!

ANGELA

In the morning!

JOHN

(*Going up, waving to* PARKER *and* CHARLOTTE.)
Good night! Good night!

PARKER   CHARLOTTE

Good night, John!   Good night!

(JOHN *exits.* ANGELA *drops off her coat.* PARKER *and* ANGELA *look at each other, and move forward.*)

CHARLOTTE

(*Putting aside the container contemptuously.*)
Stroganoff—huh!
(*She gathers the dishes and silver and exits* LEFT *into the kitchen.*)

PARKER

Hello.

ANGELA
(*Her eyes are bright.*)
Hello.
(*They embrace.*)
Oh, Park! He was right! Dion, I mean; about the rugs and the babies. I feel so—so *capable* all of a sudden!

(*They kiss.* CHARLOTTE *enters, stands in doorway, watches them for a happy moment.*)

CHARLOTTE

The well-bred thing at this point would be to leave the living room, don't you think?

(*Laughing,* PARKER *and* ANGELA *move to the stairs, and start up.* PARKER *holds back.*)

PARKER
(*A quick look at* CHARLOTTE, *then to* ANGELA.)
Go ahead, darling. I'll be with you in ten seconds. There's one thing I *have* to do.

ANGELA

Ten seconds . . .
(*Climbs the remaining stairs, turns.*)
Nine, eight, seven, six . . .

(*She backs into the bedroom.* PARKER *dashes down and into study, gets the white file box, brings it into the living room, puts it down, leafs hastily through a handful of its slips.*)

CHARLOTTE

(*Crossing into room.*)

What on earth—?

PARKER

Ah! Here it is!

(*He takes one slip, puts down the remainder, crosses* UP-STAGE *of sofa.*)

CHARLOTTE

What?

PARKER

(*Going upstairs.*)

A note to leave on my pillow in the morning! For Angie!

CHARLOTTE

(*Between sofa and coffee table.*)

Parker!

(*He stops on the landing.*)

I'm an old woman and I've had a grueling evening. Don't tease me. What does it say?

(*A beat.*)

PARKER

(*Grins, reads.*)

"Warm, vibrant, and thoroughly satisfying from first to last. The most delightful conception of the entire season!"

(*He exits into the bedroom as* CHARLOTTE *sinks onto sofa.*)

THE CURTAIN FALLS

THE END

BREAK
A LEG

INTRODUCTION

(BREAK A LEG)

Break A Leg is Ira Levin's comic gem—the most unapologetically, riotously funny of all his creations. Set long ago *somewhere* in central Europe, it concerns an embattled theater company, the critic who's routinely savaged their productions, and the creative means the company employs to drive him out of his profession and back, literally, to *Transylvania*.

The critic in question, *Johann Schiml,* is a tyrant so brutish, he berates actors on the basis of their looks, and critiques even the setting sun! (Surely Schiml's only coincidentally reminiscent of a certain past brutish theater critic, who *also* faulted actors' appearances . . .)

Levin knew personally from what *Sidney Bruhl* (of his later *Deathtrap*) referred to as *"critics peeing on"* a playwright's work. In the nearly twenty years between writing *Critic's Choice* and *Break A Leg,* both of which contemplate the theater's inner workings—and in particular the problematic nexus between the creative impulse and its critical reception—Levin had seen no less than five of his Broadway outings die untimely deaths, aided no doubt by their share of unkind reviews. Hence perhaps the shift from *Critic's Choice's critic-as-paragon* perspective, to *Break A Leg's critic-as-villain.* (Though in true Levin fashion, even the loathsome Schiml receives a fair hearing; hurtful stuffed shirt though he may be, he's still empathetically drawn, and rendered as a flesh-and-blood human—near-freezing though that blood may at first appear.)

When asked in a 1979 interview if this new work was indeed borne of any genuine ill-will towards critics, Levin related *"I think it really did start with a book review or a play review, I forget which. But I had the feeling someone should kill him . . . So I began to cook and concoct an elaborate scheme of revenge."*

Just as Sidney Bruhl served as Levin's *Deathtrap* stand-in, here his surrogate is the always *close-but-not-sufficiently-close* dramaturge *Imre Laszlo* (note the matching initials). I suspect Laszlo himself might've composed the play's succinct synopsis: *"The play, in two acts, is set long ago in Vienna or Berlin. Or Prague or Buda-Pesth. Anyway, it's not New York and not now."*

But the author of the company's efforts to send the detested *Schiml* packing is its comically-unhinged impresario, *Dietrich Merkenschrift*. And under his direction, the bedraggled troupe's actions up the ante on even *Deathtrap*'s bone-deep *metatheatricality*. Who needs to break the *fourth* wall, when you can just get rid of *all* the walls, and take your revenge vignettes *outside* the theater and *into the real world*—its parks, plazas, and other public spaces. Reality itself is Dietrich's canvas—his scenarios a kind of vindictive nineteenth-century performance art.

As uproarious as *Break A Leg*'s dealings are, the circumstances of its Broadway premiere were, ironically, about as unfunny as it gets. And here I have to inject myself into the mix, as—as one of Levin's sons—I was present for the entire production, including its out-of-town previews, which saw the company living in an upscale motel compound near the theater—a kind of highbrow gypsy encampment. My brothers and I would attend each performance, and elsewise hang out with the various company members either at the theater or back at the motel. In particular, we'd routinely drop by the show's director Charles Nelson Reilly's lair, where he'd hold us in thrall with his "always-on" persona and madcap wit; it was a real-life *Match Game*.

The story holds that Charles either would not, or could not, bring himself to give the cast the critical notes that are essential to shaping a show during previews, even with a company of pros such as *Break A Leg* was blessed with. To accommodate his reticence, the production hired an assistant to perform this sole task—which Charles mistook as an attempt to oust him from his director's chair, leading him to quit the show two days before its Broadway opening—his sole focus then appearing to be to trash the endeavor he'd spent the past several months shepherding.

I was present at what must've been the second-to-last Broadway preview when, at the very start of the second act, a booming baritone voice intoned a prolonged, full-throated *"BOOOoooooo . . . ! !"* from the back of the theater, before turning around and striding out. It could only have been an actor-colleague of Charles' "second-acting" the show (sneaking in during intermission)—as who would actually purchase a ticket, sit through the entire first act, then wait through intermission, to only *then* issue their (professionally-voiced) utterance?

Faced with the demonstrable venom Charles had for the show at that point, its producers decided (probably wisely) to cut their losses, but pronto; *Break A Leg* closed literally on opening night.

A few days later, Charles appeared on *The Tonight Show*—accompanied by an actress dressed as his nurse, to help him onstage and over to his desk-side chair—so weak and fragile was he from his recent ordeal. Claiming that the play was so bad it had been *booed* (see above), he proceeded to tell Johnny Carson (and America) what a disaster it had all been, and how rigid and unaccommodating my father had been to him. I recommend watching the clip, which is easily found online—as Charles was a genuinely funny man, and it's a hoot. (Though less so when considering that he was seeking to defend his reputation as a *director* at the expense of something far more important.)

The *irony* in all that, is that Charles was "doing" the play *in real life*—staging fake events *out in the real world*—to bring about his (perceived) oppressor's downfall. Dietrich Merkenschrift would be proud.

The saddest part (for me and my brothers, at least) was the loss of someone who—given our genuine affection for him up to that point—had been welcomed into our intimate family circle. My father had bought him a solid gold cigarette lighter as an opening night present, which he could neither give him (he'd quit) nor return (it had been engraved with Charles' initials, CNR)—so it sits on a shelf now, a symbol of the whole misadventure.

But how was the show, Mrs. Lincoln? *Hilarious*, as it happens. The *Associated Press*'s Jay Sharbutt raved that *Break A Leg* *"is one of the wildest, funniest, best-acted farces I've ever seen."* The casting certainly could not have been better. Veteran character actor Jack Weston was hysterically funny as Merkenschrift. Julie Harris (as Gertie Kessel) was every inch the star she was held up to be. And—as Johann Schiml himself—René Auberjonois was as imperious and aloof a figure as anyone from here to Carpathia.

A practical tip: If (like my father) you end up writing a play that lampoons critics, do not rely on their taking it in their stride, as Mr. Sharbutt did; they are, after all (like Schiml himself) only human.

But read *Break A Leg* for yourself; be your *own* critic. (Just go easy on the sun.)

Nicholas Levin
New York City
January, 2025

BREAK
A LEG

BREAK A LEG was first presented at the Palace Theatre, New York City, on April 29, 1979, by Stephen R. Friedman, Irwin Meyer, and Kenneth D. Laub, with the following cast:

DIETRICH MERKENSCHRIFT,
    a theatrical manager . . . . Jack Weston
FREITAG,
    his assistant . . . . Joseph Leon
PEPI LUBAUER,
    a scenic designer. . . . . Michael Connolly
IMRE LASZLO,
    a playwright . . . . .David Margulies
GERTIE KESSEL,
    an actress. . . . . .Julie Harris
JOHANN SCHIML,
    a critic . . . . .René Auberjonois
MITZI KARLÖWE, CARLO MIZZI,
    singing sweethearts. . . . . Particia O'Connell,
                                        James Cahill

ACTORS, STAGEHANDS
. . . . Patricia O'Connell
                                       James Cahill
                                    Timothy Lewis
                                  Natalie Norwick

The production was directed by Charles Nelson Reilly. Peter Larkin designed the scenery, Marc B. Weiss the lighting, and Theoni V. Aldredge the costumes. Peter Lawrence was the production stage manager.

The play, in two acts, is set long ago in Vienna or Berlin. Or Prague or Buda-Pesth. Anyway, it's not New York and not now.

ACT ONE

DIETRICH MERKENSCHRIFT'S OFFICE
A morning in spring

THE PRINCE FRIEDRICH THEATRE
A week later, afternoon

THE ROOF OF A HOUSE ON THE FELDERSTRASSE
That evening

AN APARTMENT IN THE HOUSE
Soon after

ACT TWO

THE THEATRE
A few days later, morning

"GOOD-BYE, SCHIML!"
The following week

THE ROOF OF THE HOUSE ON THE FELDERSTRASSE
Evening

THE THEATRE
The following day

THE OFFICE
Three weeks later, afternoon

THE OFFICE
Two days later, morning

ACT ONE

SCENE ONE

DIETRICH MERKENSCHRIFT*'s office. Elegant bad taste. Framed theatrical posters:* Hello, Mitzi; The Student Gypsy; The Gypsy Student; New Faces of 1904.

MERKENSCHRIFT *is seated at his desk, paralyzed with anger, his face bent to the fingertips of one hand, his eyes closed.* FREITAG, *his assistant, stands at a distance holding several newspapers, from the uppermost of which he has just finished reading aloud. He watches* MERKENSCHRIFT *with heartfelt compassion.*

MERKENSCHRIFT

Again.

FREITAG

Why torture yourself?

MERKENSCHRIFT
(*Flings his head around, glaring.*)
AGAIN!

FREITAG
(*Near tears.*)
Oh God! . . . The whole thing?

MERKENSCHRIFT

The whole thing! From the top! "Last night a stench"!

(*He thrusts his face back to his fingertips.* FREITAG *sighs, shakes his head, composes himself, reads.*)

FREITAG

"Last night a stench pervaded the city, a noxious putrescent foulness which, as reported elsewhere in these pages, is assumed to have been the product of an unfortunate confluence of air currents from the slaughterhouses in Gratz, the Bratislava sulphur works, and our own malfunctioning sewage plant. I should like to offer an alternative hypothesis. The stench originated, I would suggest, on the stage of the Prince Friedrich Theatre, where Dietrich Merkenschrift exposed to the public his new production, *Love's Vengeance*, an unfortunate confluence of one playwright, forty-six actors, and twelve sets.

    (FREITAG *looks at* MERKENSCHRIFT, *who, savoring the ignominy, gestures for more.*)

Our government is embarked on policies of doubtful merit; injustice surrounds us; the mark is unsteady. At this moment in history Mr. Merkenschrift offers us romantic melodrama by Imre Laszlo, who again demonstrates that he has only two talents: the crocheting of plots whose intricacy would be admired in any lunatic asylum, and an unfailing capacity to climax every speech with precisely the wrong words. Most of Mr. Laszlo's wrong words last night were droned by a new performer, Miss Schatzi Molendorf. Her debut can be of interest only to the orthodontists among us.

    (FREITAG *casts another look at* MERKENSCHRIFT, *who makes a weaker keep-it-coming gesture.* FREITAG *plows miserably on.*)

The sets by Pepi Lubauer harmonized effectively with the pre-
vailing atrociousness, as did the ungrammatical program notes,
the decrepit ushers, and the clogged soap dispenser in the gentlemen's washroom."

(Nothing from MERKENSCHRIFT. FREITAG switches
gamely to the other papers.)

The other reviews aren't so bad. "Occasional moments of interest . . ." "Miss Molendorf has slender wrists . . ."

(MERKENSCHRIFT *slowly raises his head.*)

MERKENSCHRIFT

Someone should kill him . . .

FREITAG

Johann Schiml?

MERKENSCHRIFT
(*Squinting, beginning to glimpse a grand design.*)

Someone should . . . no, not *kill* him . . . but do *something* to
him that . . . makes him resign and go back where he came
from . . .

FREITAG

Transylvania.

MERKENSCHRIFT

Yes, back to Transylvania . . .

FREITAG
(*A prayer to heaven.*)

Dear God, if that could only be!

> (MERKENSCHRIFT *stays as he is, squinting at his gradu-*
> *ally clarifying design.* FREITAG *pulls himself together and*
> *puts the newspapers aside.)*

Well, wishing won't sell tickets. That's our fifth production in a row he's murdered.

MERKENSCHRIFT

Get me Laszlo . . .

> (FREITAG *moves to the desk, picks up the phone, unhooks the ear-*
> *piece, jiggles the hook.)*

FREITAG

Two-thirty-nine, please.

MERKENSCHRIFT

One hires actors, builds sets, produces a play . . . Couldn't one produce . . . a *reality!?*

FREITAG

Is that you, Mr. Laszlo? Mr. Merkenschrift.

> (*He hands the phone and earpiece to* MERKENSCHRIFT, *who takes them without shifting his gaze from the vision before him.)*

MERKENSCHRIFT

Imre? Did you read Schiml's review? What? Imre, I can't understand you; you sound—
> (*Looks at the phone.*)

Oh my God, untie it!
> (*Pantomimes to* FREITAG *with his earpiece hand: rope around the neck and pop-eyed head-lolling hanging.*

FREITAG *gasps and claps his hands to his cheeks.* MERKEN-SCHRIFT *waits and addresses the phone again.*)

Now *throw it away*, Imre; *you mustn't let him do this to you.* That *garbage* about climaxing every speech with the wrong words; you *know* it's not true; you're one of the finest playwrights in Europe! He's a vicious hateful man who's *mad* with his own authority. Remember what you said the other day? "Power corrupts—and absolute power corrupts the *worst of all*"! Imre, I'm going to fix his wagon, and you're going to help me do it.

(FREITAG *listens eagerly.*)

You're going to go to that desk of yours—that desk where you wrote *Love's Vengeance* and *The Curse of the Falkenheims* and *A Good Girl's Last-Minute Triumph*—you're going to go to that desk, and you're going to sit down, and you're going to— No, not a letter to the editor, Imre. I want a *plot* from you. One of those *marvelous, intricate Laszlo plots* that Johann Schiml finds so despicable! I'm going to *cast* it, and *stage* it—but not at the Prince Friedrich, uh-uh. On a street! In a cafe! Maybe even in Schiml's own house! Wherever your genius leads us! The supporting roles are going to be played by actors, sometimes improvising, sometimes speaking Laszlo dialogue; and the *principal* role is going to be played by Johann Schiml—always improvising and never suspecting he's in a Dietrich Merken-schrift production!

(FREITAG *is wide-eyed, excited.*)

No, not to harass him, nothing that petty! To drive him out! To make him resign and send him back to Transylvania; you can do it, Imre, I know you can!

(*Withdraws a bit, with a look of put-on surprise.*)

Bubi, *you're* the plotter, *I'm* the *producer.* How did you make Baron von Falkenheim sell his daughters to the tinker?

(*Listens, smiles.*)

That's more like it, *that* sounds like Imre Laszlo! The sooner the better, sweetheart, and the budget is as high as you want to go! And Imre, listen— Imre? Work in a part for Schatzi Molendorf; we'll cover her teeth somehow; he'll never recognize her!

(*He hangs up and puts the phone down.* FREITAG, *beside himself and beside* MERKENSCHRIFT, *grabs him and tries to kiss his hand.*)

FREITAG

You're the genius, not Laszlo! You're marvelous! Magnificent! What daring! What imagination!

MERKENSCHRIFT

(*Pushing him away, rising.*)
All right, all right, don't break my concentration!

FREITAG

(*Cringing reverently.*)
Forgive me! Forgive me!

MERKENSCHRIFT

(*Pointing at* FREITAG.)
Information on Schiml! His quirks, his foibles; get it to Imre double-quick!

FREITAG

There was an article about him last month in the—

MERKENSCHRIFT

Find it! Run it over!
    (FREITAG *starts to go.*)
And make me a list!

(FREITAG *stops, turns.*)

Every actor he's ever insulted! We start casting the minute Imre has something!

(FREITAG *starts to go.*)

Close *Love's Vengeance!* The hell with it!

(FREITAG *stops, turns.* MERKENSCHRIFT *is tearing his coat off, electric with energy.*)

We'll make it up on the next show! We'll make it up on every show from here on in!

(FREITAG *starts to go and makes it this time.* MERKEN-SCHRIFT, *throwing his coat on a chair, cups his hands and bellows after him.*)

UNCLOG—THE—SOAP—DISPENSER!

(*The office set begins to fly, or slide away or whatever it does.* MERKENSCHRIFT, *in shirtsleeves, helps it.*)

Get this desk out of here, somebody! This junk was supposed to be cleared three days ago! *Frei*tag, I asked for *wa*-ter!

(*And as the house lights come up, we are in Scene Two.*)

ACT ONE

SCENE TWO

The Prince Friedrich Theatre and ours.

Busy, busy. A few STAGEHANDS *complete the striking of the office set, under the brisk supervision of* PEPI LUBAUER. ACTORS *gossip in the wings.* FREITAG, *in shirtsleeves and with a sheaf of papers and manuscripts under one arm, hurries to* MERKENSCHRIFT *with a glass of water.*

MERKENSCHRIFT

Will you clear the stage please? We're trying to hold auditions here!

    (*Drinks thirstily.*)

FREITAG

Everybody off the stage! Clear the stage, please!

MERKENSCHRIFT

    (*To* LUBAUER, *indicating the Audience.*)

Pepi, these people came here to try out for parts, they didn't come to watch you schlep scenery!

LUBAUER

Almost done, Dietrich!

MERKENSCHRIFT

(*To the Audience.*)

Just sit tight, everybody, we'll get to each one of you in due time. Including you latecomers. The call was for twelve noon, kids; you're not going to get the good parts if you keep showing up late. Freitag, where are we?

FREITAG

(*Consulting his lists.*)

We've got the girl, the locksmith, the boyhood friend of his father, both doctors, the leper—I almost forgot: Pepi found a marvelous doctor's office on the Billingstrasse, fully equipped.

LUBAUER

We can have it for as long as we want, for ten marks a day.

MERKENSCHRIFT

I'll look at it tonight. I want someplace *really seedy*. He should feel sick just setting *foot* in it.

LUBAUER

This is perfect.

FREITAG

The doctor was arrested yesterday.

MERKENSCHRIFT

Imre! Imre darling!

(IMRE LASZLO *has come onto the stage, shyly but happily.* MERKENSCHRIFT *hands the glass to* FREITAG *and goes to* LASZLO *with open arms.*)

Here he is! Here's our genius playwright!

(MERKENSCHRIFT *embraces* LASZLO. ACTORS *and* STAGEHANDS
gather round admiringly. MERKENSCHRIFT *brings* LASZLO
DOWNSTAGE; FREITAG *follows. Others watch the great men with
hushed awe.*)

LASZLO

(*On the way* DOWNSTAGE.)

How is it going?

MERKENSCHRIFT

Brilliantly! Brilliantly!

LASZLO

(DOWNSTAGE, *looking about delightedly.*)

Mmm! Twenty-six productions and still I get excited when the
words are being brought to life!

(*Hugging himself ecstatically.*)

Ai! There's *no* business—like the *theater* business!

MERKENSCHRIFT

(*To the Audience.*)

The *phrases* that *fall* from his *lips!* Imre, you've got to use that
someplace!

FREITAG

It could be a song even!

LASZLO

(*The word of the master.*)

No, no, not a song, definitely not. Mm-mm. Never.

MERKENSCHRIFT

(*Picking up a manuscript.*)

Imre, what can I tell you? Compared to what you've cooked up for Johann Schiml, Baron von Falkenheim was a carefree man!

LASZLO

There's no problem with the leper?

MERKENSCHRIFT

Putty and yellow paint, that's all. There's no problem with anything; the leper, the runaway carriage, the apparition of his mother . . . The scene in the cathedral worries me a little—I can't see them renting it even for half an hour—but we'll manage it somehow, don't worry.

LASZLO

I'd hate to have to rewrite . . .

FREITAG

Tell him the good news.

MERKENSCHRIFT

(*A hand on* LASZLO'*s shoulder.*)

The part of the girl—is going to be played—by Gertie Kessel!

LASZLO

I thought she died!

MERKENSCHRIFT

No, she *pretended* to, after Schiml reviewed her Ophelia . . . but actually she took his advice and went into a nunnery. The one

at Eggenburg. I was up there this morning trying to talk sense
to Schatzi Molendorf, and I met Gertie and—

LASZLO

Schatzi's in the nunnery?

MERKENSCHRIFT   FREITAG
Haven't you heard?   You didn't know?

LASZLO

No!

MERKENSCHRIFT

Yes! Yes.
  (*Nods sorrowfully.*)
Poor little Schatzi has taken the veil . . .
  (*A descriptive gesture.*)
Across her mouth.

LASZLO

Oh! And I wrote in a part for her! The nurse!
  (*Also with a gesture.*)
With the surgical mask!

MERKENSCHRIFT

Well *anyway*, I met Gertie up there, and as soon as she
heard there was a chance to get back at Schiml—I tell you,
you never saw a nun get out of a habit so fast in your entire
life! She'll be here any minute. Stick around. She's at the
wigmaker's.

FREITAG

Shall we go on with the auditions?

MERKENSCHRIFT

(*Looking at the list* FREITAG *holds.*)
Yes. Who are we up to now?

LASZLO

Wait a second, now just a second. I want you to know, I'm not such a big Gertie Kessel fan. You know how she always made her own little additions to the script.

MERKENSCHRIFT

Imre, relax, trust me; I'm going to—

LASZLO

(*Interrupting him.*)
No, no, no, Dietrich, no; this is the most intricate plot I've ever invented. If the girl doesn't play her part just right, Schiml's not going to believe the doctor. If he doesn't believe the *doctor*, he's not going to listen to the *fortune teller*. If he doesn't listen to the—

MERKENSCHRIFT

(*Interrupting him.*)
Imre, please, relax. Sit down, wait. As soon as Gertie gets here I'm going to stage her two scenes; you'll see how firm I'm going to be with her. The weather is perfect; we're going to play them this evening.

LASZLO

This evening?

MERKENSCHRIFT

Why not? We have to wait a few days before the doctor scene; the sooner we start, the better. Sit down, you'll see; a year in the nunnery has made her very obedient.

LASZLO

The whole conception is like a delicate chain. If anybody departs from the script *anywhere*, Schiml won't even *think* of going into his father's bakery business.

MERKENSCHRIFT

(*Encouraging* LASZLO *into a chair.*)
He'll go, he'll go; you worked it out beautifully.
(*Turning.*)
Who's next, Freitag?

FREITAG

The mysterious Frenchman.

MERKENSCHRIFT

(*To the Audience.*)
We need a mysterious Frenchman! Have we got a mysterious Frenchman here?

GERTIE

(*Coming radiantly onstage.*)
We've got a nun! Do you have any use for a nun, Dietrich?

MERKENSCHRIFT	FREITAG
Gertie.	Miss Kessel!

(GERTIE KESSEL *is a pretty, vivacious woman of thirty or so, color-fully dressed and sporting, courtesy of the wigmaker, a magnificent head of coppery hair.* MERKENSCHRIFT *goes to meet her,* FREITAG *follows,* LASZLO *rises.* MERKENSCHRIFT *and* GERTIE *embrace and kiss cheeks.*)

GERTIE

An ex-nun, I should say.

MERKENSCHRIFT

You don't look very ecclesiastical.

GERTIE

I don't feel it, darling, believe me!
> (*She has extended a hand to* FREITAG; *he kisses it and she starts.*)
Oooh! *Do* that *again!*
> (*He does.*)
Mmmm!
> (LASZLO *joins them;* GERTIE *offers her other hand.*)
Two, please.
> (LASZLO *kisses her hand twice.*)
Mmm! Heaven . . .

MERKENSCHRIFT

You remember Imre . . .

GERTIE

Mais oui.

LASZLO

I'm so happy you're still alive.

GERTIE

So am I, darling! I was *mad* shutting myself up in that nunnery because of Johann Schiml. Thank *God* you rescued me, Dietrich. When I think of all I've wasted!

> (*A gesture encompassing the three men—coquettishly cut short.*)

In terms of my work, that is.

MERKENSCHRIFT

> (*Taking her arm and leading her* DOWNSTAGE.)

Nothing's going to be wasted again, Gertie. After *this* little production I'm going to mount a *big* one for you, a welcome home—*Electra, Medea*, whatever you want. With Schiml out of the way, you'll be what you were meant to be.

GERTIE

I certainly wasn't meant to be a postulant, or whatever they called it. This is where I belong, right here on a stage!

MERKENSCHRIFT

> (*To* LASZLO.)

Tell her what you said before.

LASZLO

> (*Modest pride.*)

"There's no business like the theater business."

GERTIE

Oh! How lovely! And it's *so true!*

LASZLO
(*A helpless shrug.*)
Things come to me, that's all.

MERKENSCHRIFT
(*To* GERTIE.)
We're going to stage your two scenes right now.

GERTIE
Wonderful!

MERKENSCHRIFT
(*Notices the Audience and realizes his gaffe.*)
Oh . . .
(*Coming* DOWNSTAGE.)
Listen, kids . . . When we set up these auditions, I had no idea I'd be finding Gertie this morning and that the weather would be so perfect for the first two scenes. *Please forgive me.* Go out quickly, and be back here tomorrow morning at nine sharp. That's *nine*, you latecomers.

(*He goes* UPSTAGE *and rejoins* GERTIE *and* LASZLO. GERTIE *is removing her cape and gloves or whatever.* FREITAG *signals the Audience to get moving.*)

FREITAG
You heard him, folks. What is it? You want to stay?
(*He's surprised, but he postpones judgment with an upraised hand and goes* UPSTAGE *to* MERKENSCHRIFT.)
Sir?

MERKENSCHRIFT

What is it?

FREITAG

Excuse me, but may some of them stay?

MERKENSCHRIFT

Stay?

FREITAG

And watch while you . . .

MERKENSCHRIFT

*(Doesn't like the idea at all, but looks at the Audience and
gives in to his innate good nature. Coming* DOWNSTAGE.*)*
All right, you *may* stay, and perhaps pick up a few pointers, but
please, I beg you—ab-so-lute silence.
(To FREITAG.*)*
Take out the house lights. And get a country-girl cloak from
wardrobe.

FREITAG

Yes, sir.

(Going offstage.)
House lights out, Wolfgang!

MERKENSCHRIFT

(Going back to GERTIE.*)*
We're going to have an audience; that won't throw you, will it?

GERTIE

No, no, not at all.

(*As the house lights go down, she smiles at the people in the front row, waggles her fingers at a friend.*)
Oh hi, Lottie! Ooh you lost weight; you look marvelous! Gerhardt . . .
(*To* MERKENSCHRIFT.)
It's Old Home Week!

(LASZLO *is putting aside* GERTIE*'s cape, etc. The* STAGEHANDS, ACTORS, *and* LUBAUER *have drifted off into the wings.*)

MERKENSCHRIFT

Here's the way the whole thing begins, Gertie. Schiml is very retiring. He's got this apartment on the Felderstrasse, he hardly ever steps out of it except to go to the theater or to church. But almost every clear day he goes up on the roof to watch the sunset. This evening *you're* going to be there. You're a new tenant in the building.

LASZLO

A girl from the country; simple, friendly, no sign of disease.

MERKENSCHRIFT

I've taken an apartment on the top floor. My set designer, Pepi Lubauer, furnished it this very morning. The name on the door—is "Gretel Gesundt."

GERTIE

Gesundt . . .

LASZLO

Which is also *your* name, you understand.

GERTIE

(*Concentrating; she's really going to give this role her all.*)
Yes. I understand that.

MERKENSCHRIFT

Now basically, what happens is this. Scene One, you're on the roof with him. You say a few words about the sunset, you tell him you've just moved in from the country, and you sway dizzily.

(GERTIE *has a go at this.*)
He comes over and supports you—

(*Takes her arm.*)
You say you're not accustomed to the height—and you ask him to help you down to your apartment.

LASZLO

And he's a caught, like a rat in a box.

MERKENSCHRIFT

Scene Two is in the apartment. What happens here is very simple: *you get him to drink from the same glass you do.*

LASZLO

You ask him to bring you some wine—you're still weak from the height, you see—

MERKENSCHRIFT

He brings it from the kitchen, where wine and *one glass* is waiting for him—

LASZLO

You taste it, it doesn't taste right, you ask *him* to try it.

MERKENSCHRIFT

And that's it. You thank him for his courtesy, he exits.

LASZLO

A tiny dramatic acorn, but from it will grow—
    (*An evocative spreading gesture.*)
a mighty tree of some kind!

(FREITAG *comes onstage carrying a cloak.*)

MERKENSCHRIFT

Come, we'll stage Scene One.
    (*He goes to get chairs.* FREITAG *helps* GERTIE *on with
    the cloak, a healthy-girl-from-the-country type garment.*
    LASZLO *rummages among scripts on table.*)
The railing is about six inches higher than these chairs . . .

(*He places two chairs* DOWNSTAGE, *a good distance apart. His coat
and hat are on chair* RIGHT. LASZLO *gives* GERTIE *a few handwrit-
ten sheets.*)

LASZLO

Here are both scenes, Gertie. And please, dear, wherever you
can—*my* words, not new ones.

GERTIE

I'll improvise as little as possible.

MERKENSCHRIFT

There are chimneys there and there, and the stairs coming up
are here.
    (*Indicating* CENTER RIGHT.)

There's a housing around the stairs, and I tell you right now, Gertie, I'll be behind it, watching to see that you don't add any Gertie Kessel improvements.

GERTIE

I promise you both, I'll follow the script as closely as I can: I sway, I ask him to help me downstairs. Believe me, the nuns taught me discipline.

MERKENSCHRIFT

(*Pinches her cheek.*)

Mm, you're an angel!

(*Makes a kiss at her, takes her arm.*)

Come.

(*He leads her to the chair* LEFT. FREITAG *withdraws* RIGHT, *and* LASZLO LEFT, *watching.* MERKENSCHRIFT *puts* GERTIE's *hands on the chairback.*)

We'll get there good and early, so you'll be in position first.

(*Backs a step from her.*)

Simple, open, friendly.

LASZLO

No disease.

MERKENSCHRIFT

(*Who needs playwrights?*)

Thank you, Imre. No disease.

GERTIE

(*Beginning to act.*)

But . . . unaccustomed to heights . . .

MERKENSCHRIFT

Yes.

> (*Backs farther away.*)

Not *too* unaccustomed yet, dear; wait till he's with you. That's nice . . . lovely . . . And here comes Schiml.

> (*He enacts the following as he describes it.*)

Up the stairs—out the door. He's a bit surprised to see you—but he nods—

> (GERTIE *nods back.*)

That's right, you nod back—and he goes to the railing and watches the sunset. You wait a few seconds, and then you speak.

GERTIE

> (*Glances at the script, looks out.*)

It's a beautiful sunset, isn't it?

MERKENSCHRIFT

Yes, lovely. Maybe he just nods.

GERTIE

> (*Another glance at the script, another look out.*)

Do you often come sunset-watching here on this roof?

MERKENSCHRIFT

Every day, when the weather's clear. Or, yes I do, or whatever he says.

GERTIE

> (*Reading now.*)

I'm a new tenant in the building. I have only today moved in from the country. I have rented apartment three on the fifth floor. Oh!

> (*Sways dizzily.*)

MERKENSCHRIFT

Away from the railing, back a little.
> (GERTIE *obeys*.)

That's it.

GERTIE

. . . three on the fifth floor. Oh!
> (*Sways dizzily*.)

MERKENSCHRIFT

Is anything wrong?

GERTIE

I'm . . . not accustomed to heights . . .

(*She sways more extravagantly, a hand to her forehead.* MERKEN-SCHRIFT *hurries to her and supports her. He stops, frowns, looks to* LASZLO.)

MERKENSCHRIFT

Could she have a line here? Something to say when he comes and supports her?

LASZLO

Thank you?

MERKENSCHRIFT

No, no, something—something appealing, pathetic; something that'll make him want to help her even more.

LASZLO

Yes, yes, I see what you mean! I know exactly what you mean!

(*He throws back his head, shuts his eyes, claps a hand to his forehead. His lips move soundlessly.* MERKENSCHRIFT *waits, and gets tired of waiting.*)

MERKENSCHRIFT

Go on without it. You say the new line—

GERTIE

New line, new line, new line.

MERKENSCHRIFT

(*Enormously appealed to.*)

Is there anything more I can do to help you, Miss?

GERTIE

(*A glance at the script.*)

Please, would you assist me to my apartment? Perhaps a glass of wine will help restore me.

MERKENSCHRIFT

Of course, I'll be glad to.

(*He shepherds unsteady* GERTIE *to the imaginary stairs.* LASZLO *bends over the table and writes and crosses out.*)

And there we are. Short, clean, to the point.

GERTIE

Can we do it again?

MERKENSCHRIFT

Yes, we'll do it a *few* times. Do you have the line, Imre?

LASZLO

(*Turning, offended.*)
Please. It has to be *just—right*.

MERKENSCHRIFT

We only have a few hours.

LASZLO

I'll have it in a few *minutes*, perfectly.

(*He takes pencil and paper and goes* UPSTAGE, *the better to commune with his muse.* MERKENSCHRIFT *heaves a sigh for genius and steers* GERTIE *back toward the chair.*)

MERKENSCHRIFT

From the top again.
(*He goes to his chair. They wriggle themselves and settle into their characterizations.*)

GERTIE

It's a beautiful sunset, isn't it?

MERKENSCHRIFT

Yes, it's lovely.

GERTIE

(*After a moment.*)
Do you often come sunset-watching here on this roof?

MERKENSCHRIFT

Almost every day.

GERTIE

(*A glance at the script.*)

I'm a new tenant in the building. I have only today moved in from—

MERKENSCHRIFT

No, no, dear, off the railing now.

GERTIE

Now?

MERKENSCHRIFT

(*Taking his hat and coat from the chair and going to her.*)

Yes. If you're near the railing he doesn't feel he has to come help you; you could just hold onto the railing.

(*As he talks he puts on his hat and begins getting into his coat.* FREITAG *and* STAGEHANDS *take the chairs and table off. A sky drop is coming down.*)

So you've got to be *away* from it, and you've got to get away from it *now*, at the beginning of the speech.

(*Sections of rococo railing are sliding in from both sides.*)

GERTIE

(*Folding the script and tucking it away in a pocket of her cloak.*)

But don't I have to see the street to justify the dizziness?

MERKENSCHRIFT

Darling, you've been seeing the street long before he enters. You're dizzy *already*, but as long as you're holding the railing it's not so bad.

*(Chimneys and the stairway housing are sliding in. the sky
drop is almost down.)*
It's when you let go and step away that you feel everything begin
to spin around you.

(The railing sections meet and we are in Scene Three.)

ACT ONE

SCENE THREE

The roof of a house on the Felderstrasse. And very pretty indeed, washed as it is in warm rosiness, with a violet sky behind it.

GERTIE

Yes, that makes sense . . .

MERKENSCHRIFT

So you move away at the start of the speech, right?

GERTIE

Yes. Right.

MERKENSCHRIFT

One last time now, quickly.

(They go to the railing, in the same positions they took at the chairs. LASZLO, UPSTAGE, *watches.)*

GERTIE
(After a settling-in moment.)
It's—a *beautiful* sunset, isn't it?
(And what do you know, she's an actress.)

MERKENSCHRIFT

Lovely.

GERTIE

(*With a smile.*)
Do you often come—"sunset-watching" here on this roof?

MERKENSCHRIFT

Every day.

GERTIE

(*Moving away from the railing.*)
I'm a new tenant in the building.

MERKENSCHRIFT

That's right . . .

GERTIE

I've only today moved in from the country. I've rented apartment . . . three on the . . . fifth floor. Oh . . .
(*Sways dizzily.*)

MERKENSCHRIFT

What's wrong?

GERTIE

I'm—

FREITAG

(*Bursting breathlessly from the stairway housing.*)
He came out of his apartment!

GERTIE
(*Clasps her hands nervously.*)
Aiiiii!

MERKENSCHRIFT
Shh! It's just another opening! Now remember, in the apartment: you sit *first, then* you ask for the wine. Sit first, then wine.

GERTIE
(*Fingers to temples.*)
Sit first, then wine; sit first, then wine; sit first, then wine.

LASZLO
You remember the new line?

GERTIE
Yes, yes, yes, yes, yes! I remember everything!

MERKENSCHRIFT
Break a leg!
(*Kisses her cheek.*)

LASZLO   FREITAG
Break a leg!   Break a leg!

(*The three run and hide behind the stairway housing.* GERTIE, *biting her clenched hands, goes to her place at the railing.* LASZLO *pops from hiding.*)

LASZLO
Don't add anything!

(GERTIE *waves him away;* MERKENSCHRIFT *yanks him back.*
GERTIE *clasps her hands to her face, draws a deep breath, pulls
herself together, grasps the railing. She rearranges her cloak and
takes the railing again. She gets into the part by singing softly to
herself.*)

GERTIE

I'm just a little country girl . . . alone in the city . . . unaccustomed to heights . . . but free of disease. Just a little country
girl . . . watching the sunset . . .

(*She continues humming to herself, an open friendly country girl
watching the sunset. Free of disease. The housing door opens and*
JOHANN SCHIML *comes out on the roof. He's a bit surprised to see*
GERTIE, *but he nods, she nods back with an open friendly smile, and
he goes to his assigned position at the railing. He is in his thirties,
stiff and precise-looking; steel-rimmed glasses, carefully plastered
hair, a stiff collar. He inspects the vista before him. After a few
seconds* GERTIE *speaks.*)

GERTIE

It's—a *beautiful* sunset, isn't it?

SCHIML
(*Further scrutiny, then:*)
It would appear to be so, on first inspection.

(GERTIE *is just a trifle disconcerted, but she readies herself for her
next line.*)

GERTIE

Do—

SCHIML

A Gibraltar of cloud usurps one half the sky, its underside—an inverted meadow of gold, pink, saffron, red. The city beneath it lies—enameled; the shadowed woods beyond— invite and embrace their returning birds. And miles away, the molten sun— like the King of All Oranges—settles himself comfortably in the throne of the Alps. The effect is undeniably impressive.

> (*A pause.* GERTIE *gets ready.*)

And yet . . . Isn't that gold—too brightly gold, that red too boldly red? The cloud itself, so—so massive and unmoving, seems less the work of God than of—Manet at his worst or Turner at his best. Even the city . . .

> (MERKENSCHRIFT, *murderous with rage, comes tiptoeing out from behind the housing, his hands before him, ready to push.* LASZLO *and* FREITAG *pull desperately at him, argue with him in manic silence.* GERTIE *watches horrified.* SCHIML *goes on.*)

. . . seems unreal today, the spires too sharply tipped, the streets too picturesquely crooked. The very silence cries aloud of artifice; why not a hoofbeat, a tramcar's clatter, a bicycle bell? —why not *anything* to relieve this total unnatural nullity?

> (LASZLO *and* FREITAG *finally manage to drag the still-raging* MERKENSCHRIFT *back into hiding.* GERTIE *tries to compose herself. She begins listening again to* SCHIML.)

The Alps look flat and two-dimensional; the sun has many an evening appeared to better advantage. And so, taking all in all, one must say, with regret, no, *not* a beautiful sunset. Merely—an adequate one.

(GERTIE *waits a good long time. He's through, all right.*)

GERTIE

(*Venomously.*)

Do you often come sunset-watching here on the roof?

SCHIML

(*Looks at her.*)

Every day, when the weather's clear. Haven't we met somewhere?

GERTIE

(*Hastily resuming her role.*)

Oh no, no, that's not possible. I've only today moved in from the country. I'm a new—

(*Realizes she shouldn't be holding the railing, moves quickly away from it.*)

I'm a new tenant in the building. I've—

SCHIML

A very pretty one, may I say.

(*Hastily, embarrassed.*)

Or rather, one who—gives a first impression of extreme prettiness.

GERTIE

Well—thank you. I've rented—

SCHIML

May I—excuse me.

GERTIE

No, go ahead, it's all right.

SCHIML

May I ask you—an unusual question? One that's of consider-able importance to me?

(GERTIE *glances uncertainly at the housing, then nods.*
SCHIML *moves away from the railing and a bit closer to*
GERTIE.)
Would you tell me, please, quite honestly, what first impression I give to *you?* Do you find me pleasant, unpleasant, ugly, attractive, menacing, harmless—what?

GERTIE

(*At sea.*)
Well—not *menacing.* Pleasant . . . attractive . . . polite.
(*A gesture toward the sunset.*)
Wordy.

SCHIML

Yes, yes that, yes.

GERTIE

Austere, I think I would say. And sort of— interestingly *monastic.*

SCHIML

(*Considers that quite carefully.*)
Thank you.

(*He turns away and takes from an inner pocket a notebook and pencil. He opens the notebook, licks the pencil, and writes.* MERKEN-SCHRIFT *and* LASZLO *appear, signaling* GERTIE *to do her swaying. Helplessly, she signals that* SCHIML *is writing. They smite their brows and vanish.*)

GERTIE

You're—writing what I said?

SCHIML

Yes.

GERTIE

(*A puzzled pause.*)

Why?

SCHIML

(*Finished writing, facing her candidly.*)

I engage in very little—social intercourse, and am curious therefore—rather morbidly so, I confess—about the sort of impression I present. By writing down such comments as yours, I am able to study them at my leisure, in an attempt at objective self-appraisal.

(*He shows the open notebook to* GERTIE. *She leans forward, squints at it. He moves closer.*)

Those *were* your words, correct?

GERTIE

Yes. There were no exclamation points, though.

SCHIML

(*Taking aback.*)

No exclamation points?

GERTIE

No.

SCHIML

(*Withdrawing.*)

The tone of your voice certainly implied them.

GERTIE

Not intentionally. "Austere," period. "Interestingly monastic," period.

SCHIML

(*A "so be it" gesture.*)
It's hardly worth arguing about.
(*Makes two little crosses in the notebook, closes it, returns it with the pencil to his pocket, bows.*)
Thank you for your graciousness and I wish—

GERTIE

Oh!
(*Sways dizzily.*)

SCHIML

What's the matter?

GERTIE

I'm . . . not accustomed to heights . . .

(*She sways more extravagantly, a hand to her forehead.* SCHIML *hurries to her and supports her.*)

SCHIML

It's all right! It's all right, I have you.

GERTIE

(*Leaning against him; appealingly.*)
Whoever you are . . . I have always depended . . . on the kindness of . . . people I don't know who happen to be around when something happens to me.

SCHIML

(*Touched and tense.*)

Then permit me to introduce myself, though I hope you'll continue to—depend on my kindness. I am Johann Schiml.

GERTIE

How do you do. I'm—

(*Looks away; what a name!*)

Gretel Gesundt.

SCHIML

Gesundt?

(GERTIE *nods;* SCHIML *smiles.*)

Forgive me for smiling, but a girl with the name "Gesundt" should be immune to all illness, even vertigo.

GERTIE

I am! I *am* immune! To everything except vertigo.

(*Desperate to get on safe ground again.*)

Please, would you assist me to my apartment? Perhaps a glass of wine will help restore me.

SCHIML

Of course, I'll be glad to.

(*He shepherds unsteady* GERTIE *toward the housing.*)

GERTIE

(*Still sounding harried.*)

It's apartment three on the fifth floor. I've *only today* moved in from the country.

(*They exit. After a moment* MERKENSCHRIFT, LASZLO *and* FREITAG *come out from behind the housing. They go stealthily to the door, listen, and then* MERKENSCHRIFT *whirls on* LASZLO *and* FREITAG, *driving them toward the railing.*)

MERKENSCHRIFT

Why didn't you let me do it? What did you stop me for?
(*A gesture over the railing.*)
He could be lying down there *now*—splattered! Still talking about the sunset, but *splattered!*

LASZLO

Dietrich . . .

MERKENSCHRIFT

The swine! The opinionated wretch!
(*In* SCHIML'S *position, caricaturing his gestures.*)
"Even the city seems unreal today; the spires are too sharp, the streets are too crooked"!
(*Smites his brow with his fists.*)
Ooooh! And that *superior Transylvanian accent!* Oh my *God!*

FREITAG

If only you could have rehearsed *him* a little!

MERKENSCHRIFT

If only the two of you hadn't butted in!
(*Pushes a phantom* SCHIML, *with a suitable sound effect.*)
Everything would have been over.
(*Rests his elbows on the railing, shakes his head.*)
Ai . . .

LASZLO

But wasn't *Gertie* marvelous? The way she kept bringing him back to the script! I take back everything I ever said about her!

MERKENSCHRIFT

She's changed; I told you so.

LASZLO

The new line went well, don't you think?

MERKENSCHRIFT

(*A noncommittal head-wag.*)

Hmm-hmm . . .

(*The lights are dimming.*)

FREITAG

How long does the *apartment* scene run?

MERKENSCHRIFT

About three minutes. Unless he has a long opinion about the *wine*, that is. She'll be up as soon as he's gone.

LASZLO

Have you found a doctor's office?

MERKENSCHRIFT

I'm going to look at it tonight. You can come along if you want.

(LASZLO *nods, and rests his elbows on the railing beside* MERKEN-SCHRIFT *and* FREITAG.)

LASZLO

Mmm! Is he something!

MERKENSCHRIFT

(*Shakes his head.*)

Mmm!

FREITAG

(*Shakes his head.*)

Mmm!

(*The lights dim further.*)

LASZLO

There goes the sun . . .

MERKENSCHRIFT

(*Nods, watches.*)

With a review like that I'm not surprised.

(*Night falls instantly, ending Scene Three.*)

ACT ONE

SCENE FOUR

In the darkness, we hear voices:

GERTIE

This wine doesn't taste right to me. Would you try it, please?

SCHIML

Yes. I'd be glad to.

GERTIE

(*A moment's pause.*)
You don't mind— drinking from my glass this way?

SCHIML

No. Why should I?

(*A good question, since, as the lights come up, we find* GERTIE *and* SCHIML *naked in bed together,* GERTIE *lolling comfortably on a mass of pillows,* SCHIML *sitting beside her, judiciously wine-sipping. The apartment is a bed-sitting room, charmingly furnished and decorated: bed,* CENTER RIGHT; *settee, chairs, table, book-shelves, etc.,* CENTER LEFT. *Entrance,* UPSTAGE LEFT. *Discarded clothing everywhere.*)

GERTIE

What do you think?

SCHIML

Brittle, insipid, certainly underaged and probably overpriced.

GERTIE

(*Taking the glass.*)
That's what *I* thought.
          (*She puts the glass on a bedside table.* SCHIML *turns from
          her, finds his underpants on the floor and gets into them.*)
I hate to rush you out this way, but I have so much scrubbing
and embroidery to do.

SCHIML

(*Finds his undershirt, shakes it out thoughtfully.*)
How was it?

GERTIE

How was what?

SCHIML

(*Not looking at her, a gesture.*)
Us.

GERTIE

Oh.
          (*Surprised he has to ask.*)
It was— wonderful.

(*He puts on the undershirt. She reaches to the floor and finds a
chemise or something. He broods. She untangles the garment.*)

SCHIML

That's a meaningless word.
(*She looks at him.*)
It's vague. It's inexact.

GERTIE

(*A pause.*)
Look. *You* came, *I* came; it was *wonderful*.

(*She puts on the chemise. He puts on a sock— still brooding, and getting resentful.*)

SCHIML

People who use vague and inexact words are themselves vague and inexact.
(*Turning to her.*)
They touch, but they don't feel; they look, but they don't see. Their lives leak through them, while they sit around saying "Wonderful! Awful! Marvelous!"

GERTIE

All right, just wait a minute! Just wait now. Wait. Just wait a minute . . .
(*Sitting there in the bed, she puts her hands to her face and thinks furiously.* SCHIML *waits, watching her. She lowers her hands, sits back, thinks for another moment, and speaks.*)
This evening, in an apartment on the Felderstrasse, Mr. Johann Schiml made love to Miss—Gretel Gesundt. The deft stroking of his manicured fingers brought swift excitation to the inexperienced country girl, an excitation that Mr. Schiml reinforced and heightened by skillful kisses administered to her face, lips, ears, throat—

(She pinpoints in the air before her the relative locations of the next three.)

etc., etc., etc.

*(*SCHIML *is memorizing every word, and* GERTIE *is beginning to find her critic's role engaging.)*

In the later stages of the action, Mr. Schiml comported himself with unfailing vigor and efficacy, the happy outcome of which was the elevation of Miss Gesundt—despite her inexperience—to a peak of transfixing pleasure where she remained gasping for an infinity of blissful moments. Mr. Schiml is, beyond a doubt, an able and most gratifying performer.

(She gives him a "There, are you satisfied?" look and swings her legs out of bed and begins putting on her stockings. SCHIML *stays sitting on the bed for a few moments, overwhelmed, and then he gets up and goes one-socked to the chair where his coat lies. He takes from it his notebook and pencil, returns, finds his glasses somewhere, puts them on and sits on the corner of the bed. He licks his pencil and sets to work.* GERTIE, *done with her stockings, turns and sees him writing. She watches with astonishment and then with growing malice. She licks her lips and looks up in space.)*

And yet . . .

(The pencil freezes. SCHIML *looks up, large-eyed. Impaled on the spear of "And yet," he slowly turns and stares at* GERTIE. *She blinks coolly into space, considers.)*

. . . those deft strokings, those skillful kisses, seemed motivated—less by desire than by desire to please. That unfailing vigor and—efficacy?—

*(*SCHIML *nods.)*

efficacy, was unfailingly accompanied by a certain cool detachment, as if Mr. Schiml's *ultimate* objective was neither his own

gratification *nor* Miss Gesundt's, but rather the acquisition of
a favorable comment to inscribe in his everpresent notebook.

(SCHIML *glances down guiltily at the notebook and pencil.*
GERTIE, *watching him, relents; she raises a hand and smiles
magnanimously at him.*)

But— *this is mere carping.* The strokings *were* strokings, the
kisses *were* kisses, the outcome was *indeed* an outcome. In what
has been, God *knows*, a dry and arid season—the occasion may
fairly be termed—a thumping success!

(*She leans back against the pillows, quite pleased with herself.*
SCHIML *looks again at his notebook and pencil—and puts them
away from him. He rises and moves from the bed, troubled, roiled
in his depths. He moves* LEFT, *stops, turns toward* GERTIE.)

SCHIML

"Motivated—less by desire than be desire to please"?

GERTIE

(Nodding archly, knowingly.)

Mm-hmm . . .

SCHIML

My ultimate objective . . . was a favorable comment . . .

GERTIE

(*The same nod.*)

That's my impression; I'm sorry, but it is.

(SCHIML *stands for a moment, racked by intense and unaccustomed
emotion. He looks at himself, looks at* GERTIE. *He can scarcely
speak, but manages to.*)

SCHIML

I love you.

>(GERTIE *stares at him.*)

I do! Oh God, *my whole heart is unlocking inside me!*

>(*Running to the bed.*)

I love you! I love you! I love you!

>(*Flings himself on it, seizes* GERTIE's *hand.*)

All my life I have dreamed of a woman who could see me as clearly as I see others!

(He kisses her hand, her arm, any part of her he can manage to get hold of. She struggles to get free of him.)

SCHIML

I love you! I love you! I love you! I love you! I love you! I love you! I love you! I love you! I love you!

GERTIE

Oh, my God! Listen, it's late, it's very late. You've got to go now. Will you *stop* that, please? You've got to *go!*

SCHIML

Oh, clear-eyed country maiden who measures the very soul of me!

GERTIE

I've got *scrubbing* and *embroidery*—

SCHIML

Oh love-dream-woman who speaks only truth, truth, truth!

GERTIE

Will you please get dressed and get out of here?

SCHIML

I'm yours forever! I swear it! I swear it! Command and I obey!
I love you! I love you!
> (*Kissing again.*)

I love you! I love you! Command and I obey!

GERTIE

Now *honestly, you can't stay any longer!* I—

(*Gradually she's given pause.* SCHIML *goes on kissing.*)

SCHIML

I love you! I love you!

GERTIE

I—command, and you—obey?

SCHIML

> (*Kissing.*)

Yes, yes, yes! I swear it! I love you! All my life I've—

GERTIE

> (*A nervous laugh.*)

But you *really* can't *mean* that; I *mean*—

SCHIML

I do! I do! I swear it, my angel! I love you! I *love* you!

GERTIE

But, well, I *mean*—suppose I were to command you to—well,
to change *jobs* or something—

SCHIML

I would *do* it! I would *do* it! I swear it! I would *do* it! Where's your Bible? Where's your Bible?

(*Looking on the bedside table, unsuccessfully.*)

Where's your Bible? *Where's your Bible?*

GERTIE

Oh God, I don't *know!*

SCHIML

(*Rising, hurrying to the bookshelves.*)

Your Bible, the Bible, the Bible, the Bible. I swear that I mean it, command and I obey!

(*Racing a finger over the rows of books.*)

The Bible, the Bible, the Bible, the Bible . . .

GERTIE

Is that it up on the—

SCHIML

Here it is!

(*He yanks at a book, turns.*)

I swear on this Bible I'll—

(*And finds that he's holding an entire shelf of book-spines.*)

do whatever you—

(GERTIE *sinks her face to her hand.* SCHIML *looks at the panel of book-spines, at the empty shelf behind him, at the panel, at* GERTIE, *at the panel again. He glances at the back of it, sees something printed there, turns it over, reads.*)

"Property of Dietrich Merkenschrift"? "Do not remove from theater"?

(*He looks about, nonplussed; touches other rows of books*

*and finds that they too are panels of spines. He turns and
his distracted gaze falls on a chair before him.)*
This chair . . . It was in— it was in—
          (Slaps his forehead rapidly, eyes shut.)
A Good Girl's Last-Minute Triumph! And the settee! The bed! The—
          (Looks around, taking in the apartment as a whole.)
Why is the furniture *arranged* this way? *Everything facing the
one blank wall!*

GERTIE
          (Raising her head.)
I rented the place *furnished!* It's *late;* you'd better go now.
          (SCHIML *stares at her. She tries authority.)*
I command you.

SCHIML
          (Stares at her, points.)
Ophelia . . . You're *Ophelia* . . . ! The one that slapped Hamlet
in the face!

GERTIE
          (Her last line of defense.)
I have only today moved in from the country! I thank you for
your neighborly courtesy and trust we shall meet again!

SCHIML
          (Dizzily, a hand to his forehead.)
What kind of—*plot* is this? What kind of *scheme?* You rub against
me in the doorway, I must open your dress so you can breathe
more easily—*what are you doing to me?*
          (Hurls the panel away.)
Blackmail, is that what you're up to? Or—no, no, I'm to give
up my post for love of you! That's it, isn't it?

(*Advancing on* GERTIE.)
I'm to give up my post!

GERTIE

(*Backing* RIGHT *off the bed.*)
Please, there's been a mistake . . .

SCHIML

(*Coming around the foot of the bed.*)
Admit it, you liar, *that* was the game, wasn't it?
(GERTIE *scrambles over the bed but* SCHIML *doubles back and catches her.*)
You lying, deceiving, bitch of an actress!
(*Flings her to the bed.*)

GERTIE

(*Screaming.*)
Dietrich! Dietrich!

(SCHIML *throws himself on her and tries to get her by the throat. She screams and struggles.*)

SCHIML

So he's in on it too! Of *course* he is; I should have *guessed* it!

GERTIE

He's killing me! Dietrich!

SCHIML

Yes! Yes! Killing you for deceiving me! Killing you for lying! Killing you! You lying bitch of an actress!

(*Pounding at the* UPSTAGE LEFT *door, and it's flung open—by* MERKENSCHRIFT, *with* LASZLO *and* FREITAG *close behind him.* GERTIE *screams and hits* SCHIML *as he tries to strangle her.* LASZLO *and* FREITAG *rush forward but* MERKENSCHRIFT *catches them by the arms and restrains them.*)

MERKENSCHRIFT

Wait! Wait! *Wait!*

LASZLO

He's killing her!

MERKENSCHRIFT

So he kills her! He *hangs*; it's *gorgeous!*

(FREITAG *sees the wisdom of this, but* LASZLO *struggles to get free.*)

LASZLO

For God's sake, Dietrich!

MERKENSCHRIFT

She changed your lines, didn't she? Doesn't she deserve to be pun-ished?

LASZLO

Let *go* of me!
          (*He breaks free and rushes to the bed.* MERKENSCHRIFT
          is in a fury. LASZLO *takes a firm stance behind* SCHIML.)
Unhand that woman at once, sir, or by all that's holy, I'll thrash you very, very hard!

SCHIML

Imre Laszlo!
> (*He stops strangling* GERTIE *and turns.* LASZLO *is surprised and flattered.*)

LASZLO

You know me?

(SCHIML *gets off* GERTIE *and off the bed.* GERTIE *groans, moans, lifts herself partway.* SCHIML *stares at* MERKENSCHRIFT.)

SCHIML

And *you* are—

MERKENSCHRIFT
> (*A click of the heels, a bow.*)

Captain Schwartz of the Homicide Bureau, at your service. I strongly suggest that you leave the city. I give you this opportunity to escape only because I like your face and I have a heavy work load.

SCHIML

You're Dietrich Merkenschrift!

MERKENSCHRIFT

No, Captain Schwartz.
> (*Patting his pockets.*)

I left my badge in my other suit, but I think I have a card here from the Policeman's Humanitarian and Social—

SCHIML

You're Dietrich Merkenschrift!
> (*Going to him.*)

You've engineered this whole deception and you're going to be
sorry you ever did, I promise you that! All of you shall be sorry!
(*He begins gathering his clothes.* GERTIE *sits up on the bed,
rubbing her throat.* LASZLO *moves near her solicitously.*)
I fall in love with her, I quit my post; she commands, I obey.
Cleverly done! Wait, just wait, you'll see how I repay you!

MERKENSCHRIFT

(*To* FREITAG, *gesturing at* SCHIML.)
My God, this isn't Reinhold!
(*To* SCHIML, *accompanying him as he collects his clothes.*)
We were playing a joke on this friend of ours, Reinhold
Schwartz—no, not Schwartz; I forget his last name. He watches
the sunset on the roof of the house next door.
(*To* GERTIE.)
You went to the *wrong house, dumbbell!* A thousand pardons for
this inconvenience, sir! Yes, I'm Dietrich Merkenschrift, and I'd
like to offer you free tickets to all my future productions. May
I have the honor of knowing to whom I'm speaking?

FREITAG

He looks a lot like Reinhold!

MERKENSCHRIFT

Doesn't he? It's amazing!

SCHIML

(*A cold majestic pause, his arms full of shoes and clothing.*)
You are speaking, as you very well know, to Johann Schiml,
who will make every effort to *judge* those future productions
with his customary fairness and objectivity, unswayed by the
fact that you are a *toad and a cockroach!* You wish me to change

my job, "Miss Gesundt"? I was thinking of doing just that, of going back home and writing for a year.

(*To* MERKENSCHRIFT, *with chilly pleasantness.*)
Another rival newspaper is near closing, you know. My growing power makes me more and more uncomfortable.

(*A chilly smile all around.*)
But no, I'm a critic, not a playwright. I think I'll stay on—for five more years at least. Your dialogue this evening showed improvement, Mr. Laszlo. Keep up the good work.

LASZLO

(*Confused.*)
Well, thank you.

SCHIML

Miss—Kessel, is it not? —I advised you last year to "get thee to a nunnery." This year I should suggest a different species of all-female establishment. Good evening, gentlemen. Thank you for the entertainment.

(*Carrying his armload of clothes, he makes a firm proud underwear-and-one-sock exit.* MERKENSCHRIFT *sinks to the settee, stunned.*)

MERKENSCHRIFT

Five years . . . !

(GERTIE, *crushed, picks up from the bed beside her* SCHIML'*s notebook.* LASZLO *comes and confronts her angrily.*)

LASZLO

Point out to me, please, where it says in the script she goes to bed with him!

GERTIE

I—I thought it would be—a bigger dramatic acorn.

MERKENSCHRIFT

(*Turns, glaring.*)
You thought it would be! Look what you've *done*, you—you—
you—*IMBECILE!*
(*Rising, to* LASZLO.)
I TOLD you to let him strangle her! But NO . . . !
(GERTIE *begins weeping.* MERKENSCHRIFT *paces,
raging.*)
Five years! I'll be bankrupt in five *months* with him out to get
me! And another *paper's* closing! He's going to be practically the
only critic in town! I might as well sell the—
(*He stops short as* SCHIML *comes marching in, bath-
robed and slippered. He goes to* GERTIE *and holds out
his hand. She looks at him tearfully but proudly and
gives him the notebook. Trembling, he opens it, finds
a certain page and carefully tears it out. He offers it to
her but she won't take it. He crumples it, throws it to
the floor and turns and marches out.* GERTIE *weeps.*
MERKENSCHRIFT *picks up the page, uncrumples it, reads,
frowns.*)
"Comported himself with vigor and efficacy"? "An able and
gratifying performer"? —three exclamation points?
(*Turns the page over.*)
"Austere . . . Interestingly monastic . . ."
(*Looks at both sides of the pages again.*)
The son of a bitch doesn't know if he's a hit or a flop!
(*Turning to* LASZLO.)
Imre . . .

LASZLO

(*Moving to him.*)

What?

MERKENSCHRIFT

You're going back to that desk of yours.

LASZLO

I am?

MERKENSCHRIFT

(*Pacing, plotting.*)

I want a whole new script from you. About a critic—who wants criticism—and gets so much of it—

LASZLO

—that he goes crazy!

MERKENSCHRIFT

Right!

LASZLO

I see what you mean! I know exactly what you mean!

MERKENSCHRIFT

Good! Get going! Freitag, pack up this junk! We rented this place by the hour!

(LASZLO *is hurrying out the door.* FREITAG *starts piling the furniture.* MERKENSCHRIFT *is heading* DOWNSTAGE. GERTIE, *on the bed, calls after him.*)

GERTIE

What are you going to do to him, Dietrich?

MERKENSCHRIFT

None, of your business, Miss Hot Pants!

GERTIE

(*Rising.*)

Dietrich! Leave him alone!

MERKENSCHRIFT

(*To the Audience.*)

I know I told you to come back, but I'm sorry kids, I've got to kick you out again.

(*House lights begin fading up.*)

There's going to be a slight delay in production; that's the theater business. Be back here the day after tomorrow at exactly the same time—or maybe fifteen minutes later. Believe me, we're going to get Schiml. *There's nothing to worry about.* As Imre Laszlo put it so beautifully in the curtain line of *A Good Girl's Last-Minute Triumph*—"The only thing we have to fear—is actually being afraid."

(*He steps back behind the falling curtain as the lights come up to full.*)

END OF ACT ONE

ACT TWO

SCENE ONE

When most of the Audience has returned to its seats, the curtain rises. MERKENSCHRIFT, *beaming and enthusiastic, comes* DOWNSTAGE. *The stage is hung with a large banner bearing a picture of disdainful* SCHIML *and the title* Good-bye, Schiml!

LASZLO *and* FREITAG *sit at a table* DOWNSTAGE LEFT, LASZLO *holding a manuscript,* FREITAG *behind stacks of excerpts.*

MERKENSCHRIFT

That's it, that's it. Come on in, come in. It's wonderful that you're all getting here so promptly. *Take any seats!*

(*The house lights begin to fade.*)

It doesn't matter where you sit, you're all going to get parts! No auditions this time; there are parts for everybody! Hello, Heinrich . . . There are two seats over there. That's right, you people take them. Let them through, please. Bertha! You really dressed up, didn't you! That's right, everybody in. You folks upstairs, move down and fill in the holes, will you? That's right.

(*Ushers are going up the aisles handing out fliers.*)

Our ushers are passing out pictures of Schiml. We don't want any slip-ups. Those of you who don't get one now can pick one up when you're leaving the theater. Let's all settle down now, please.

(*The house lights are down, the ushers are gone up the aisles.* MERKENSCHRIFT *addresses the audience gravely.*)

This is the largest cast I've ever assembled. Except for *The Gypsy Student*. I want to thank you all for getting here so promptly, and for seating yourselves in such an orderly manner. It's cooperation like this that's going to make *Good-bye, Schiml!* by Imre Laszlo—

    (*A gesture at* LASZLO.)

into the big success we all so desperately want it to be. Can you hear me up there? It's a big theater and the acoustics aren't that great. The other day we chose some of you for parts in a relatively small production designed to send Mr. Schiml back to his father's bakery business. Unfortunately that production was torpedoed—to coin a word—by one of your colleagues, a former nun who's a disgrace to *both* her professions. Today, however, we're embarking on a much bigger production, one that can't possibly fail. Mr. Schiml has a little notebook that he carries around with him, and he jots down in it whatever comments anyone makes about him. We're going to give him so many comments to jot— so many *totally contradictory* comments—that in two or three weeks, a month at the most, he isn't going to have an opinion on *anything*. He's going to be a quivering jelly! They're going to need *spoons* to get him into the lunatic asylum! Let me give you an idea of what I'm talking about. Freitag, who plays the painter?

FREITAG
    (*Consulting a list.*)
Hugo Graubermann.

MERKENSCHRIFT
Hugo Graubermann. Where are you?

GERTIE
    (*Coming down the aisle.*)
May I speak to you, Dietrich? May I speak to you for a minute?

MERKENSCHRIFT

Who let *you* in?

(*He mouths "She's the one" to the Audience, pointing at* GERTIE, *who's coming up onto the stage.*)

GERTIE

May I speak to you in private?

MERKENSCHRIFT

There's no part for you in *this* production, Gertie Kessel.

GERTIE

I don't want one, thank you. I'm *doing* a part, for Otto Schlegel. I'm playing a Japanese pearl fisher, under the name of Mitsuko Shibui. I never liked "Gertie Kessel" anyway.

(MERKENSCHRIFT *makes a derisive sound.*)

Isn't it easier simply to change our names and hope he doesn't recognize us?

MERKENSCHRIFT

And what am I supposed to do with the theater? Paint it blue and push it over to the Krottenbachstrasse?

(LUBAUER *comes onstage and silently supervises the setting up of a flat or two representing the wings.*)

GERTIE

(*To the Audience.*)

I know you think that Johann Schiml is a monster, but he really isn't. Wanda, how can you be part of a plot to drive someone mad? How can any of you? Don't you—

MERKENSCHRIFT
(*Interrupting her, taking her by the arm.*)
All right, all right, we're not doing Joan of Arc. Go wait for me
in the wings.
(*He sends* GERTIE UPSTAGE, *and addresses the Audience.*)
I'm going to speak to this traitor in private for a moment. While
I'm gone, you ladies take those pictures of Schiml and stick your
hatpins in them; it may just work.

(LASZLO *and* FREITAG, *shaking their heads disapprovingly, withdraw
and exit* LEFT; *stagehands remove the table as* MERKENSCHRIFT *goes*
UPSTAGE *to join* GERTIE.)

GERTIE
You really will drive him mad, Dietrich! He gives so much weight
to whatever is said about him!

MERKENSCHRIFT
It's not enough that you went to bed with him? Now you're
feeling sorry for him?

GERTIE
He's human, Dietrich; he's a human being!

MERKENSCHRIFT
(*A long scornful look at the heretic.*)
Get out of here. Go back to the nunnery and pray for forgive-
ness. Incredible! Absolutely fantastic!

GERTIE
It's wrong, Dietrich, and if you go ahead with it—I'm going to
tell him. I will!

MERKENSCHRIFT

Now you listen to me, you—*A*, he won't let you come within
ten feet of him, or read anything you write; have you forgotten
his last words of advice to you? *B*, you're *Gertie Kessel*, not Mit-
suki Pearl-Fisher! It's him or you; face the facts! It's him or *us*.
All right, you messed things up; they're better now than they
were before. Go away for a few weeks; when you come back,
he'll be gone.

  (*Putting an arm around her shoulder.*)
I'm going to do a big revival of *The Student Gypsy*, to pay off
my debts, and then—I'll do your welcome-home.

GERTIE

I told you, I'm working for Otto Schlegel.

MERKENSCHRIFT

Gertie, Gertie, Gertie, think for a minute, will you? In any given
season, how many good parts are there for Japanese women?
Even in *Japan* there aren't that many, and *they* all go to the *men*.
Come on, go find an inn or a spa; read plays, decide which one
you want to do.

  (GERTIE *looks uncertain.* MERKENSCHRIFT *gets out his*
  wallet.)
You need money? I'll give you an advance on your salary.

GERTIE

Thanks for your generosity.

MERKENSCHRIFT

All right, it's a present. Here.
  (*Puts a bill in her hand.*)
Go pick a play.

(GERTIE *looks wryly at the bill, and puts it in her purse.*
MERKENSCHRIFT *pockets his wallet.*)
You're a crazy warm-hearted woman and I love you.
(*Kisses her cheek.*)

GERTIE

I'm a shit like you and I hate us both.

MERKENSCHRIFT

All right, let's not split hairs. Have a good time.
(*A pat on her rear to send her on her way.*)
Let me know where you are, hm? Maybe I can get away for a
day or two.

GERTIE

For a hundred marks? Mm-mm.

(*She shakes her head and exits.* MERKENSCHRIFT *turns with a "You-
can't-win-'em-all" shrug, rubs his hands, and comes* DOWNSTAGE
to the Audience, smiling. The curtain falls behind him.)

MERKENSCHRIFT

Okay! Did you make lots of little pinholes?
(LASZLO *and* FREITAG *are coming back onstage, accom-
panied by an* ACTOR.)
Where are we?

FREITAG

Hugo Graubermann.

MERKENSCHRIFT

Oh yes.

(*Bringing the* ACTOR *forward.*)

Hello, Hugo. I guess you've never forgiven Schiml for that cruel remark he made about your nostrils.

ACTOR

No, I haven't.

MERKENSCHRIFT

Good. Hugo, you're going to be a painter on the roof of Schiml's building. He goes up there every evening to watch the sunset. You'll bump into him, flick a tiny drop of paint on his shoulder, and then you'll fall to your knees trembling and say—What are the exact words, Imre?

LASZLO

(*Acting it enthusiastically.*)

"Oh, please, sir, don't hit me! It's only a drop of paint! You're so big and strong and manly, you could kill me with a blow! Please, sir, I beg you! Oh, thank you, thank you, thank you!"

MERKENSCHRIFT

Thank *you*, Imre.

LASZLO

(*To the Audience.*)

"Big and strong and manly." But a little girl in the street will cry because "that short ugly man"—Schiml—"scared me." And at the theater, the couple behind Schiml will talk pointedly about the increasing number of obvious sexual deviants around.

MERKENSCHRIFT

Hundreds of comments on all sides of him! There are parts for all of you. Most of you are doubling, in fact. And some of you are even tripling.

(LASZLO, FREITAG, *and the* ACTOR *are going offstage.*)

When your name is called, you'll come up here on the stage. I'll rehearse your scenes and then you'll go downstairs and see Hedy, our wardrobe mistress. *Good-bye, Schiml!* begins its run tomorrow. You've got to be at your assigned places on time, fully made up so you won't be recognized; you've got to play your scenes sharply and clearly; and above all—and I can't stress enough how crucially important this is—you're to make *ABSOLUTELY NO ADDITIONS TO THE SCRIPT!* Mr. Laszlo has done his job, I'm going to do mine, and if you people do yours—and I know full well you will—in a very short time Mr. Johann Schiml is going to be a total wreck. So let's bring up the curtain on the most important production of your career—

(*The curtain rises to reveal a projection screen, and on it, a picture of* SCHIML, *sternly disapproving.*)

Good-bye, Schiml!

(*Blackout—except for the projected picture.*)

ACT TWO

SCENE TWO

Voices of actors and actresses are heard.

ACTRESS ONE

Carries himself well, doesn't he?

ACTOR ONE

God, I'd give anything to have a build like that!

ACTRESS TWO

Watch where you're going, Fatso.

(*The projected picture changes—to a matching one of* SCHIML *looking taken aback.*)

ACTOR TWO

May I touch your hump for luck?

(*The picture changes;* SCHIML *looks surprised and puzzled.*)

ACTRESS TWO

I can't see the stage with this hulk in front of me.

ACTOR ONE

Want me to help you across the street, grandpa?

ACTOR TWO

There's a bar down the street that caters to our kind.

(*The picture changes;* SCHIML *looks alarmed.*)

ACTOR TWO

It *can't* be Lord Byron; he's been dead for ages.

ACTRESS TWO

Handsome, isn't he?

(*The picture changes;* SCHIML *is relieved, hopeful.*)

ACTRESS ONE

Homely, isn't he?

(SCHIML *is panicking.*)

ACTOR TWO

How about that nose?

ACTOR ONE

Out pretty late for a kid that age.

ACTRESS TWO

Don't look now, Fritz, but speaking of midgets . . .

(SCHIML*'s panic grows . . .*)

ACTRESS ONE

If only some people would use cologne!

ACTOR ONE

What a break that the seat in front of us is empty!

(*. . . and grows . . .*)

ACTOR TWO

Typical criminal forehead.

ACTRESS TWO

Obvious gigolo.

ACTRESS ONE
(*Screaming.*)
EEeeeeeahhh!

(SCHIML, *is wild-eyed, tearing his hair.*)

ACTRESS TWO

Oh Daddy, that short ugly man scared me!

ACTRESS ONE

Handsome profile.

ACTOR TWO

Poor old beggar.

ACTRESS TWO

Now *there's* a beautiful toupee!

(SCHIML *is in the final stage of a nervous breakdown.*)

ACTOR TWO

Looks like Napoleon!

ACTRESS ONE

Looks like Wellington!

ACTRESS TWO

Looks like Josephine!

(*The projection screen is rising.*)

ACTOR ONE

Oh, please, sir, don't hit me! It's only a drop of paint! You're so big and strong and manly, you could kill me with a blow! Please, sir, I beg you! Oh, thank you, thank you, thank you! How lucky I am that a rugged and powerful man like you can also be merciful! Thank you, thank you, thank you . . .

ACT TWO

SCENE THREE

The roof of the house on the Felderstrasse, evening. Another adequate sunset, maybe even a bit more adequate than the first one.

Out of the stairway housing bursts SCHIML, *moaning with anguish, his hands to his head, the right shoulder and arm of his suit covered with white paint. He runs in circles, a wretch pursued by demons.*

He tries to compose himself but can't. He runs to the housing door and closes it, runs back to CENTER STAGE, *tries again to master his agony. This time he partly succeeds. He gets out his notebook, leafs rapidly through the pages looking for a blank one. He stuffs the notebook away and gets out his new notebook, leafs, leafs, and finally finds a page. Licking his pencil, he stabs his tongue. He takes a deep breath, and manages, despite the quavering of his hand, to write.*

He compares what he has written with entries on other pages, and is hopelessly mired in confusion. He stuffs the book and pencil away, tries to shake some of the paint off his arm, wipes his face with both hands, smooths his hair. He goes to the railing and clutches it, his eyes shut tight. He opens them, looks—and his gaze is drawn irresistibly downward. He leans forward—but by dint of a massive effort, fights off the impulse. He looks at the sunset, holds the railing again. By degrees he calms down, but God, it's not easy. He breathes deeply, brushes a tear from his eye, and watches his one solace, the sunset.

Is this a tinkling sound that he hears from the stairway housing? More madness? He turns. Yes, there is a tinkling sound, and footsteps. The housing door opens, and onto the roof, rather awkwardly, steps an elaborately costumed JAPANESE WOMAN. *With her arms folded in her kimono sleeves, she bows to* SCHIML *and advances with tiny shuffling steps to the railing near him, her silver-belled headdress tinkling musically. She bows to the sunset and proceeds to watch it.* SCHIML, *all but totally paralyzed, has turned, following her movement. He stares at the* JAPANESE WOMAN, *inscrutably watching the sunset—and he knows he's crackers. He backs away from her, wondering if he can get to the stairway before he falls into pieces. The* JAPANESE WOMAN *raises her hand and speaks. We give away what would have been a big surprise and refer to her as* GERTIE.

GERTIE

Please do not leave, honorable sir!

    (SCHIML *freezes, petrified.* GERTIE *stows her hand in her sleeve and bows to him.*)

Humble Mitsuko brings important message for you. You are Johann Schiml, is not so?

    (SCHIML *gives the smallest nod ever nodded.* GERTIE *bows.*)

Is not also so that people have been making contradictory comments about you?

    (SCHIML *looks about, preparatory to flight.* GERTIE *quickly raises her hand.*)

Please! Listen!

    (SCHIML *does.*)

They are not *real people!* They are actors and actresses, engaged by a man who seeks to destroy your mental faculties!

    (SCHIML *stares at her.*)

Actors and actresses are making the comments! Engaged by a man who—doesn't like you.

SCHIML
(*A stunned whisper.*)
Merkenschrift . . . ?

GERTIE
(*Hands in sleeves, inscrutable.*)
I name no names.

(*She turns to the sunset again.* SCHIML *stares at her. It takes him a while to find his tongue.*)

SCHIML

Who—are you?

GERTIE

Mitsuko, a humble pearl fisher.

SCHIML

A what?

GERTIE

Pearl fisher. Pearl. Pearl.
(*Shows him an imaginary necklace, or maybe a real one.*)

SCHIML

A *pearl* fisher?
(*Looks at the city.*)
Here??

GERTIE
(*Thinks about that.*)
Unemployed pearl fisher.

SCHIML

And these—these people who have been saying all these—these different things about me—on all sides of me—men, women, children, policemen—

GERTIE.

Actors and actresses, all of them. Not real people.

SCHIML

My *God*, I was—I was on the edge of— madness! Just now I almost—

(*A gesture toward the railing.*)

GERTIE

(*A sharp intake of breath.*)
Sssssss! Mitsuko is glad she came in time.

SCHIML

(*Moving closer to her, anxiously.*)
But *how* did you come? How do you *know* about this?

GERTIE

A lady send me. A lady who knows you despise her. A beautiful lady.

SCHIML

A—beautiful lady who—

GERTIE

(*Turns to him, bows.*)
Mitsuko must go now. Good evening, Honorable Sir. Humble Mitsuko is glad she could help you.

SCHIML

Wait, wait, please!
(*Touches her arm, briefly.*)
Please stay! Only a minute!
(*An entreating gesture.*)
Watch the sunset!

GERTIE

(*Hesitates, bows.*)
Only a minute.

(*She resumes her sunset-watching position.* SCHIML *takes the railing beside her.*)

SCHIML

Dietrich Merkenschrift . . . ? By God, he'll pay for this! I swear on my *soul* he'll pay for it! It *is* Merkenschrift, *isn't* it!?

GERTIE

I name no names.

SCHIML

Who is the lady? Tell me that! Please, you must! I'm indebted to her! I want to thank her for sending you!

GERTIE

I name no names. I only watch the sunset.

(*She watches.* SCHIML *does too, thinking desperately. He turns to* GERTIE.)

SCHIML

Could it be—

(*And turns away.*)
No, not *she*, not *that* one, though God knows she's beautiful
and God knows I despise her!

(*They watch the sunset.* GERTIE *surreptitiously wipes a tear from
her eye. She tries to bear up.*)

GERTIE

Sunset is . . . also beautiful . . .

SCHIML

(*Nods distractedly.*)
Lovely . . .

GERTIE

Do you often come sunset-watching here on—
     (*Oops. She stays very still.* SCHIML *turns slowly, wide-eyed.*
     GERTIE *backs from him, bowing.*)
Minute up. Mitsuko go now.

(*She backs shufflingly toward the stairs, but* SCHIML *grabs her,
and holds her, dislodging her headdress and wig. She struggles in
his grasp.*)

GERTIE	SCHIML
Please! Please, Sir! Please! Let go of me!	"Mitsuko," is it? We'll see if you're—

(SCHIML *withdraws from her, looks at her exposed hair.*)

SCHIML

It's you again!

GERTIE

Only half Japanese!

SCHIML

(*Clutching his head.*)
Oh God in heaven, I can't STAND any more!

(*He throws himself at the railing and starts over it.* GERTIE *grabs him and drags him back.*)

GERTIE

No! No! Don't! Oh God! No!
You mustn't!

SCHIML

I *can't!* I *can't!* Let go! Let go
of me!

(*Considerable struggle and finally* GERTIE *succeeds in thrusting* SCHIML *well away from the railing. He stands weaving dazedly.* GERTIE *is breathless, her headdress askew.*)

GERTIE

I came here to help you! To *help* you!

SCHIML

Oh Lord . . . !

(GERTIE *tears off her headdress and wig, strips of tape and her own short hair are underneath.*)

GERTIE

You wouldn't have listened if I'd come as myself!

SCHIML

Is Imre Laszlo writing this?

GERTIE

No! He's writing the *comments!* I'm *improvising!* I'm supposed to
be at a *spa*, picking a play for my *welcome-home* production . . .
                (*Pokes irritably at the headdress.*)
But I kept worrying about *you*, being driven *mad . . .*

SCHIML

                (*Going to the railing, his hands over his ears.*)
Please! I can't stand those BELLS!

GERTIE

                (*Lowers the headdress to her side, looks away. After a
                moment:*)
I was improvising in our other scene too.

SCHIML

                (*Takes his hands from his ears, looks at her.*)
What?

GERTIE

                (*Looks at him.*)
I *said*, I was improvising in our other scene too. Downstairs.

SCHIML

                (*A pause. Lowers his hands.*)
You were?

GERTIE

Yes.
                (*Looks away.*)
All I was supposed to do was get you to *drink from my glass . . .*

SCHIML
(*Looks away, decides.*)
Un*disc*iplined . . . !

GERTIE
(*Turns to him.*)
I'd been a year in a *nunnery*, thanks to *you!*

SCHIML
(*Turns to her.*)
You *went?*

GERTIE
I went.

SCHIML
Good God! How could you pay such attention to a—*a random comment?*
(*She glares at him. He looks away concedingly.*)
I suppose I'm—not the one to ask that.

GERTIE
You certainly are not.
(*Peevishly, she adjusts his pocket flaps, straightens his tie. He smooths his hair.*)
There. Now you're—"interestingly monastic" again.
(SCHIML *holds the railing, looks away.*)
Aren't you going to write it down?
(SCHIML *disdains to react.*)
Why are you painting your suit?

SCHIML

A workman in the hall did it. A big stupid— an *actor*, of course.

GERTIE

(*Touching near the paint.*)

It's ruined . . .

SCHIML

Merkenschrift shall pay for it . . .

       (GERTIE *turns to the railing, holds it. The lights dim a*
       trifle.)

So he wishes to drive me out, does he? Well perhaps he shall,
and perhaps my replacement will be more to his liking.

GERTIE

What are you thinking of?

SCHIML

A matter of honor.

GERTIE

Oh dear . . .

       (*Sighs, and looks out.*)

What a rotten sunset.

(SCHIML *turns and looks at her. After a moment, he touches*
a sprig of her hair. She slaps his hand away. He keeps looking
at her.)

SCHIML

Do you swear to me that *this, now*, the two of us, is *real*, is
happening?

(She turns, looks at him, raises her hand and nods. He puts his hands to his eyes, sighs, shakes his head.)
I don't know where I am. I can scarcely breathe.

GERTIE
(Takes his elbow.)
Come. Let's go to your apartment.

SCHIML
(Lowers his hands, nods.)
Yes.
(They leave the railing.)
Perhaps a glass of wine will help restore me.

(As they reach the door of the housing, the lights fade to darkness and the curtain falls, ending Scene Three.)

ACT TWO

SCENE FOUR

FREITAG *comes out onstage, lists in hand.*

FREITAG

There are even more parts *this* week, so when I call your name, come up quickly please. Gerhardt Ehrhardt. Heinrich Mitteldorf. Hilde—

MERKENSCHRIFT
(*Interrupting him.*)
Hold it, Freitag! Hold it right there!
(*He has come hurrying onstage, a letter in his hand.*)
Is somebody on the spot? Who's up there? Hit me with the spot, whoever you are!
(*A spotlight comes on and finds him. He gives the thumb-and-forefinger sign of approval.*)
That's it . . .
(*To the Audience.*)
For this I want the spotlight!
(*He savors the joyful news for a moment, and then, leaning forward with his hands on his knees, gets ready to share it.*)
Kids . . . You've done it. You've *done* it! *You've DONE it! That's RIGHT, he's GONE, he's QUIT, he's gone HOME TO*

TRANSYLVANIA! He *has!* He *has!* He *has!* That *is,* they *say* he's gone home to Transylvania; where he's *really* gone, I'm willing to bet you, is into a little padded cell somewhere! You've done it. You're real troupers, every last one of you.

(*Makes a big kiss at them.*)

God bless you! I got the news early this morning, and I sent a note and a case of champagne to the newcomer who's replacing him. This letter was just delivered to me. I'd like to share it with you.

(*Angles himself toward the light.*)

"Dear Mr. Merkenschrift: What a pleasure to receive a free case of champagne, and what an unexpected honor to hold in my hand a note written by Dietrich Merkenschrift himself. It goes right in my scrapbook. Thank you for your good wishes. Being appointed drama critic of the most influential newspaper in the city is, *for a stagestruck fellow like me,* a dream come true. I hear you are planning a revival of my favorite operetta, *The Student Gypsy.* I know you will give it the lavish, unstinting production it deserves, and I know I will adore every second of it. Thank you for the champagne, and especially for the note. Ever your admirer"—are you ready?—"Melchior Schnook." So help me God!

(*Shows the letter to the front rows.*)

Look! Melchior Schnook! Right there, as big as life! Look! Look! See? You see it? You see?

(*To* EVERYONE.)

Isn't that gorgeous? Melchior Schnook!

(*Kisses the letter passionately, folds it and tucks it away.*)

This goes in *my* scrapbook! What else is there to say? In three weeks we raise our curtain—that's why we lowered it just now, ha-ha—in three weeks we raise it on the biggest, most lavish *Student Gypsy* that's ever been seen, starring those singing

sweethearts of *Countess Trudi*, Mitzi Karlöwe and Carlo Mizzi!*
Stay right where you are! These three weeks are going to pass
like a flash!

*(He snaps his fingers, and the curtain rises on the office set, ending
Scene Four.)*

* Which is pronounced, of course, "Mitzi."

ACT TWO

SCENE FIVE

MERKENSCHRIFT *goes* UPSTAGE *into the office, where* FREITAG, LUBAUER, MITZI, *and* CARLO *are waiting, glasses of champagne in hand.* MERKENSCHRIFT *picks up a glass too.*

MITZI

Those three weeks certainly passed like a flash, Dietrich!

CARLO

Those three weeks certainly passed like a flash, Dietrich!

MERKENSCHRIFT

Didn't they? It's amazing!
    (*Raising his glass.*)
To Melchior Schnook!

OTHERS

Melchior Schnook!

(EVERYONE *drinks.*)

FREITAG

I can't get over the way he keeps sending you those encouraging letters!

MERKENSCHRIFT

It's marvelous, isn't it? He's *got* to be the greatest living *Student Gypsy* fan!

LUBAUER

Well, he certainly won't be disappointed *tonight*, at least not in the scenery department.

(*The telephone rings.*)

MERKENSCHRIFT

Not in the *anything* department.
　　(*Picks up the telephone.*)
I'll pay you at the end of the week.
　　(*Puts the phone down.*)

FREITAG

　　(*Looking at a newspaper.*)
And his every review the same thing: "A pretty good show, but not the lavish tuneful operetta we're all waiting for."

MITZI	CARLO
Has anyone gotten a good look at him yet?	Has anyone gotten a good look at him yet?

MERKENSCHRIFT

No, he moves even faster than the other critics. He knocked down a woman in the lobby of the Athena last week; all she saw was a black beard and paint in his right ear.

LUBAUER

Sounds peculiar, even for a critic.
　　(*The telephone rings.*)

MERKENSCHRIFT

Well, he's A-number-one in *my* book!
(*Picks up the phone.*)
I'll pay you at the end of the week!

(*He puts the phone down.* LASZLO *taps at the door, looking in.*)

LASZLO

Dietrich?

MERKENSCHRIFT

Imre, darling Come on in! Have some champagne with us!
(LASZLO *comes in, says hellos all around and gets answering hellos plus a simultaneous "Hello there, Imre!" from* MITZI *and* CARLO.)
Got another glass, Freitag?

FREITAG

Yes sir, right here!

(*He fills a glass.* LASZLO *looks around, a bit surprised.*)

LASZLO

You're not rehearsing?

MERKENSCHRIFT

Rehearsing! Rehearsing! We've been rehearsing three weeks; it's enough already.

LUBAUER

The avalanche works like a dream.

(FREITAG *gives champagne to* LASZLO, *who thanks him.*)

MERKENSCHRIFT

And wait till you see what we do in Act *Four! Mmm!* You're coming tonight, aren't you?

(*The telephone rings.* MERKENSCHRIFT *signals to* FREITAG.)

LASZLO

I don't think so. Bella's gout is acting up.

MERKENSCHRIFT

Ah, that's a shame . . .

FREITAG

(*On the phone.*)
He'll pay you at the end of the week.
(*Puts the phone down.*)

MERKENSCHRIFT

Leave it off the hook!
(*To* LASZLO.)
You can't come alone?

(FREITAG *sets the earpiece on the desk.*)

LASZLO

Maybe, I'll see. Guess what? I got a letter from Melchior Schnook!

MERKENSCHRIFT

You too?

LASZLO

I'm his favorite living playwright. My only fault is I punch my lines a little too hard.

MERKENSCHRIFT

I've had *four* letters! *Four*, mind you! Each one telling me how great I am, and begging me to go all out on *The Student Gypsy!*

LASZLO

It's wonderful when a critic takes a real interest.

MERKENSCHRIFT

Isn't it?

FREITAG

(*Having gone* RIGHT, *he is looking out the door.*)
Yes, sir? Is there anything I can do for you?
(*Exits.*)

MERKENSCHRIFT

(*Shouting.*)
I'll pay you at the end of the week!

LASZLO

You're in debt?

MERKENSCHRIFT

Only till tomorrow; don't worry.
(*Goes to the desk, picks up a bottle.*)
Look, leave Bella at home with her gout, come tonight—
(*Refilling his glass.*)
you'll see the biggest, most expensive production you ever saw in your entire life. I guarantee it! A quarter of a million—

FREITAG
(*Coming in, closing the door behind him; a wide-eyed whisper.*)
Mr. Merkenschrift!

MERKENSCHRIFT
(*Alarmed.*)
What? What is it?

FREITAG
He's here! Melchior Schnook!

MERKENSCHRIFT
Oh my God!
(*Those who are sitting rise; all stare at* FREITAG.)
Show him in! Show him in!
(FREITAG *goes out.* EVERYONE *neatens himself.* MITZI *and* CARLO *neaten each other. Whispers of excited speculation.*)
Shhh! Shhh! Don't fawn on him!
(*Goes beamingly* RIGHT.)
Mr. Schnook! Mr. Schnook! At last we meet! Come in! Come in!

(MELCHIOR SCHNOOK *enters, with* FREITAG *behind him.* MERKENSCHRIFT *pumps* SCHNOOK*'s hand. Above his suit,* SCHNOOK *consists of black hair, black spectacles, and a bushy black beard. Guess who.*)

SCHIML
(*In a well-disguised voice.*)
What a *pleasure*, Mr. Merkenschrift! Are you *sure* I'm not intruding?

MERKENSCHRIFT

Oh, no, no, no, not at *all!* Come in! Have some champagne
with us! Meet everybody!

SCHIML

I was passing by, and at the risk of being presumptuous I
thought I—

MERKENSCHRIFT

Presumptuous? You? Are you *serious? We're* presumptuous! Please!
Let me introduce everybody! This is Imre Laszlo . . .

SCHIML

Oh, what joy!

(*He and* LASZLO *shake hands.*)

LASZLO

Thank you so much for your letter! It went right in my scrapbook!

(MERKENSCHRIFT *leads* SCHIML LEFT *to* MITZI *and* CARLO, *standing arm in arm.*)

MERKENSCHRIFT

And the stars of *The Student Gypsy*, Mitzi Karlöwe and Carlo
Mizzi . . .

SCHIML

Miss Karlöwe . . .
        (*Takes her* RIGHT *hand, kisses it.*)
Mr. Mizzi . . .
        (*Shakes* CARLO's LEFT *hand.*)

MITZI

Call me Mitzi.

CARLO

Call me Carlo.

MERKENSCHRIFT

My assistant, Mann Freitag . . .

SCHIML

How do you do?

(*They shake hands.*)

FREITAG

It's an honor, sir!

MERKENSCHRIFT

And my scenic designer, Pepi Lubauer.

SCHIML

(*Arms wide with admiration.*)
The Master of the Waterfall!

(*He and* LUBAUER *shake hands.*)

LUBAUER

You have quite a treat in store for you tonight, sir, if I do say so myself. Specially laid conduits—from the river, right in through the back wall!

SCHIML

(*To* MERKENSCHRIFT.)
So you've really gone "all out," have you?

MERKENSCHRIFT

Oh yes, yes indeed. One hundred and twelve actors, fourteen sets, two floods, and an avalanche.

SCHIML

I'm glad you can afford such an expensive production.

MERKENSCHRIFT

(*Laughs.*)

Between us, I can't. That's why the phone is off the hook! I owe money to everybody in the city. But I wasn't going to disappoint a big *Student Gypsy* fan like you, was I? Mm-mmn! By the end of the week, I expect, we'll have those nice long lines at the box office and I'll start paying everyone back.

SCHIML

Yes . . . everyone shall be paid back . . .

(MERKENSCHRIFT *smiles and raises his eyebrows to the* OTHERS. SCHIML *chuckles softly to himself.*)

MERKENSCHRIFT

You're laughing?

SCHIML

Yes. I'm thinking of my predecessor, Johann Schiml.

MERKENSCHRIFT

He was nothing to laugh about, believe me!

(*The others cluck sympathetically.*)

SCHIML

I was just thinking of what *he* would have written tonight. He hates *The Student Gypsy*, you know.

MITZI

Oh, how *could* he!?

CARLO

Oh, how *could* he!?

MERKENSCHRIFT

(*Raises a hand.*)
No, no, I'm not surprised. I'm not the least little bit surprised.

SCHIML

(*Sips his champagne.*)
I hear you had a hand in his—departure, Mr. Merkenschrift.

MERKENSCHRIFT

Oh well, rumors float around—

SCHIML

No, no, don't be modest. I feel there's so much that I owe you!

MERKENSCHRIFT

Well yes, I *did* do a little—small-scale maneuvering.

SCHIML

I hear it was more like a grand-scale game of chess: innocent-seeming pawns gradually encircling him—and then check and mate.

MERKENSCHRIFT

(*Proudly.*)
Well, sort of!

SCHIML

(*Drains his glass and sets it precisely on the desk.*)
Two can play that game, Mr. Merkenschrift.

MERKENSCHRIFT

(*A puzzled pause.*)
I know. One takes the white, one takes the black.

SCHIML

(*Rising, going* DOWNSTAGE RIGHT.)
The game I refer to isn't chess. The game I refer to is deception
and disguise, the destruction of one's enemies.

(*He takes off his wig, beard and glasses and turns and faces* MERKEN-
SCHRIFT, *who starts and stares. Simultaneous gasps from* MITZI *and*
CARLO; LASZLO *and* LUBAUER *rise;* FREITAG *drops a bottle.*)

MERKENSCHRIFT

No. No. No.
(*Clutches the edge of the desk, shakes his head.*)
No. No. No. No. No. No. No.
(*Looks beseechingly at the* OTHERS.)
No. No. No. No. No. No. No.
(*And again at* SCHIML, *who comes slowly to the desk.*)
No. No. No. No. No.

SCHIML

(*In his own voice.*)
Yes, Mr. Merkenschrift.

MERKENSCHRIFT

No.

SCHIML

(*Puts his disguise gear on the desk.*)

Johann Schiml returns to his post this evening, just in time for *The Student Gypsy*.

MERKENSCHRIFT

No . . .

SCHIML

(*Unpocketing his regular glasses and putting them on.*)

There will be no long lines of ticket buyers; rather, I think, large mobs of creditors, don't you?

MERKENSCHRIFT

No. Yes. No . . .

SCHIML

(*Takes an envelope from an inner pocket.*)

A letter for you, from my wife.

(*Puts it on the desk.*)

Good day, sir.

(*Nods all around.*)

Miss Karlöwe. Mr. Mizzi. Mr. Lubauer. Mr. Freitag. Mr. Laszlo.

(*Goes to the door, turns and smiles poisonously at* MERKEN-

SCHRIFT.)

Break—a *leg*.

(*He goes. Hubbub and discussion;* EVERYONE *gathers around the desk;* MERKENSCHRIFT *sits stunned.*)

MERKENSCHRIFT

No.

LASZLO
(*Picking up the envelope.*)
He must have just gotten married.

MERKENSCHRIFT
Open it.

(LASZLO *does so, while the* OTHERS *talk excitedly.*)

LASZLO
A hundred marks!

MERKENSCHRIFT
Gimme!
(*Grabs the bill and pockets it, still stunned.*)

LASZLO
"Dear Dietrich: It wasn't him *or* me, it was him *and* me." It's
from Gertie! "Gertrude Kessel Schiml"!

MERKENSCHRIFT
The bitch . . .

LASZLO
She *told* him, and he *married* her . . .
(*A startled realization.*)
It's *A Good Girl's Last-Minute Triumph!*

MERKENSCHRIFT
Like HELL it is! Get back, everybody!
(*Waves them away.*)
Get back! I've got to think! Get back and be quiet! Unless you
have a good idea.

(*He claps his hands to his face and thinks ferociously.* EVERYONE *draws away from him.* MITZI *and* CARLO, *watching him anxiously, sit* LEFT *and automatically assume their arm-in-arm position.* LASZLO *puts the letter down and sits* RIGHT *of desk.* LUBAUER *and* FREITAG *sit* RIGHT. *Silence.*)

LUBAUER

Couldn't your lawyer *bar* him somehow?

FREITAG

We've tried that six times.

(*More silence, more thinking.*)

MITZI

Why doesn't he like it?

CARLO

It's such a good show!

(MERKENSCHRIFT *gives them a disgusted look.* EVERYONE *thinks.*)

LASZLO
(*Giving slow birth to the idea.*)
When the ticket-taker . . . tears his ticket in half . . . could he maybe keep both halves?

MERKENSCHRIFT
(*A disgusted hand-wave.*)
No, that's no good! Once he's through the door we're finished! I've got to find a way to keep him *outside the theater*, to stop him right at the threshold!

(EVERYONE *thinks another while—and then* LUBAUER *feels something growing.*)

LUBAUER

We build another theater, just a false front—

MERKENSCHRIFT

We've got FOUR HOURS, PEPI!

FREITAG

(*Gets out his watch.*)
Three hours and— forty-three minutes.

(EVERYONE *thinks.*)

LASZLO

I just thought of something.

MERKENSCHRIFT

What?

LASZLO

Who wrote *The Student Gypsy?*

(MERKENSCHRIFT *can't remember; he looks to* FREITAG.)

FREITAG

Siegfried Kleiner.

LASZLO

So why am *I* sitting here dying?
(*Gets up.*)

I'm going to go out and get some pastry. Anybody want anything?

>   (*He looks to* MITZI *and* CARLO; *they shake their heads.*)
Dietrich? Sugar is energy.

MERKENSCHRIFT

All right, bring me something.

LASZLO

You boys?

LUBAUER

No, thanks.

(FREITAG *shakes his head.* LASZLO *goes out.* EVERYONE *thinks.*)

MERKENSCHRIFT

It's no use. He's got me, the bastard! A quarter of a million
marks! I'm going to have to sell *everything:* my house, the Prince
Friedrich, my—

(*And he stops, arrested by thought.* FREITAG *stares at him.*)

LUBAUER

Do you think you—

FREITAG

SHHH!

(EVERYONE *watches* MERKENSCHRIFT. *Is the Master getting an
idea? Yes, yes, it's coming! He squints at it this way and that:
it's so farfetched, and yet maybe, just maybe . . .* EVERYONE

watches breathlessly. Finally MERKENSCHRIFT *lets it out through his lips.)*

MERKENSCHRIFT

Suppose . . . I call . . . Prince Friedrich.
　　(*Silence.*)
The theater is *named* for him, isn't it? In his youth he was an avid theatergoer. I remember when I was a stagehand, he used to come backstage after every opening and feel the actresses.

FREITAG

Could you get through to him?

LUBAUER

And what could he do?

MERKENSCHRIFT

I don't know. *Some*thing. He's a *prince*, isn't he?

MITZI	CARLO
Try it!	Try it!

FREITAG

(*Moving to the chair* RIGHT *of desk, sitting on the edge of it.*)
There's nothing to lose, sir!

(MERKENSCHRIFT *thinks about it for a moment, then carefully lifts the phone's earpiece from the desk. He raises the phone and ever so lightly jiggles the hook.*)

MERKENSCHRIFT

Please, would you tell me the phone number at the Royal Palace?

Thank you.
>   (*Presses the hook.*)
One . . .
>   (*He thinks some more. God, what a momentous decision!*
> FREITAG *leans toward him.*)

FREITAG

Do it, sir! Do it! Ride with your vision!

(MERKENSCHRIFT *looks at* FREITAG, *then off at that vision. He draws a breath, looks at the phone, takes his finger from the hook, holds the earpiece to his ear.*)

MERKENSCHRIFT

One please. It's ringing . . . Good afternoon, this is Dietrich Merkenschrift, of the Prince Friedrich Theatre. Returning His Highness's phone call. I will. Thank you.
>   (FREITAG *whips out a handkerchief and pats* MERKEN-
> SCHRIFT'S *brow.* MERKENSCHRIFT *thanks him silently.*)
Good afternoon! M-E-R, K-E-N, S-C-H, R-I-F-T. *F. F* as in— Friedrich. Look, this is an emergency. It's about the survival of the theater that bears His Highness's name. Would you just tell him that, please? *The theater that bears his name.* Please. Tell him that.
>   (*Looks around gravely at* EVERYONE *while he waits.*)
Footsteps. I think he's coming! Your Highness?
>   (*He rises. So does* EVERYONE *else.*)
Merkenschrift, the owner and manager of the theater that so proudly bears Your Highness's name! Thank you for speaking to me, Prince Friedrich! I wouldn't—Yes, I remember, I do! I was a stagehand then!
>   (*Listens, laughs.*)

Yes, yes, they certainly were!

    (*Covers mouthpiece; to* OTHERS.)

Wonderful old man!

    (*Uncovers mouthpiece.*)

The theater is in peril, Your Highness! Have you heard of a critic named Johann Schiml? Yes, that's the one, yes!

    (*Covers mouthpiece.*)

Hates him! He *hates* him!

    (EVERYONE *comes closer to* MERKENSCHRIFT, *suddenly hopeful.*)

That's just what *I've* said, Your Highness! *Nothing* satisfies the son of a bitch! But he *isn't* gone, that's the trouble! He only *pretended* to go, to trap me into this fantastically expensive production, Mitzi Karlöwe and Carlo Mizzi in *The— Student Gypsy.*

    (*Slowly, getting devious.*)

And *incidentally*, Your Highness, Miss Karlöwe is *dying* to meet you.

    (MITZI *and* CARLO *nod cooperatively.*)

Mm-hmm. She has a picture of you in her dressing room—

    (*Turns away from* MITZI *and* CARLO, *lowers his voice a bit.*)

and I hear she does some pretty strange things in front of it. Your Highness, he's going to *kill* us! We open tonight and by the end of the week I'll have to sell the theater—to—to *God*-knows-who, developers who'll smash it down and put up houses in its place! No, he's from Transylvania . . . A—Writ of *Banishment? Would you?*

    (*What wide eyes all around!*)

Bailiffs at every entrance?

(*What excitement!* MITZI *and* CARLO *start waltzing and singing.*)

MITZI

"You are a student!
I am a gypsy!
We are imprudent and
    tipsy
With love!"

La-da-dee-da-da,
La-da-dee-da-da . . .

CARLO

"I am a student!
You are a gypsy!
We are imprudent and
    tipsy
With love!"

La-da-dee-da-da,
La-da-dee-da-da . . .

MERKENSCHRIFT

Oh, Your Highness! Oh, God bless you, Prince Friedrich!

(*Listens, laughs.*)

Yes, yes, *I'd* love to see his face too! I *will* see it; I'm going to be there watching! I'll call you tomorrow and tell you about it!

(FREITAG *and* LUBAUER *join in the waltzing and singing.* MERKENSCHRIFT *laughs more.*)

Yes, yes!

(*Covers mouthpiece.*)

He's laughing, he's laughing! He *loves* the idea!

(EVERYONE *kisses* MERKENSCHRIFT, *hugs him. Laughing, he listens again.*)

He's *still* laughing!

(EVERYONE *lifts* MERKENSCHRIFT *and swings him to and fro, laughing and la-dee-da-ing. He listens again.*)

He's *still* laughing! No, now he's coughing! He's coughing. He's coughing. He's coughing.

(*They stop swinging him and put him down.*)

It's all right, he stopped.

(*Sighs of relief all around.*)

Someone's crying.

(Gasps of fear, bitten lips. MERKENSCHRIFT *listens and then, staring straight ahead, glazed, lowers the phone.)*
He's dead . . .
(He looks incredulously at the telephone in his hands; looks at the OTHERS.*)*
I killed Prince Friedrich . . . !

(He drops the phone. LUBAUER *sinks into his chair, then* FREITAG, *then* MERKENSCHRIFT. MITZI *slowly crosses herself and* CARLO *with a single split-down-the-middle cross, and they too sit. After a long moment,* FREITAG *realizes something.)*

FREITAG

There'll be a period of mourning. No theater for thirty days.

MERKENSCHRIFT

Oh my God . . . !
(He covers his face and cries and who can blame him? He makes wordless gestures at the telephone, cries more, turns to FREITAG.*)*
"Ride with your vision! Ride with your vision!"

(He cries more. FREITAG *gets up and goes back to where he sat earlier.* EVERYONE *sinks into the very bowels of depression.* MERKENSCHRIFT *still quakes with an occasional sob.* MITZI *dabs at her eyes with a handkerchief.* LASZLO *comes in, rather briskly, with a small white paper bag. He slows a bit and shakes his head when he sees how depressed* EVERYONE *is. He goes to the desk, puts the bag down, carefully opens it and lifts out a little pink pastry. He offers it to* MERKENSCHRIFT *who, his face in his hand, waves it away.)*

LASZLO

You told me to bring you something.

> (MERKENSCHRIFT *waves it away more vehemently.*)

Mitzi?

> (*She shakes her head.*)

Carlo? Anybody?

(NOBODY *wants it.* LASZLO *shrugs. He looks at the pastry in the bag, and decides on the one he's holding. He sits down* RIGHT *of desk, takes out his pocket handkerchief, spreads it on his lap and begins eating the pastry. Neat bites, careful chewing. It's delicious, but he's a little annoyed by the way* EVERYONE *has surrendered to despair.* BBBBONNNNGGGGG! *A tremendous bell tolls, a foundation-and-roof shaker,* LASZLO *looks up, surprised. The* OTHERS *sink lower in their seats. After a moment—BBBBONNNNGGGGG!* LASZLO *looks around thoughtfully, pastry in hand, trying to figure out what might have happened. The death knell keeps slowly tolling as the lights fade to darkness, ending Scene Five.*)

ACT TWO

SCENE SIX

The death knell continues tolling in the darkness—slow, solemn, unremitting.

Finally it remits, and the lights come up on the office, draped with yards of black crepe. MERKENSCHRIFT, *standing by the desk, is putting on* SCHIML*'s bushy black beard.* FREITAG, *beside him, holds the wig and dark glasses.* MERKENSCHRIFT *adjusts the beard, looking in a makeup mirror on the desk. The phone is off the hook. Both* MERKENSCHRIFT *and* FREITAG *wear wide black armbands.*

FREITAG *gives* MERKENSCHRIFT *the wig. He puts it on; and then the dark glasses. He shows his face, or his nose, rather, to* FREITAG.

FREITAG

If you walk fast they'll never know it's you.

MERKENSCHRIFT

(*Walking, groping with both hands.*)
Who can walk fast in these things? How did he see?

(*He stumbles over a chair.* FREITAG *steadies him.* LASZLO *enters with a suitcase. He too wears a black armband. He stops short.*)

LASZLO

Ooh my God!

MERKENSCHRIFT

(*Whirls.*)
Who is it? Who *are* you?
(*Tears off the glasses.*)
Oh.

LASZLO

I thought it was him!

MERKENSCHRIFT

I thought it was *them!*

LASZLO

(*Putting down the suitcase.*)
There are more of them out there than yesterday, and in an uglier mood.

FREITAG

It's a good thing they respect those military uniforms.

MERKENSCHRIFT

And that they don't know it's Mitzi and Carlo wearing them.
(*To* LASZLO.)
Did you get everything?

LASZLO

Two suits, shirts, pajamas, underwear, five hundred Norwegian Kröner, and a ticket on the Oslo Express. One thing I couldn't get . . .

MERKENSCHRIFT

What?

LASZLO

Your passport.

MERKENSCHRIFT

I *told you*; the top drawer under the handkerchiefs!

LASZLO

Your manservant wouldn't let me have it; he says you owe him two thousand marks.

MERKENSCHRIFT

How do you like that! Ten years of free passes and this is how he repays me! How am I going to get out of the country without a passport?

FREITAG

We have some prop ones.

MERKENSCHRIFT

What good is a *prop passport*, idiot?

LAZSLO

Could you dress up as a train conductor?

GERTIE

(*She enters.*)

Hello, Dietrich. Imre, Mann . . . Mitzi let us through the barricade.

MERKENSCHRIFT

(*Snatching off the beard and wig.*)

What do *you* want?

GERTIE

To give you the best play you've ever produced.

(*She beckons towards the doorway.* SCHIML *enters, somewhat reluctantly. Both he and* GERTIE *wear mourning insignia on their costumes.*)

SCHIML

Gentlemen . . .

(MERKENSCHRIFT *lunges at him, but* LASZLO *and* FREITAG *catch his arms, restraining him.*)

GERTIE

Go ahead, Johann.
    (SCHIML *hesitates.*)
I command you.

SCHIML

    (*Heaves a sigh.*)
As the deaths of Romeo and Juliet brought an end to the feud between the Montagues and the Capulets, perhaps the death of our beloved Prince Friedrich can bring an end to the feud between you and me.

GERTIE

I cried for two hours. Isn't it awful?

MERKENSCHRIFT

    (*Throws off* LASZLO'*s and* FREITAG'*s hands, in command of himself once more.*)
Yes, yes, tragic, really tragic. Do they know what caused it?

GERTIE

They say there was a threatening phone call.

SCHIML

The entire palace to be smashed down and replaced with houses
for workers.

MERKENSCHRIFT

They stop at nothing, these Bolsheviks!

GERTIE

He was such a *nice* person too! He visited me backstage after
my first performance.

SCHIML

Did he? I didn't know that.

GERTIE

Oh sweetheart—I forgot to mention it.

MERKENSCHRIFT

(*Looking meaningfully at* LASZLO *and* FREITAG.)
Yes, His Highness was an avid theatergoer . . .

GERTIE

(*Eager to change the subject.*)
Go on, Johann.

SCHIML

Sobered by his untimely passing, and finding myself with no
professional duties in the month ahead—and softened too by
the love of my darling Gertie—I've decided to follow my earlier intention and return to my home in Transylvania, to work
on a play I've been thinking of.

GERTIE

A romantic comedy!

SCHIML

With social implications, of course.

LASZLO

You're going to write a play?

SCHIML

One watches, one learns.
> (*To* MERKENSCHRIFT, *with a gesture at the beard and wig.*)
I'm sure you can—elude your creditors for a month, and then you can open *The Student Gypsy* to the unbiased appraisal that every show deserves.

MERKENSCHRIFT

You mean—you're *really quitting?*

GERTIE

He's done it!

SCHIML

We've just come from the newspaper.

MERKENSCHRIFT

Really?

SCHIML

Really.

MERKENSCHRIFT

May I ask who's replacing you?

SCHIML

They're not sure yet. Either the gardening editor or the boy who proofreads the want ads.

> (MERKENSCHRIFT, LASZLO, *and* FREITAG *shake hands and embrace, delighted.*)

GERTIE

Dietrich, his play is going to be *marvelous!*

SCHIML

That's an inexact word.

GERTIE

Oh, hush! The girl is a flower seller, almost illiterate, with a terrible peasant accent, dirt all over her face, awful! "Buy ein flower, sir? Buy ein flower?"

SCHIML

And the man—is a professor of phonetics! Very superior, very rude and arrogant.

> (*To* MERKENSCHRIFT, *pointing at* GERTIE.)

"Listen to that creature!"

MERKENSCHRIFT

"Ooy, how she talks!"

SCHIML

Yes!

MERKENSCHRIFT

I love it!

LASZLO

It's a good beginning, I have to admit.

FREITAG

What happens?

SCHIML

He takes her in to live with him! Not for romantic reasons. He's
going to teach her how to speak and make a *lady* of her.

MERKENSCHRIFT

That's wonderful!

GERTIE

You'll produce it and I'll star! Next season!

LASZLO

What's the rest of it?

GERTIE

Six months later—

SCHIML

(*Interrupting her.*)
No, no, dear; I don't want to give away *all* my surprises.

MERKENSCHRIFT

Oh come on, come on, friend Schiml; tell us!

<table>
<tr><td>LASZLO</td><td>FREITAG</td></tr>
<tr><td>Yes, tell us!</td><td>Tell us, please!</td></tr>
</table>

SCHIML

Well, I really shouldn't, but it's so satisfying and delightful and theatrically correct . . . He works day and night teaching her proper pronunciation; "The fog in Prague—"

GERTIE

"—stays mainly in the bog . . ."

SCHIML

And six months later—

MERKENSCHRIFT , LASZLO, AND FREITAG

Yes!

SCHIML

HE'S talking as badly as SHE is!

(MERKENSCHRIFT *pumps* SCHIML's *hand enthusiastically and* GERTIE *hugs and kisses them both.* FREITAG *beams, but* LASZLO *moves away scratching his head doubtfully as the curtain falls.*)

THE END

CANTORIAL

INTRODUCTION

(*CANTORIAL*)

Unlike the other two plays in this volume, which are straight-ahead comedies, *Cantorial* is a *seriocomic* work—melding an earnest human drama onto a succession of genuine laughs.

It's also partly a suspense play, as protagonist *Warren Ives* struggles to tease out his true identity. It's also part ghost story, and also part *musical*—incorporating as it does its powerfully emotive *cantorial* singing. (The Phantom of the Synagogue, if you will.) If you don't know a *cantor* from a cantaloupe, don't worry—the play was written for audiences of all beliefs and backgrounds, with Levin seeing it as *"a mainstream comedy with religious overtones."*

The above serenading was recorded for in-performance playback (*"ingeniously projected in stereo around the theater,"—The New York Times*) by renowned cantor Paul Zim—who would touchingly sing decades later at Levin's funeral.

In a 1989 interview, Levin related that he'd toyed with the idea of writing a novel about a haunted synagogue for some time, finally concluding that *". . . if a synagogue is going to be* haunted, *it should be haunted by a* cantor—*whose singing would be very exciting to hear in a theater."* That realization, he said, made it a play. *"Once I had the idea of the cantor, one thing led to another. I asked myself, 'Why is this cantor haunting the syna-gogue?' and eventually the synagogue became a* former *synagogue."*

Eerily, on the night Levin made the above realization, he was working further on the idea by candlelight—so as not to wake his sleeping wife—when he noticed that on the wall opposite their bed there had appeared the life-sized silhouette of a singing cantor. *"I went ice cold, and I pinched myself to see if I was still awake."* he later told *The New York Times*. He soon realized it was just the shadow of his bedside lamp's finial and other parts casting the image. Still, he woke his wife (who didn't know he was working on such an idea)—and asked her what the shadows resembled. *"A singing cantor"* she replied immediately, before returning to sleep. The author took this as the most positive of omens.

Levin has described *Cantorial* as "*. . . probably the warmest thing I've ever written.*" That's no doubt true (though an argument could be made for *Drat! The Cat!* as a contender—itself an *actual* musical—Levin's only one). It was not until he was working on *Cantorial*'s third and final pass that Levin recalled a boyhood excursion he'd taken with his father to the Bronx's *Ascot Theatre* (demolished in 2016) to see the Yiddish-language film *The Cantor's Son*, which itself featured cantorial singing. *"[It] was an especially good day between us,"* Levin shared—and that positive memory (of a sometimes thorny relationship) surely informs some of the play's warmth, as well as its strong father–son contours.

The play's warmheartedness is also reflected in the host of autobiographical references present. The character of *Morris Lipkind* refers at one point to a former cantor by the name of *Isaac Schlansky*—Schlansky was Levin's mother's maiden name. As Morris further explains: *"They was all from Russia, the ones what built the [synagogue]. From a* shtetl *in the Ukraine, a little village. Like in* Fiddler on the Roof.*"* Levin's parents' families had in fact both emigrated generations earlier from (coincidentally) the same Russian *shtetl* as one another; and Levin's mother grew up on *Cantorial's* setting of the Lower East Side.

Numerous other autobiographical tidbits abound. The names of various family friends and relations are woven throughout. A family is referenced in *King's Point,* Long Island—the very town where Levin had just set up home with his (sleep-deprived) second wife, and written the play. Even the featured *chopped herring* and *Lorna Doone* cookies were Levin household staples.

Cantorial premiered in 1984 at Connecticut's *Hartman Theatre.* Levin continued to hone the play, and in 1988 a revised version was produced at off-Broadway's *Jewish Repertory Theatre* (the same theater where *Crossing Delancey* premiered). The production transferred a year later to the Times Square–adjacent *Lamb's Theatre.*

Of its 1988 Jewish Rep run, *The New York Times* wrote: *"Cantorial may be the most melodic nonmusical in town. What's more, it strikes the right note theatrically almost to the very end: good staging, attractive casting, inventive idea, and crisp dialogue."* The *Christian Science Monitor* praised the *"genial new comedy"* and its *"well-tempered mix of the mystical and whimsical."*

By turns spiritual, comic, suspenseful, mystical, and *musical...* here is *Cantorial.*

Nicholas Levin
New York City
January, 2025

CANTORIAL

CANTORIAL was first presented in New York City at the Jewish Repertory Theatre on October 27, 1988, with the following cast and crew:

WARREN IVES . . . . Anthony Fusco

LESLEY ROSEN . . . . Lesly Kahn

MORRIS LIPKIND . . . . Woody Romoff

PHILIP QUINN . . . . James DeMarse

DONNA QUINN . . . . Joan Howe

WILLIAM IVES . . . . Robert Nichols

Director . . . . Charles Maryan
Sets. . . . . Atkin Pace
Costumes . . . . Lana Fritz
Lights. . . . . Brian Nason
Sound . . . . Gary & Timmy Harris
Production
     Stage Manager . . . . Catherine A. Heusel
Stage Manager . . . . Mimi Moyer
Casting. . . . . Jim DeMeaux
Press Rep . . . . Shirley Herz Associates

Featuring the voice of Paul Zim

TIME

ACT ONE—Late summer, early fall of 1989
ACT TWO—Late fall, early winter

SETTING

The play is set in a home that formerly was a synagogue, on the Lower East Side of Manhattan.

ACT ONE

SCENE: *A home that formerly was a synagogue, on the Lower East Side of Manhattan. A small synagogue but a spacious home—a handsome contemporary habitat with track lighting, clear glass windows, and a staircase spiraling up to a sleeping loft* RIGHT *(originally the gallery), under which a compact open kitchen has been installed.*

The UPSTAGE *wall was the synagogue's front wall. The stripped-down Ark remains as a large shelved recess at its center, with a platform extending before it. Stereo speakers have been installed above.*

Double doors RIGHT *open onto a vestibule and the street entrance (offstage* RIGHT*). A single door* DOWNSTAGE RIGHT *leads to the bathroom, and another* LEFT *to the basement stairs. Beyond the upper windows can be seen the bottom of a Spanish-language billboard.*

Furnishings change during the course of the play and are described in the text.

AT RISE: *the luminous moment before sunset.* WARREN IVES, *29, in T-shirt and shorts, is on the platform connecting stereo components on shelves in the recess. A 20" TV and VCR are already in place. A sectional sofa is backed against the* DOWNSTAGE *end of the platform, facing a coffee table and low side chairs. A table and chairs* CENTER RIGHT *before the kitchen, a desk* LEFT *with telephone. Miscellaneous other contemporary furniture. Pictures leaning against the walls, wrappings and cartons about, garment bags on the bed upstairs. An upper window* LEFT *is open; street sounds are heard.* WARREN *works on . . .*

LESLEY ROSEN *enters* DOWNSTAGE RIGHT, *closing the door. She's 27, also in T-shirt and shorts.* WARREN *smiles at her.*

WARREN

Music in two minutes.

LESLEY

(*Looks about.*)
Oh God, Warren, it's going to be so beautiful!

WARREN

They *said* it looked even better at night.
(*Switches track lighting on.*)

LESLEY

And *your* furniture loves *my* furniture . . .

WARREN

How could it not?
(LESLEY *joins him on the platform. They hug and kiss.*)
Glad now?

LESLEY

I wasn't *not glad*, I just had butterflies.

WARREN

(*Gives her another kiss.*)
Almost done.
(*He resumes work. She watches.*)

Everything fits right in. With the acoustics in here it's going to sound fantastic.

LESLEY

This must have been the *Ark* . . . It's where they keep the Torahs.

WARREN

I know.

LESLEY

(*Indicating the platform.*)
And this was the—ooh, wait a second, wait—the beema! That's what it's called. This platform. They unroll the Torahs and read from them, on a—table or something.

WARREN

I thought Ryan and Thad built it in.

LESLEY

No, it's from before, it must be . . .
(*Looks about, thinking.*)
When did they say it was built?

WARREN

Eighteen ninety-six.

LESLEY

(*Thinks.*)
Do you know my great-grandparents could have gone here? They lived on Attorney Street—I remember the name from my grandmother's stories—and they'd have gone someplace within walking distance. You're not supposed to ride on the

Sabbath . . . Wouldn't that be weird, if I'm co-owner of the synagogue they attended?

WARREN

Any way you can find out?

LESLEY

My Aunt Rose might know . . .
  (*Going off the platform and into the kitchen.*)
She's my great-aunt really. You met her at Denise and Mark's
wedding. Tiny? Blue hair?

WARREN

Oh, yeh.

LESLEY

I'll have to call her . . .
  (*A faint phrase of tenor singing is heard.* LESLEY *unwraps
  things and puts them away.*)
Have you ever *been* in a synagogue?

WARREN

Oh, sure. Whenever my father was trying to get elected. I've been
in every house of worship in Detroit. Dressed up, not fidget-
ing . . . Jeez, I hated it when he ran. Ungrateful little bastard . . .

LESLEY

Honey . . .

WARREN

It's the truth. Whenever he was running for something, which
was always, I felt their main reason for adopting me, his anyway,

was to have a kid to show to the voters. Which made me an "ungrateful little bastard."

LESLEY
(*Holding up a pitcher.*)
This is beautiful! Where'd you get it?

WARREN
(*Smiles at her.*)
I don't know. I think someone gave it to me when I moved into my old place.

(*He makes a kiss at her; she returns it. The phrase of singing—Hebraic—is heard, louder.*)

LESLEY
What's that?

WARREN
Somebody's radio.

(*He homes connected components.* LESLEY *grows uncomfortable.*)

LESLEY
Hey, I'm exhausted. Let's knock off.

WARREN
Okay.

LESLEY
(*Coming out of the kitchen.*)
We don't have to do everything today.

WARREN

(*Finishing.*)
Want to try the Jacuzzi?

LESLEY

Yes!

WARREN

And the *mirrors*?

LESLEY

I don't like them. I felt like the Rockettes in there, all of us sitting down in a line.

WARREN

That's because you didn't have any champagne . . .

(*As they are about to kiss, the phrase is sung:* "B'NAY BASE-CHOH K'VOT CHEE-LOHHHHH.")

LESLEY

That's in here.

WARREN

It sure sounded like it . . .
    (*They look around, and at each other.*)
It *must* have been from outside. The acoustics.

(*He goes* UPSTAGE LEFT, *takes a hooked window pole, and closes the upper window.* LESLEY *watches. Street sounds fade out.*)

LESLEY

I think it was—Hebrew.

WARREN
(*Laughs as he replaces the pole.*)
Don't start imagining things.

LESLEY
Could somebody be in the basement?

WARREN
No. I checked the whole place to make sure they got the junk out.
(*They wait hand in hand, listening.* WARREN *smiles reassuringly.*)
It was from outside. A passing Jew.

(*Laughing with relief, they hug and kiss.*)

LESLEY
I thought for a minute we—

(*Louder: "B'NAY BASE-CHOH K'VOT CHEE-LOHHHH."*)

LESLEY
(*Overlapping.*)
What's that?

WARREN
They left a present for us. Ryan and Thad. A tape, and a player, and a timer.

LESLEY
Where?

WARREN

(*Looking about.*)
Somewhere.

LESLEY

We'd have found it. We found the mousetrap.

WARREN

It's somewhere. It's got to be. You look *up*stairs, I'll look down.
(*Heading* LEFT.)
This is gay humor.

(*He exits* LEFT *and goes downstairs.* LESLEY *hesitates a moment then goes
quickly up the stairs to the loft. As she starts to search, singing begins.*)

LESLEY

Warren!

(WARREN *races in* LEFT *and across the platform into the kitchen as
the singing continues.* LESLEY *hurries down the stairs as* WARREN
opens a wall panel, flips switches.)

LESLEY

What are you doing?

(*Lights go out.*)

WARREN

Cutting off the power!

(*Faint light from the street remains. The singing continues, a
poignant Hebrew appeal sung in a strong, beautiful tenor voice.*

WARREN *and* LESLEY *find and hold each other, looking up and about in the near-dark.*)

WARREN

Holy Christmas!

LESLEY

It's moving!

WARREN

Everything's shut off!

(*They listen as the song continues to its end. They look at each other, and* WARREN *finds his way back to the panel and flips the switches. Lights come on as before. He closes the panel, looks at* LESLEY.)

LESLEY

Some tape.

WARREN

It's got to be. It's on batteries.

(*Urgently: "B'NAY BASE-CHOH K'VOT CHEE-LOH!"* WARREN *draws an angry breath and goes to the desk* LEFT, *finds an address book and looks for a number.*)

LESLEY

Who are you calling?

WARREN
                (*Tapping phone buttons.*)
Guess.

LESLEY

Who?

WARREN

Them! . . . Thad? It worked beautifully, we had a big laugh.
Where is it? . . . Warren Ives! . . . You know damn *well* what!
The tape and the player! . . . *The singing! The rabbi!*

LESLEY

It's a cantor.

WARREN

Hold on. What?

LESLEY

It's a cantor. The cantor sings. The rabbi read and speaks.

WARREN

(*Looks at her a moment.*)
Thanks. Look, Thad, a joke's a joke and . . . There's a whole
Jewish concert going on! . . . We're not smoking *anything*; we
haven't even opened the champagne! . . . All right, somebody
else must have rigged it. I'm sorry.

LESLEY

Who else?

WARREN

Not thoroughly, but I'm going to, from the roof to the basement.
Oh, I saw you got the junk out. Thank you . . . . Yeh, I will.
(*Hangs up.*)

LESLEY

Nobody else was *in* here. Just the movers. In and out . . .

(They look at each other for a moment, at a loss. "B'NAY BASE-CHOH K'VOT CHEELOHHHHH.")

WARREN

(Overlapping.)
Thanks for waiting till I got off the phone!

LESLEY

It *did* wait . . .

(They look uneasily at each other, and upward.)

WARREN

Hey, knock it off, will ya? It's not a synagogue any more!

LESLEY

It hasn't been for years now!

WARREN

Seven!

LESLEY

Please! Don't bother us!

(Silence. Then pleadingly: "B'NAY BASE-CHOH K'VOT CHEE-LOHHH!")

WARREN

What does that *mean?*

LESLEY

I don't know . . .

WARREN

It's asking for something . . .

LESLEY

The man in the deli would know. He said he was a member here.

WARREN

Maybe it's him, throwing his voice.

LESLEY

He'd only get it halfway across the street. It was all he could do to cut the sandwiches.

WARREN

Maybe he's still there. Take a look.

(LESLEY, *nearer* RIGHT, *goes out into the vestibule.* WARREN, *waiting, makes a cross of his forefingers and shows it to various parts of the roof. He assumes a casual pose as* LESLEY *returns.*)

LESLEY

It's closed up.

(*She goes to* WARREN*'s side. He puts his arm around her and they look up. Low: "B'NAY BASE-CHOH K'VOT CHEE-LOHHHHH."*)

WARREN

There's a rational explanation.

LESLEY

I know . . .

(They look uncertainly at each other as the lights fade to darkness . . .

The cantor sings a brief lament.

As the singing ends, the lights come up: again, before sunset. Car-
tons and wrappings are gone, pictures still leaning, lamps and track
lighting on. From the vestibule, WARREN *and* LESLEY, *in jeans and*
shirts, usher in MORRIS LIPKIND, *near 80. It's his first time in*
the transformed synagogue, and as he moves effortfully about and
mounts the platform, all that he sees pains him. Especially the elec-
tronic Ark. WARREN *and* LESLEY *watch as* MORRIS *turns his back*
on it and makes his way to the front of the platform.)

MORRIS

Here was . . . mahogany, railings with carving. And posts, here
and here, with lights, candelabras . . . bulbs in glass flowers.
The Ark too, mahogany. A velvet curtain in fron' a' the doors,
purple velvet, embroidered. Carving all around . . .
　　(Pointing at the loft's facing.)
Along there, also mahogany. More carving. Panels.
　　(Coming down off the platform.)
Cushions in the pews. Us, and the Kalvarier Shul on Pike Street,
cushions. And the *windows!* The windows was . . .
　　(Looks, turns back, waves.)
Forget the windows. I could sit?

WARREN   LESLEY
Sure, right here!   Of course! Please!

(WARREN *offers the low chair* RIGHT *of the coffee table.* MORRIS *eyes it dubiously.*)

MORRIS

You have somet'ing harder, with a straight back?

WARREN

One of these?
(*Indicating chairs by the table.*)

MORRIS

Perfect. I'm sorry to be a bother.

WARREN

(*Bringing one over.*)
No bother. Here you go . . .

MORRIS

Thanks.
(*Glances at the Ark, moves the back of the chair toward it, sits.*)

LESLEY

Would you like something to drink?

MORRIS

You have tea?

LESLEY

Tons of it, from both our old places.
(*Heads for the kitchen.*)
Warren? Want some tea?

WARREN

Sure.

MORRIS

(*Rubbing his thighs.*)

Ei . . . Don't go into the grocery business.

WARREN

(*Sitting on the sofa.*)

Too late, I'm in it. Soy beans, cocoa beans, coffee . . . I'm with Shearson Lehman, in commodities.

MORRIS

Ohh . . . !

WARREN

Lesley's with Harper and Row. Publishers.

MORRIS

(*Turning.*)

You're a writer?

LESLEY

Only of publicity releases.

MORRIS

My kid brother, alav 'asholem, was a writer. You wouldn'a heard of him. Simon Lipkind? Books on t'eology, philosophy?

LESLEY

No . . .

MORRIS

Taught fifteen years at CCNY.

WARREN

That's *great*.

MORRIS

(*Takes another look around.*)
Your friends did this?

(WARREN *nods.* MORRIS, *too.*)

MORRIS

Ya' gotta give 'em credit . . . Someplace else it would be beautiful.
(*Settles himself.*)
So where's the chahzin?

WARREN

Excuse me?

MORRIS

The chahzin, the singer.

WARREN

I thought he was a cantor.

MORRIS

Uptown a cantor, here a chahzin.

(WARREN*'s confused.*)

MORRIS

It's the word in Yiddish.

WARREN

Oh.

MORRIS

So?

WARREN

He's been quiet since we got back from work, but this is when he started last night.

LESLEY

(*Joining them, perching on the arm of the sofa.*)
We searched the place from top to bottom. There's no tape or radio or anything.

MORRIS

Whole songs he sings?

WARREN	LESLEY
Yes.	Yes.

WARREN

Plus this one line over and over, last night and this morning.

LESLEY

The commercial.

MORRIS

(*Wagging his head.*)
Tt, tt, tt. Hmm!

WARREN

Who *was* the—kahzin here?

MORRIS

Shainowitz. Irving P. Shainowitz.

WARREN

When did he die?

MORRIS

He didn't. He's in Fort Lauderdale.

LESLEY

He must have died in the past few days.
> (*To* WARREN.)
That's why Ryan and Thad never heard him.

MORRIS

And he come here to haunt? Naaah . . . Half the time he didn't
show up when he was alive.
> (*Thinks.*)
But taka . . . this could be his punishment. Ahhh! How d'ya like
that! Day and night he's gotta be here, no alibis, no excuses . . .
> (*Upward.*)
Hey, Shainowitz! He gotcha, didn't He, you momser!
> (*Chuckles delightedly.*)
I'm so glad you invited me!

LESLEY

> (*Rises with a smile at* WARREN *and heads for the kitchen.*)
How do you take your tea?

MORRIS

Milk and sugar, please. Heavy on both.

WARREN

Lesley's great-grandparents may have worshiped here.

MORRIS

Oh?

WARREN

They lived on Attorney Street.

MORRIS

(*Turns away toward* LESLEY.)

What was the name? Maybe I'll know them from the yortzeit plaques.

(WARREN *is puzzled.*)

LESLEY

Levy.

MORRIS

The first names?

LESLEY

Etta . . . and Aaron.

MORRIS

Levys . . .

(*Thinks, points to the wall.*)

. . . there was a bunch over there. Aaron and Etta . . . I don't t'ink. But this don't mean they didn't pray here.

LESLEY

I'm going to ask a great-aunt of mine.

(WARREN *clears space on the coffee table as* LESLEY *brings a tray.
She puts it down.*)

MORRIS

Oh, I *forgot* you bought Lorna Doones . . .

(LESLEY *gives him a mug and offers a plate of cookies.*)

MORRIS

Thanks.

(WARREN *has taken a mug.* LESLEY *sits next to him.*)

LESLEY

Where do *you* pray, now that—
          (*A gesture at the place.*)

MORRIS

Don't ask. On Pitt Street, a room upstairs. Over a penny arcade,
with the guns and the rockets. Under a place, they cut pipe to mea-
sure. It's a good thing we pray to God; nobody else can hear us.

(*Singing begins softly.*)

LESLEY

How many are you?

MORRIS

A couple a' dozen, and dropping like flies. This year alone—

WARREN

(*Interrupting.*)

Shh, shh. There he goes. Excuse me.

(*The singing, a prayer, grows louder. They listen as it swells, echoing.*)

MORRIS

Isn't that *wonderful . . .* ! You're sure it's no trick?

WARREN	LESLEY
It can't be.	We searched thoroughly.

(*They listen.*)

MORRIS

Damn it!

WARREN	LESLEY
What is it?	What's the matter?

MORRIS

That's not *Shainowitz!*

WARREN

Are you sure?

MORRIS

(*Listens, shakes his head.*)

In his *mother's ears* he never sang like this.

WARREN

Who is it then?

(MORRIS *shrugs, listens.*)

LESLEY

Who was the cantor before him?

MORRIS

Lubell.
    (*Considers.*)
Better than *Shainowitz* . . . But not in this league. No . . .

WARREN

Well, whoever it is, our—

MORRIS

    (*Interrupting with a raised hand.*)
Shh. Wait. Please.
    (*Listens intently.*)
I t'ink . . . I know . . . who you got here. Before Shainowitz, and before Lubell, before I was coming here, was the *first*
chahzin, from when they built the shul. I joined, he was dead
maybe ten years.

WARREN

When was that?

MORRIS

'Fifty-five. He died say in 'forty-five. Still they raved about him.
Singing on Yom Kippur that could break God's heart, another
Rosenblatt, so on and so fort'. I'll tell you the truth, I took it

with a grain a' salt. A great chahzin in a shul so small? They were lucky they had Lubell.

(*He sips. The singing ends.*)

I'll bet you that's who it is. He helped build the place, I t'ink. A carpenter, maybe a stonecutter, one a' the trades. And he lived here, downstairs.

(*He takes a bite of cookie. "B'NAY BASE-CHOH K'VOT CHEE-LOHHHHH".*)

LESLEY

That was it.

WARREN

What does it mean?

MORRIS

I didn't hear. I was chewing.

(*He puts the remaining piece of cookie down and looks up. They wait, listening.*)

LESLEY

He lived here?

MORRIS

I t'ink that's what they said. Details I could get from Teirstein, a friend a' mine in Sarasota. He goes *way* back.

WARREN

You don't have to bother.

MORRIS

It's all right, I owe him a letter.

(*They wait, listening.*)

WARREN

Frankly, our main concern is getting him out.

MORRIS

(*Taken aback, but . . .*)
Yeh, I could understand . . .

(*"B'NAY BASE-CHOH K'VOT CHEE-LOHHHHH."* WARREN
and LESLEY *look at him.*)

MORRIS

B'nay base-choh k'vot chee-loh . . .
(*Realizes the import.*)
This is from the Musaf, a special prayer we say on holy days. It
means—"Build your house . . . the way it was."

(WARREN *and* LESLEY *look at each other.*)

MORRIS

Asking God to build again the Temple. That was destroyed in
Jerusalem.

(*Louder, imploring: "B'NAY BASE-CHOH K'VOT CHEE-LOH!"*
WARREN *rises, looking upward;* LESLEY *too, holding his hand.*)

WARREN

This house . . .

LESLEY

He wants us—to make it a synagogue again . . . !

MORRIS

That's how it looks.

WARREN

Sorry! No way!

LESLEY

I hope he can't break things.

MORRIS

He can't, don't worry, he can't.

(*They look at him.*)

LESLEY

How do you know?

MORRIS

(*Gives her a tolerant look.*)
If he could break t'ings, dear . . . your TV would be broken.

(LESLEY *looks* UPSTAGE, *and is disconcerted.* WARREN *goes to* MORRIS.)

WARREN

You speak to him. Tell him you're—one of the people from here. Ask him to stop bothering us and get out.

(MORRIS *frowns.* LESLEY *moves to his side.*)

LESLEY

We don't want to be in the middle of a media event, reporters outside, mobs. And we can't have him *singing* at us all the time!

(MORRIS *starts to rise.*)

LESLEY

Please!

MORRIS

(*Rising.*)
I'll speak, I'll speak! Lemme t'ink first . . .

(*He broods a little.* "B'NAY BASE-CHOH K'VOT CHEE-LOHHHHH".)

MORRIS

By the bell it says Ives-Rosen, with a dash between. You're one one and one the other or both both?

WARREN

What has *that* got to do with it?

MORRIS

I wanna know. I'm your lawyer like.

LESLEY

He's Ives, I'm Rosen.

MORRIS

Jewish, gentile.

LESLEY   WARREN
Yes.   Yes.

MORRIS

(*Nodding.*)

No wonder he wants it back.

WARREN

Look, if you don't think we're worthy of living here—

MORRIS

(*Interrupting.*)

I said I would speak, didn't I? I know, I know. It's a different world today, it's totally different . . .

(*Sighs, looks up and around.*)

Where should I aim?

WARREN   LESLEY
Anywhere.   Just speak.

MORRIS

(*Clears his throat, addresses the roof respectfully.*)

Chahzin? Mein nummen is Morris Lipkind. Dee grocery gesheft oif yenner zeit foon der gaas balangt zu meer. Ich bin geven a mitgleed foon der shul foon Neintzen-finf-oond-fufzig biz dee tzeit ven men hut duss gemoozt farmachn.

(*He gestures toward* WARREN *and* LESLEY, *who with confused looks are trying to follow along.*)

Duh zeinen tzvay feineh kinnder. Ess is emmess oz zay zeinen nisht ferhayret . . . abber hinetiggeh tzeiten zayt men duss zayer oft. Oond oz zee is a Yiddisheh maidel oond err is a goy . . .

(*That they understand, and* WARREN *is annoyed.* LESLEY *squeezes his hand.* MORRIS *shrugs roofward.*)

MORRIS

. . . nebbuch, is oich nisht ungehvenlich. Farvoss zollen mir zay shterren oond machen oomglicklich? Der plotz vet *kaynmoll veeder zine a shul.* Ess zeinen nor a por Yidden ibbergehblib-ben. Marestens zeinen duh Spanisheh oond Puerto Ricans! . . . Bitteh, hairt oif freggen, vill ess vet nisht helfin, oond ihr macht dee kinnder—meshugeh. Zeit gezundt. Gayt rooig, v'shalom.
(*He waits, then looks at* WARREN *and* LESLEY.)

WARREN

Thanks.

LESLEY

Thank you.

MORRIS

I hope it works.

(*Loud, insistent:* "B'NAY BASE-CHOH K'VOT CHEE-LOH!")

WARREN

Damn it!

(MORRIS *turns his hands out helplessly.*)

LESLEY

Is there any ritual of exorcism in the Jewish religion? To drive out a—spirit?

WARREN

A ghost. We've got a ghost here. Let's not mince words, Lesley.
(*Moving away.*)
We've got a *ghost!* This is a *haunted house!*

LESLEY

Warren . . . Is there a ritual?

MORRIS

I don't t'ink so, but I' no aut'ority.

LESLEY

Could you find out?

MORRIS

Sure, I got my brother's books behind the store, his whole liberry.
Come in in a couple a' days.
(*Moving toward the door.*)
I'm goin' back, I'm gonna write to Teirstein; *I* want to know
about this fella even if *you* don't.

WARREN

(*Going to him.*)
Thanks for coming over and trying to help. We appreciate it.

(*They shake hands.*)

MORRIS

Please . . .

LESLEY

You did help. At least now we know what he wants.

(*She shakes his hand, too. "B'NAY BASE-CHOH K'VOT CHEE-
LOHHH." They all look ruefully upward.*)

MORRIS

Maybe he'll get tired and stop by himself. I hope so. And I wish
you healt' and happiness in—your new home.

(*With as much of a smile as he can muster, he goes out.* WARREN *follows him into the vestibule.* LESLEY *sighs, and with a bitter upward
glance, goes to gather the tea things. The outer door is heard closing
and the vestibule light goes off.* WARREN *comes back in as* LESLEY,
with the tray, heads for the kitchen.)

WARREN

We need experts, not a—grocer with his brother's books.

LESLEY

There's a Psychic Research Society . . .

WARREN

They probably have a hot-line to the *Enquirer*.
   (*He replaces the chair* MORRIS *sat in as* LESLEY *comes out
   of the kitchen. "B'NAY BASE-CHOH K'VOT CHEE-
   LOHHHH."* WARREN *shouts over it.*)
Shut up, Kahzin! I've got six damn reports I've got to read!

(LESLEY *winces, then thinks as* WARREN *goes* RIGHT, *picks up an
attaché case, and brings it* LEFT *to the desk.*)

LESLEY

Hey . . .

WARREN

What?

LESLEY

(*Going for her attaché case.*)
One of the galleys I have to read is a book on psychic phenom-
ena, debunking them, by a professor at St. John's.

WARREN

(*Unlatching his case.*)
So what's he going to do, come here and tell him he doesn't exist?

LESLEY

He probably knows people in the field . . .
(*Singing begins as she brings her case to the sofa.*)

WARREN

Here we go.

LESLEY

Damn!

WARREN

(*Looking up, a sheaf of computer printouts in his hand.*)
Welcome to the Amityville Synagogue . . .

(*The lights fade to darkness as the singing grows louder and
continues . . .*

*As the song nears its end, the singing loses volume and resonance.
The lights come up.* WARREN, *in jacket and jeans, stands by the
stereo watching* PHILIP QUINN, *early 30s, who stands with a glass*

of white wine CENTER RIGHT, *listening restlessly. Stereo lights twinkle.* DONNA QUINN, *late 20s and pregnant, sits at the* LEFT *end of the sofa sipping soda and nibbling snacks. Night outside. Pictures are hung, flowers have appeared, wine in a dry cooler stands on the coffee table. The song ends and* WARREN *switches the stereo off as* LESLEY, *in a light dress, brings a plate of hors d'oeuvres from the kitchen.)*

WARREN

The real thing has much more color and presence . . .
            (*Picks up his wine and comes* DOWNSTAGE.)

PHILIP

I hope we get to hear it. I don't mean that sarcastically. Inside me there's still an eight-year-old kid, hunkered down by the campfire *longing* to be scared witless by a genuine apparition. Paradoxical, isn't it?

(WARREN *already in a bad mood, nods.* PHILIP *takes from the plate* LESLEY *offers.)*

PHILIP

Thanks.

(WARREN *passes—they exchange frustrated looks—and* LESLEY *heads for the coffee table as* PHILIP *swallows.)*

PHILIP

I suspect that's the underlying reason for my work in the supernatural, the hope that I'll encounter a phenomenon that I *can't* explain rationally. The restoration of primal innocence, as it were.

WARREN

Tonight's the night.

(*He goes to the sofa, where* LESLEY *is sitting, and sits on the arm by her.* PHILIP *sits in the chair* RIGHT. *All wait.*)

LESLEY

Maybe he's worn out from last night . . .

(WARREN *gives a puzzled shrug.*)

DONNA

What happened last night?

LESLEY

That was when my family was here.

DONNA

Oh.

LESLEY

He was on his third encore by now.

PHILIP

How many nights has it been?

WARREN   LESLEY

Five . . .   Five.

(PHILIP *sighs.* DONNA *pats herself.*)

DONNA

Cut it out. Quiet.
          (*Smiles at* LESLEY.)
They're *both* kicking.

(LESLEY *smiles, and thoughtfully sips her wine.* WARREN *rises and moves* DOWNSTAGE RIGHT, *looking up.*)

PHILIP

Is twenty thousand really considered a large printing?

LESLEY

Oh yes, for a first book, definitely.

(PHILIP *worries.* DONNA *eats.*)

WARREN

He's here . . .
          (*Looks at* LESLEY.)
Don't you feel him?

LESLEY

(*Tries to, shakes her head.*)
No.

WARREN

What's he holding back for . . . ?

(PHILIP *gives* DONNA *a skeptical look.* LESLEY *catches it.*)

LESLEY

Do you know anyone who could get rid of him for us? Without fanfare?

PHILIP

I know a few people who *claim* they've performed exorcisms, one in my own department. They'd be as anxious as you are to avoid publicity, they're all academics . . .

(WARREN *goes onto the platform.*)

LESLEY

Would you give us their names, please?

PHILIP

(*Hesitates, smiles.*)

Why not?

(*Takes out a memo pad and pen.*)

Of course if they ask me, I'll have to say I didn't actually hear him myself.

WARREN

Come on, damn you!

(*Sings.*)

B'nay base-koh k'vot kee-lohhhhh!

(*They look at him.*)

WARREN

(*Turns.*)

He's here!

(*He stays facing them, then goes off the platform and stands* DOWN-STAGE RIGHT *looking away, exasperated.* LESLEY *makes a smile at* PHILIP. *He leans forward as he writes.*)

PHILIP

You didn't mention you sing in Hebrew . . .

(WARREN *turns, stares at him.*)

LESLEY

That was the line I told you about. We've heard it a hundred times.

WARREN

You think that was *me* on that tape?

PHILIP

Of course not. It was a trained voice. I was simply remarking . . .

(*He writes on.* WARREN *simmers.*)

DONNA

We went to this house in New Jersey where there was supposed to be a poltergeist, and it turned out it—

PHILIP

Donna . . .

WARREN

It turned out *what*?

PHILIP

That it wasn't a—

WARREN

(*Interrupting.*)
Could Donna answer the question, please?

LESLEY

Hey, Warren . . .

WARREN

It turned out *what*, Donna?

DONNA

That . . . . it was the woman doing things herself but she was
unaware of it . . .

PHILIP

She had a history of schizophrenia.

WARREN

Ah. I see.

(*He draws a breath and turns away again.* PHILIP *tears a page
from the pad and gives it to* LESLEY.)

PHILIP

Try Flexner first. I'm sure he'll be interested.

LESLEY

Thanks.

PHILIP

(*Signals to* DONNA, *rising.*)
We really have to go. It's a long drive.

LESLEY

Thanks for coming. Good luck, Donna.

DONNA
(Getting to her feet.)
Thanks.

(WARREN turns. PHILIP smiles and offers his hand.)

PHILIP
Warren. Nice meeting you.

WARREN
(Shaking it.)
Philip. Shalom, shalom. Shalom, Donna. Mazel tov, too. Mazel tov.
    (She gives him a confused smile and follows as LESLEY hustles PHILIP into the vestibule. WARREN waves.)

WARREN
B'nay base-koh k'vot kee-loh!

DONNA
What does it mean?

WARREN
Build your house . . . the way it was.

DONNA
    (Smiles at him.)
We're *adding* a room.
    (She goes.)

WARREN
(Shakes his fist at the roof.)
Damn you!

(LESLEY *comes in, sighs.*)

WARREN

He thought I'm nuts! He thought that was *me*!

LESLEY

He didn't.

WARREN

He *did*!

LESLEY

He gave us the names, what difference does it make?

(*She kisses him. He hugs her. They sigh.*)

LESLEY

Maybe we won't need them. Maybe he got tired and quit, the way Morris said.

WARREN

I'm telling you, Les, he's *here*. I don't know why he stopped singing but he's—

(*Loud: "B'NAY BASE-CHOH K'VOT CHEE-LOH!" Overlapping.*)

WARREN

What'd I tell you?
    (*He turns out. Offstage* RIGHT.)
Maybe I can catch them!

(*The front door is heard opening.* LESLEY *clenches her fists and glares at the roof!*)

LESLEY

We're getting an exorcist!

("B'NAY BASE-CHOH K'VOT CHEE-LOH!" LESLEY *fumes.
The front door slams.* WARREN *rushes in, limping.)*

LESLEY

What happened?

WARREN

Kid on a bike.
  (Jumps onto the platform.)
Now you listen, and you listen good, Kahzin!

("B'NAY BASE-CHOH K'VOT CHEE-LOH!" WARREN *out-
shouts it.)*

WARREN

THIS IS *our home!* IT BELONGS TO *us* NOW! It's not gonna
be a synagogue ever again! TV in the Ark, not a Torah! And
that's the way it's gonna stay!
  (Inspiration strikes.)
If you're lucky . . . ! *IF you're lucky!* You hear me, Kahzin? If you
sing one more note *we're gonna sell!* WE CAN'T LIVE HERE
WITH YOU!
  (He waits. Silence.)
If we have to sell, Mister . . .
  (Raises his RIGHT *hand.)*
. . . as God is my witness . . . *we're selling to MOSLEMS!* I kid
you not! There's every ethnic group you can dream of in this
city and there are Moslems here too, you can bet your *tookus!*

LESLEY

There's a community in Brooklyn!

WARREN

You hear that? A community in Brooklyn! Overcrowded! *Dying to move into Manhattan if only they can find someplace to pray!* And oh, are we ever gonna make them a tempting offer! . . . *You hear me?*

>   (*He races up the spiral stairs, and leaning at the roof from the topmost curve, sings cantorially.*)

M a a a a a a a a a a z z z z z z z l e m m m m m m m m m m s ! Maaaaaaaaaaaaaaaazzzleh-eh-eh-eh-eh-eh-eh-eh-ehem-mmmmmms!

>   (*Finds his breath, pulls himself together.*)

Just one more note. As God is my witness.

(*He waits a moment, listening, then draws a breath and comes down the stairs.* LESLEY *steps up on the platform to meet him. They join hands, look up, around, at each other.* LESLEY *mouths,* "You were wonderful!" WARREN *nods, and goes and smacks the TV on, looking up tauntingly. A car chase comes up on the screen.* WARREN, *watching the roof, comes back to* LESLEY. *They step down off the platform, look about, listening—and look hopefully, happily at each other.* WARREN *picks up the bottle of wine and offers his elbow.*)

WARREN

Bath time?

LESLEY

>   (*Taking it.*)

You bet.

(*They exit* DOWNSTAGE RIGHT. *Cars pile up on the TV as the lights fade to darkness.*)

(*Mellow rock music fades in. It rises as the lights come up. A sunny morning.* WARREN *in T-shirt and jeans,* DOWNSTAGE CENTER, *is carefully repairing an antique wooden rocking chair. The doorbell rings.* WARREN *frowns, puts a tool down, and goes out into the vestibule. He returns with* MORRIS *and heads for the platform.*)

MORRIS

Lesley went out by herself before. You're all right?

WARREN

(*Switching the stereo off.*)
I'm fine. How are you?

MORRIS

(*Shrugs, looking at the chair.*)
Living. Shearson Lehman is closed today?

WARREN

(*Returning.*)
I'm playing hooky. Lesley's birthday is next week. She fell in love with this in an antique shop a few months ago.

MORRIS

It's nice . . .

WARREN

I've been hiding it downstairs. I took a good look at it last night, and you see? It's coming apart. It's got to be reglued and reinforced in here. Can't work on it when she's around—

MORRIS

Oho . . .

WARREN

—so I developed this awful backache. What's up?

MORRIS

(*Shows an envelope.*)
Teirstein, in Sarasota. About the chahzin.

WARREN

Oh, good.

MORRIS

You're here now so I hung up the back-in-five-minutes. I close
early today.

WARREN

Oh, Friday, right. Let me see.

MORRIS

(*Pulling a chair out.*)
Seeing wouldn't help you; it's in Yiddish.
(*Sits and begins exchanging eyeglasses.*)

WARREN

You want some tea? I can—

MORRIS

(*Interrupting.*)
No, no, don't bother. A glass water maybe?

WARREN
(*Going into the kitchen.*)
Sure. Perrier?

MORRIS
(*Shrugs.*)
Perrier . . .
(*Polishes reading glasses.*)
Still quiet?

WARREN
Not a peep all week.

MORRIS
That must'a been *some* shouting you gave him.

(WARREN *returns with a glass.*)

MORRIS
He was a stubborn character. Thanks.

WARREN
(*Leans close.*)
It wasn't the volume, it was the content. I told him if he sang
one more note we would sell to Moslems.

MORRIS
Ohhh . . . ! No wonder . . . !

(WARREN *straightens.* MORRIS *looks up at him uneasily.*)

MORRIS
You wouldn't *do* that, would you?

WARREN

*Absolutely. The minute he opens his mouth. I've already contacted
the Brooklyn community just in case.*

MORRIS

Oh, that's good! They was interested?

WARREN

Yes indeed, very much so.
        (*Winks.*)

MORRIS

        (*Beckons him close.*)
He's still here?

WARREN

I don't know. Sometimes I think yes, sometimes no. Better safe
than sorry. Go ahead.

(MORRIS *puts his glasses on, and as* WARREN *tinkers with the rocking chair, draws from the envelope a thick wad of pages.*)

WARREN

That looks like a book!

MORRIS

He writes big. And there's a lot about his hip replacement.
        (*Leafs through the pages.*)
He's ninety-three, kinneh horeh.

WARREN

What does that mean?

MORRIS

Kinneh horeh?

(*Has to think a moment.*)

Really it means, no evil eye. No one should give him one, back when they believed in them. So it's like nothing bad should happen to him. He should live and be well.

WARREN

I get it.

MORRIS

(*Pleased with himself, he finds the right page.*)

Here. "You asked about our first chahzin Isaac Schlansky. Such beautiful singing with such—feeling from the heart, you never heard in your life." I didn't *tell* him we heard. From him the whole Sun Belt would know.

(*Finds his place.*)

"He was a—a mixed package. The good was the singing and the work he did. The bad was he was such a—a stickler about the religious laws, that he could drive you nuts. He was a cabinet maker by trade with a shop on Canal Street. By himself he made all the woodwork in the shul, the synagogue." Remember, I told you? The panels there? The carving by the Ark?

(WARREN *nods.*)

Beautiful work. Posts, railings . . . Mmmm! "His—personal life was a sad story. His wife—

(*Shifts to the next page.*)

—ran away and left him with a boy Reuben, may he rest in peace. Reuben and I was friends. A runaway horse killed him when he was nine."

(*Shakes his head, looks at* WARREN.)

You t'ink traffic is bad with cars? It was worse with horses, believe me. My own father, alav 'asholem. A fire wagon. Never walked again.

(*Thinks, and back to the letter.* WARREN *listens intently.*)
So . . . "After that he gave up the shop and moved in downstairs in the shul." You hear? "My mother, may she rest in peace, tried to—fix him up with my Aunt Hannah, may *she* rest in peace, but he wasn't buying. He thought always the wife would come back. He became a pest—

(*Next page.*)
—telling everybody how to do everyt'ing the right way, but on accoun' a' the singing, and how he made the place so beautiful, we put up with his"—his quirks, his craziness, his—

WARREN

Mishagaas?

MORRIS

That's it! That's the word exactly! That's what he says!
(*Shows him.*)
This right here is mishagaas . . .

WARREN

Hmm.

MORRIS

(*Gives him an approving nod, then skims.*)
More from the singing . . . "To get in on Yom Kippur you needed a shoehorn . . . ." And here, get this. "The shuls uptown made him big offers"—to be the chahzin there—"*but never would he leave Ahavat Zedek.*" Hmm? That's Hebrew, the name here. Means Lovers of Righteousness.

WARREN

Ahavat—

MORRIS

Zedek. "He died in his sleep—
          (*Points downward.*)
—in 1943, still a young man, sixty-six. It was this time a' year,
before the High Holy Days. May he rest in peace."

(*They look at each other.*)

WARREN

But he didn't.

MORRIS

No.
          (*Sighs and refolds the pages.*)
That's it. The rest a' the letter is a widow chasing him.
          (*Takes a drink.*)

WARREN

What's his name?

MORRIS

Leon Teirstein.

WARREN

The kahzin, I mean.

MORRIS

Chahzin. Chuh, chuh.
          (*Unfolding, looking.*)

WARREN

Khhahzin.

MORRIS

Chuh!

WARREN

*Chhhhh*ahzin.

MORRIS

Not so much . . . Isaac Schlansky.
        (*Refolding the letter and putting it in the envelope.*)
They was all from Russia, the ones what built the place. From
a shtetl in the Ukraine, a little village. Like in "Fiddler on the
roof." You seen it?

WARREN

Yes.

MORRIS

Good.
        (*Exchanging his glasses.*)
Well, I got a lady comes in for a corn muffin around now . . .

WARREN

(*Watches him a moment.*)
Do you make anything over there?

MORRIS

A nickle a week clear profit.

WARREN

How come you don't retire? Couldn't you manage on Social Security? Or is that a stupid question.

MORRIS

No, I could manage. I got a couple a' bucks put by. And my daughter is always hocking me to go live with them. In Tucson. Her husband has asthma.

 (*Rising.*)

I'll tell you the truth, I'm scared to quit. A person like me, working since the age twelve—when my father, alav 'asholem, had the accident—the body gets used to it. You quit and you're dead; I seen it happen time and again. So . . .

 (*Shrugs, starts toward* RIGHT.)

WARREN

Thanks for bringing the letter, and happy New Year.

MORRIS

Thanks. You too, and Lesley.

WARREN

When is it?

MORRIS

Tonight it starts.

WARREN

Tonight's Yom Kippur?

MORRIS

Rosh Hashonah. Yom Kippur's the Monday after next.

WARREN

Oh.

MORRIS

Thanks for the Perrier.
          (*Turns at the door, discomforted.*)
Listen . . . Save yourself money. Regular seltzer, the same t'ing.

(*He goes out.* WARREN *moves to the door, watches him off, and turns, smiling. He stands a moment, and goes up onto the platform. He starts to turn on the stereo, stops, lowers his hand. He turns, thinking. He moves toward the front of the platform. Thinks more . . . His gaze moves upward.*)

WARREN

You there? You can sing—on Yom Kippur.

(*He looks about as the lights fade to darkness . . .*

Growing out of the darkness comes the prolonged opening note of "KOL NIDRE" . . . After the first majestic measures the lights slowly come up: sunset. Glowing tinted spots on the tracks. WARREN *and* LESLEY, *in jeans and light sweaters, recline arm in arm on the sofa, her head on his shoulder, his on the edge of the platform, their feet on the coffee table. The rocking chair has been given a place* DOWNSTAGE RIGHT. *They listen . . .* WARREN *sighs.*)

WARREN

My natural parents must have been Jewish . . .

(LESLEY *smiles. The phone rings.*)

<table>
<tr><td>WARREN</td><td>LESLEY</td></tr>
<tr><td>Oh hell.</td><td>Damn.</td></tr>
</table>

(*She moves; he holds her.*)

WARREN

Let it ring.

LESLEY

(*Watches uncomfortably as the phone rings.*)
It could be important.

WARREN

They'll call again.

(LESLEY *reluctantly settles back. The phone rings. She wants to move;* WARREN *holds her. The singing continues, plaintive, melodic. They wait, sigh with relief, and listen . . .*)

LESLEY

I never did that before . . . Did *you*?

WARREN

Not answer the phone? Sure.

LESLEY

I think it's a true gender difference.

(*They listen . . .*)

WARREN

It's possible.

LESLEY

I don't think so, not really.

WARREN

I mean that I'm Jewish . . . I've got the right trimming, haven't I? No pun intended.

LESLEY
(*Smiles.*)
You've got the wrong face.

(*She kisses it. They listen . . .*)

WARREN

A Wasp father for the face and a Jewish mother. The determining factor is the mother's religion, right?

LESLEY

Twenty-nine years ago, in Detroit, there were very few unwed Jewish mothers.

WARREN

One's enough. And they got me in Chicago. Supposedly I'm a purebred Protestant, but that's if you trust a lawyer in the adoption business.

(*They listen. She glances at him.*)

LESLEY

I guess it could be . . .
(*They listen.*)
Wait'll I tell my parents.
(*They listen.*)

WARREN

It would explain why I—*feel* him . . .
> (*Thinks, sits up.*)

And it would explain why he thought we might do it in the
first place.

LESLEY

Do what?

WARREN

Build the house the way it was. He didn't ask Ryan and Thad,
did he?

LESLEY
> (*Thinks, and rises, patting his hand.*)

I'm going to get us something to eat.
> (*She goes into the kitchen.*)

WARREN
> (*Frowns.*)

I thought you're supposed to fast.

LESLEY
> (*Gives him a cold look.*)

You want to fast, fast. *I'm hungry.*

(WARREN *broods.* LESLEY *peeks into a container.*)

LESLEY

Ooh yummy!

(*She closes the refrigerator and gets a fork while* WARREN *rises and moves* LEFT, *thinking, looking up and listening to the continuing singing.* LESLEY *comes out of the kitchen eating from the container. They look at each other.)*

WARREN

He didn't sing once in the whole seven years . . .

LESLEY

Maybe they lied, and that's why they wanted to sell.

WARREN

Them? Are you kidding? They'd have been selling tickets.

(LESLEY *sits in the rocking chair.* WARREN *goes onto the platform.)*

WARREN

And he didn't sing when your Professor—Quinn and his wife were here either . . . Maybe he won't sing for non-Jews. The letter said he was—dogmatic.

LESLEY

He sounds like a royal pain.

WARREN

He was. But the singing made up for it. And the woodworking . . .

LESLEY

I hope you made it clear this is a one-night stand.

(*She eats.* WARREN *listens as the repeat of "KOL NIDRE" begins. He looks about the front of the platform.)*

WARREN

The posts and the railing were down there . . . Ryan thought they had value . . . I said they were junk, they should get them out.

(*Looks at her.*)

I was ashamed to tell Morris. And you.

LESLEY

They couldn't have been all that special.

WARREN

They were dusty. I didn't even look.

LESLEY

(*Rises, showing the container.*)

You sure you don't—?

WARREN

I had some before.

(LESLEY *goes into the kitchen. She puts the container in the refrigerator and looks for something else as* WARREN *looks about. The singing, pleading, grows louder.*)

WARREN

That's what was there . . . The posts with the candelabras, and the railings. And junk that was junk . . . No panels from there, no carving from the Ark . . .

(*He moves* UPSTAGE *and touches the wall* LEFT *of the recess. He raps on it, and turns as* LESLEY *comes out with another container.*)

WARREN

They didn't take all of it out . . .
(*Raps again.*)
Some they just covered over.

LESLEY

(*An edge of wariness.*)
It was probably easier . . .

WARREN

(*Examines the return of the section.*)
Wallboard . . . Butted and nailed. Rotten job . . .

(*He picks at the joint.* LESLEY *puts the container down and goes
onto the platform.*)

LESLEY

Hey, listen, this goes on forever. Let's go out.

WARREN

No . . .

LESLEY

It's stuffy. We'll get some air. Come on.

WARREN

No. You go ahead.

(*They look at each other.*)

LESLEY

I have a feeling I'll come back and find a synagogue.

(WARREN *laughs. They hug and kiss. He nuzzles her.*)

WARREN

Don't you want to see it?

LESLEY

Are you serious?

WARREN

Yes. Carving done almost a hundred years ago? By *him*, singing to us now?

LESLEY

(*Drawing away.*)
He's singing to God, not us. No, I *don't* want to see it.

WARREN

(*Strokes the wall.*)
I'll put it back and touch it up. Better than they did.

LESLEY

Warren, you're not a carpenter!

WARREN

I fixed the rocking chair. It was falling apart.

LESLEY

Warren—

WARREN

I took shop.

LESLEY

You're *not* going to rip out a wall!

(*The phone rings.*)

LESLEY

Oh . . . No! It's out of the question!
        (*Backs away.*)
Just put it out of your mind.

(*The phone rings.*)

LESLEY

Forget it. No.
        (*She turns, and glaring at the louder singing, goes off the
        platform and to the desk. As the phone rings she picks it
        up, jams a finger in her ear.*)
Hello? . . . Oh hi . . .

(WARREN *goes* UPSTAGE LEFT *and gets the window pole.*)

LESLEY

Karen. Karen, listen, I can't talk now.

(*He returns to the platform and pries at the joint with the pole's hook.*)

LESLEY

I can't talk! I'll call you back in—oh *no!*
        (*She hangs up, races onto the platform and tries to wrest
        the pole from* WARREN.)
Stop it! Stop! *Warren!*

WARREN

I want to see it!

LESLEY

No! That's *half mine*, damn it! Stop! *It's half mine!*

(WARREN *thrusts her away and attacks the joint again as the singing grows louder.* LESLEY *turns and cries upward, fists to ear.*)

LESLEY

Shut up!

(WARREN *drops the pole, grasps the edge of the wall, and pulls. A six-foot section comes away with a flurry of plaster dust; he swings it to the floor, revealing dark dusty carving as the singing grows louder.*)

WARREN

Look at it! Look!
       (*Upward.*)
LOOK AT IT!

(LESLEY *cringes as he picks up the pole and steps over the downed wall. He lances and jabs at the loft's facing.*)

LESLEY

Warren!

(*A foot-square piece falls. Dark carving behind it.* WARREN *drops the pole and grabs* LESLEY *joyously as* "KOL NIDRE" *reaches its climax.*)

WARREN
Listen to him! He knows! He knows, Lesley! HE KNOWS I DID IT!
(He kisses her—she's petrified—as)

THE CURTAIN FALLS

END OF ACT ONE

ACT TWO

*AT RISE: In darkness the chahzin sings a happy rhythmic exten-
sion of "B'NAY BASE-CHOH." As he repeats it, the curtain rises.
Warm lighting within, night outside. Handsome mahogany carving gleams around the empty unshelved Ark and along the loft's
facing. WARREN is on the platform at an improvised workbench,
sandpapering decorative pieces fixed to a raw wood panel. MORRIS
sits snoring by the table CENTER RIGHT, an ancient book open on
his lap, his shoes on the floor beside him. On the table, other books,
a mug, a box of Lorna Doones. The TV, VCR, and stereo equip-
ment have been relocated on stands LEFT. The singing ends with a
cantorial flourish that causes WARREN to look up with amusement
and MORRIS to stir and waken. He blinks at the book, adjusts
his glasses.*

MORRIS

How long was I out?

WARREN

Fifteen minutes or so.

MORRIS

Ei . . . You got the point I was making?

WARREN

The questions are what count, not the answers.

MORRIS

Asking the questions. If all these great rabbis can't agree on the answers, you and I ain't gonna find 'em. But studying Torah, asking *anyway*—that at least gets us in on the conversation.

WARREN

Got it.

(*He brings the panel to the Ark as* MORRIS *puts a slip of paper in the book and closes it.*)

MORRIS

So where's Lesley? I thought it was over at eight o'clock.

WARREN

Those things always go on longer than they're supposed to. What do you think?

(*He holds the panel in place. It covers half the opening, the decorative pieces similar to the design of the loft panels.* MORRIS *changes his glasses, looks.*)

MORRIS

It's gonna be beautiful, Warren. Just like the real doors.

WARREN

I don't know, these prefab pieces look crappy alongside *his* work . . . Maybe they'll be all right when they're stained.

(*He lowers the panel, leans it there, and returns to the workbench as* MORRIS *starts putting his shoes on.*)

MORRIS

Whenever I was gonna spring something on Rifka, aleya 'asholem, something I knew she wouldn't be crazy about . . . I took her someplace fancy where she couldn't yell.

WARREN

(*Laughs.*)
That's not a bad idea.

MORRIS

It's a *good* idea, believe me.

WARREN

(*Marking measurements on a fresh panel.*)
Maybe I'll give it a try.

MORRIS

How long did they give ya?

WARREN

Just till the weekend. That's when they do most of their business.

(*Singing begins.*)

WARREN

Oh, this is a great one!

(*They listen.*)

WARREN

He sang it the other night. What is it?

MORRIS

"Atoh Chonane." It's asking God to give us understanding, knowledge.

(*They listen. The front door is heard opening.*)

WARREN

Lesley?

LESLEY

(*Offstage* RIGHT.)

Hi!

WARREN

Hi!

(LESLEY *enters, in a light coat and carrying a handbag and her attaché case. She puts them aside as* WARREN *comes off the platform and* MORRIS *turns in his chair.*)

LESLEY

Hi, Morris.

MORRIS

Hello, darling.

LESLEY

(*Upward, drily.*)

Hi.

WARREN
(*Goes to her and they kiss.*)
How'd it go?

LESLEY
Fine.

MORRIS
It was a nice party?

LESLEY
(*Taking her coat off.*)
Nothing special. Publishing parties are all the same. The same people, the same hors d'oeuvres. The book that's lying around is different.

WARREN
(*Heading for the workbench.*)
The jacket is. Inside it's the same book.

LESLEY
I wouldn't go *that* far.
(*Puts the coat down, follows him.*)
Hey, that looks terrific, Warren.

WARREN
Do you think so?
(*Lifting the decorated panel.*)
Next to the real thing?

(MORRIS *rises.*)

LESLEY

It will when you've got it stained and polished. It's great.
> (*Turning.*)
Don't you think—oh, Morris, don't go yet.

MORRIS

I got my shoes on already.

LESLEY

Oh. That settles that.
> (*Going to him.*)
Don't you think it looks great?
> (*Gives him a hug.*)

MORRIS

I told him, just like the real doors. I could leave here the books?

LESLEY

Of course.

(*The singing ends.*)

MORRIS

No sense schlepping them every time.

WARREN

> (*Busy marking measurements.*)
Tomorrow, Morris?

LESLEY

We've got Annie and Bill.

WARREN

That's right, I forgot. We have a dinner date.

MORRIS

Another time. Good night, dear.

LESLEY

Good night.

(*She kisses his cheek. He points to the kitchen.*)

MORRIS

Chopped herring.

LESLEY

Honestly, Morris . . .

MORRIS

Good night, Warren!

WARREN

Good night! Thanks for everything!

MORRIS

What everything? Please. Stay, darling, I'll go myself.

(*He goes out.* LESLEY *takes her coat and hangs it in the vestibule as the front door opens and closes.*)

WARREN

He only brought a pound this time. And some dried apricots.

LESLEY

We're going to be able to open a store and compete with him.

WARREN

Denise called. We're invited for Thanksgiving.

LESLEY

(*Going onto the platform.*)
She's going to make it?

WARREN

That's what she says.

LESLEY

That'll be laughs.
(*She hugs* WARREN *from behind and watches as he measures.*)
How was work?

WARREN

(*Heaves a sigh.*)
Don't ask . . .
(*Puts his pencil down, turns, and holds her.*)
Hey, I've got a great idea.

LESLEY

What, she asked naively.

WARREN

No, later. First . . . I'm going to put on some decent clothes and we'll go check out that place on Delancy Street.

LESLEY

Oh, gosh, I'm up to here with mesquite-grilled shrimp. Didn't you eat?

WARREN

A little. We could just have dessert and coffee . . .

LESLEY

Let's go Saturday, huh? Or tomorrow with Annie and Bill. They love new places.

WARREN

Okay.

LESLEY

I've got a ton of reading.
            (*Gives him a kiss.*)
Have some chopped herring.

(*She goes off the platform. He follows her.*)

WARREN

Lesley—

(*She turns. He points toward the Ark.*)

WARREN

Do you really like it? All of it, I mean?

LESLEY

I *told* you I do, Warren. It's beautiful woodwork and you fixed it up beautifully. It reminds me of my heritage. Once the doors are done and everything's back where it belongs, the place is going to be sensational. *Sunday Times Magazine.*

WARREN

The railing's in Stamford. At a kind of glorified junk yard.

(LESLEY *stares at him as he goes back onto the platform.*)

WARREN

They sold the posts the day they got 'em—they must have been something, huh?—but the railing is still there. They described it to me on the phone. There's a long piece, from here, and two short ones.
          (*Indicates the sides, crouches.*)
These lighter are places all around—you see—that's where the sockets were that they were set into. It should be a snap to open them up again . . .

(LESLEY *sits hollowly on the sofa.* WARREN *comes down onto it beside her.*)

WARREN

It would look just as good as everything else, and it would complete it all. *Architectural Digest.*

(*He smiles. She doesn't.*)

WARREN

They're holding them till the weekend. After that . . .

(*He shrugs. She looks at him.*)

LESLEY

The doors were supposed to complete it.

WARREN

I know . . . But the railing *really* would.

LESLEY

Except for the posts.

WARREN

The posts are gone. I told you.
(*Watches her.*)
What do you say? I can always take it out again if it doesn't look good.

LESLEY

(*Thinks a moment.*)
Darling . . . I did a lot of thinking before I agreed to this, and I do truly like it . . .

WARREN

But . . .

LESLEY

I think you were more troubled than you realized about not knowing who your natural parents are, and what your real background is. You've latched on to the idea that you're Jewish, and you're trying to prove it by—

WARREN

(*Interrupting.*)
I'm not trying to *prove*—

LESLEY

(*Over him.*)

To yourself! You're trying to prove it to yourself. So you're finally certain. By doing this, and by having Morris come read from his books, and by *wallowing* in the singing instead of trying to get rid of it, the way we should.

WARREN

Why should we get rid of it? It's beautiful.

LESLEY

Warren, you can't stand Muzak in elevators and you're kvelling over a cantor in your living room!

WARREN

(*Considers uneasily a moment.*)

Kvelling?

LESLEY

Ask Morris!

(*She rises and moves away. Singing begins softly.*)

WARREN

I'm not *proving* anything. I know it: My mother was Jewish and I am.

LESLEY

There are X million Jews in the world, and *one* who's turning his home into a synagogue.

WARREN

(*Rising.*)

Lesley, all we're talking about is a few pieces of railing! Beautiful antique railing!

LESLEY

(*Shouts upward.*)
Could we have a little privacy, please! Damn it, I can't—

(*She turns way, rubs her brow desperately.* WARREN *comes up behind her, embraces her, kisses her head soothingly. The singing continues, softly insistent.*)

WARREN

Ahh . . .
		(*Kiss, kiss.*)
Honey, please . . .

LESLEY

Warren, don't . . .

WARREN

Come on . . . Let me put it in . . .
		(*Laughing, rubbing against her.*)
I mean the railing.

LESLEY

(*Pulls away, amused but not very.*)
Come on, Warren, it's nothing to kid about. Really.

WARREN

Who's kidding? I want to. Both.

LESLEY

We're talking about one thing here, Warren. The railing. No. You can't . . . Not unless—

WARREN

What.

LESLEY

You see someone first.

WARREN

(*Looks at her.*)
A shrink?

LESLEY

A psychiatrist. Or psychologist.

(*He turns away, thinking. She moves nearer.*)

LESLEY

Just to help you . . . understand things better . . .

WARREN

(*Thinks more, turns.*)
I'll buy your half . . . ?

LESLEY

(*Looks at him.*)
Are you kidding again?

WARREN

No. I can afford to.

LESLEY

Then what happens? I get to do all the housework?

WARREN

You pay a reasonable rent. Nothing else changes.

LESLEY

Just the decor. And the landlord too. Warren, you don't keep up with reports any more, you haven't *opened* your—

WARREN

(*Interrupting.*)

How about it? I mean it. Do you want to sell? Pay back what your father lent you? Relieve your guilt?

(*They look at each other.*)

LESLEY

I'll live with it. No. I'm co-owner. You can't put in the railing unless you see someone. Buy it. Put it in the basement. See someone for—at least six months, and—

WARREN

Six months?

LESLEY

Six months! They don't do things in one visit! They're not barbers! Then if you still want the railing there . . . I'll help you polish it.

(*They look at each other, as the singing softly continues.*)

WARREN

Six months?

LESLEY

Six months.

(*They hold the look, and* LESLEY *turns and gets her attaché case.
She starts up the stairs.*)

WARREN

No.
             (LESLEY *stops.*)
This is the most—fulfilling thing I've ever done. Working with
my hands this way, making something. Beside money. I won't
put it on hold that long.

(LESLEY *resumes going up.* WARREN *goes onto the platform and picks up
his steel rule as the singing continues.* LESLEY *puts her case on the bed,
holds the loft rail, and looks down as* WARREN *measures and marks.*)

LESLEY

Four months.

WARREN

I'm not seeing a shrink, period.
             (*Draws a line.*)
The offer is open . . .
             (*He measures, marks.*)

LESLEY

             (*Looks up at the singing, down at* WARREN.)
I can't *imagine* why his wife ran away . . .

(*He looks up at her. She meets the look, and turns and moves away.
He cranes up.*)

WARREN

Hey, honey . . . ? Don't say things like that . . .

(*The lights fade to darkness. The singing grows louder, sorrow-ful now . . .*

The singing fades low again as the lights come up. Night. Propped up where the sofa, coffee table, and side chairs were is an upended section of mahogany railing. Two sections are in place on the sides of the platform, leaving passage space UPSTAGE. *Ark doors, stained and polished, match the surrounding woodwork fairly well.* MORRIS, *in a topcoat, and* WARREN, *holding a bag of groceries, enter from the vestibule.*)

WARREN

You're just in time. I need a hand.

(*He brings the bag into the kitchen.* MORRIS *stares in dismay as the singing fades.* WARREN *puts things in the refrigerator.*)

WARREN

What do I owe you?

MORRIS

What *happened?* Lesley took her furniture?

WARREN

No. I moved some of the stuff downstairs. How much?

MORRIS

Twelve . . . What'd you do *that* for?

WARREN
(*Coming out of the kitchen opening a wallet.*)
To make some room.

MORRIS
Oy! What kind a' foolishness is that? She ain't gonna come back
with the furniture downstairs! Are you crazy?
(*Clapping his cheeks.*)
Ooy, a goyisheh kupp!

WARREN
Knock it off! Just knock that off, Morris! I don't like those
racist remarks!
(*Gives him bills, pockets the wallet.*)
She isn't coming back. I'm buying her half. We had lunch the
other day and decided. She needs the money to get something
else. She's uncomfortable at her parents' and the commute is a
pain. Take your coat off. Come on, I need a hand.

MORRIS
A *head* you need!
(*He pockets the bills and takes his coat off while* WARREN
readies things by the upended railing.)
She'd 'a seen it and liked it and come back! Furniture in the
basement, she'll spit in your eye!

WARREN
Are you gonna help me or hock me? Which is it gonna be?

MORRIS
Both!
(*Moves grudgingly to the railing.*)

WARREN

Just hold it steady. I've got to shave down this piece. They bashed
it so, it won't fit in the socket . . .

(MORRIS *holds the railing and watches sourly as* WARREN *begins
working at an end foot.*)

WARREN

Can you hold it tighter?

(MORRIS *does.* WARREN *works.*)

MORRIS

You could'a just pushed t'ings over. You don't need so much
room.

WARREN

Didn't you see the fliers?

MORRIS

Fliers?

WARREN

On the lampposts all around. Notices.

MORRIS

No . . .

WARREN

I spoke to Ryan Wylie. When they did the job, they sold the
fixtures to a dealer and put the rest of the stuff outside, and
people took. So I've got fliers up offering to buy back anything

that came from here. "Restoration of Ahavat Zedek Synagogue."
Right up there with the reward for the golden retriever named
Sam. That's why I need room. I already heard from a woman
with one of the pews.

                    MORRIS
          (*Stares at him a moment.*)
Everyt'ing you wanna do?

                    WARREN
Yep. I think I can. I *know* I can. Jeez, I sound like *The Little
Engine That Could.*
          (*Smiles at himself, then.*)
I can do it, Morris. Not exactly, of course, but pretty close. You'll
have to tell me when I'm going wrong. Listen, they must have
kept records here, didn't they? Who was—

                    MORRIS
          (*Interrupting.*)
I'll tell ya when you're goin' wrong. *Right now, sonny, right this
minute! Here, now, this is when you're goin' wrong!*

(WARREN *looks at him, draws a breath, and works on.*)

                    MORRIS
Why? Because he wants it?

                    WARREN
Because *I* want it.

                    MORRIS
So much you chase away Lesley?

WARREN

She chose to go, I didn't chase her.

MORRIS

Warren, please . . . She bought into a house, not a shul. She moved in with a Shearson Lehman . . . not with a—a restorenik.

WARREN

The reason people live together without being married is so they're free to change and grow.

MORRIS

Grow. You let a girl like that get away from you, and what you're growing is meshugeh. In case ya forgot, that—

WARREN

(*Interrupting.*)
I know! I know! I knew it *long* ago!
(*Leans closer to him.*)
Morris, do you know what I deal with all day over there? Cocoa-bean futures, orange-juice futures.

MORRIS

What's that?

WARREN

Exactly. Vut's dat. The most meaningless, intangible *nothing* the mind can conceive of. Computer projections of rainfall the spring after next. Political reports on islands the size of your pinky. And why? To make money for people who've *got* money. *That's* meshugeh, Morris; this is sane.

(*He resumes work.* MORRIS *looks at the installed railing.*)

MORRIS

You stayed out today.

WARREN

Mm-hmm.

MORRIS

They'll fire you!

WARREN

No they won't. When I'm there I'm so smart you could die.
          (*Checks the work.*)
That should do it. Now you get on board and I'll swing it up.

MORRIS

Oy . . .

(*Shaking his head,* MORRIS *goes onto the platform.* WARREN *braces the railing against the edge and starts lifting it upright—not an easy job.* MORRIS *reaches.*)

WARREN

Wait, wait—

(*He gets the railing upright on the platform,* MORRIS *grasping its top.*)

WARREN

Okay, hold it—

(*He hurries onto the platform and begins lodging the railing's feet in sockets.* MORRIS *helps a little.*)

WARREN

Ah! Perfect! Yeh, that's right. There. Keep holding it. I've got to put pegs in.

(MORRIS, *with mixed feelings, touches the railing and looks about while* WARREN *collects things at the workbench.*)

WARREN

They kept records here, didn't they? Who was born, who got married, who died?
 (*Returning, he crouches at an end of the railing and sets to work.*)

MORRIS

Yeh, sure . . . The pinnkas, the minutes of the shul. Big books, from the beginning.

WARREN

What became of them when the place closed down?

MORRIS

 (*Thinks.*)
Search me . . .

WARREN

Somebody must have taken them. You don't throw away something like that, or leave them behind . . . Would what's-his-name in Sarasota know?

MORRIS

Teirstein? No. He was already down there. What d'ya want
them for?

WARREN

(*On his way to secure the other end of the railing, he puts
his hand on* MORRIS'*s shoulder.*)
To figure out the names and dates that belong on the plaques.
On the walls. You can let go now.

(*He goes and crouches down.* MORRIS, *watching him, lets go—but
has to hold on again.* WARREN *works.*)

WARREN

What do you call them?

MORRIS

Yortzeit plaques . . .

WARREN

Meaning memorial?

MORRIS

Yeh . . .

WARREN

One of them is bound to turn up and I'll be able to make copies,
or get 'em made. What were they like?

MORRIS

(*Is silent a moment.*)
I got Rifka's . . .

WARREN

You do? Oh that's great, Morris! You see? She'll be the first one
back up. Where was she?

MORRIS

(*Swallows, points.*)
Behind the icebox . . .

WARREN

Well . . . she may have to wait awhile, but sooner or later she'll
be back in the light again. Who was keeping the minutes when
the place closed down? Maybe *he's* got the books.

MORRIS

(*Hesitates, then to himself.*)
Busman, then Kaplan . . .
(*To* WARREN.)
In the end, the rabbi did it himself. Max Pearlman.

WARREN

Do you—

MORRIS

Alav 'asholem.

WARREN

Damn. When?

MORRIS

A couple a' years ago.

(*Finished,* WARREN *returns to the workbench, shaking his head.*
MORRIS *wrestles inwardly, then.*)

MORRIS

The widow's in Miami Beach . . .

WARREN

Oh, good! Could you get in touch with her? Ask her if—

(*A window is smashed upstairs* RIGHT. MORRIS *winces.* WARREN *jumps.*)

WARREN

What the hell . . . !

(*He backs to the* DOWNSTAGE LEFT *corner of the platform, looking up.* MORRIS *turns to him.*)

MORRIS

You're surprised? They're helping you make it a shul again!

WARREN

(*Stares at him, understands.*)
Oh, no . . . !

(*Another smash of breaking glass.* WARREN *pulls* MORRIS'*s hands away and runs off the platform and out* RIGHT. MORRIS *shakes his head and moans. The front door is ripped open.* WARREN *cries offstage* RIGHT.)

WARREN

GET OUT OF HERE, DAMN YOU! RUN! RUN!

MORRIS

(*To the roof.*)

You had to ask? You didn't remember?

WARREN
(*Offstage* RIGHT.)
YOU LOUSY LITTLE BASTARDS! *RUN!*

MORRIS
You almost sold *me* on it, damn you . . . !

WARREN
(*Hurries back in, distraught.*)
Black spray paint . . .

MORRIS
Oy . . .

WARREN
(*Going into the kitchen.*)
I've got to get it off before it sets . . .
(*Crouches at a cabinet.*)
Kids! Maybe fourteen years old!

MORRIS
I'll get steel wool.

WARREN
Yes. Please. All you've got.

(*Singing begins as* MORRIS *takes his coat and starts* RIGHT.)

WARREN
Do you have any turpentine?

MORRIS

No.

WARREN

Whatever cleaners you've got, bring 'em!

(MORRIS, *with a bitter look at the singing, goes out* RIGHT. WARREN *comes out of the kitchen with a scrub brush and a bottle of cleaner. He hurries onto the platform and gets rags, steel wool, a can of paint remover. The singing, anguished, imploring, grows louder and the lights begin to dim as* WARREN, *hands full, hurries toward* RIGHT. *He turns and calls upward.*)

WARREN

I'll get it off! Don't worry!

(*He goes out. The lights remain at a low level as the singing continues, pleading for pity…*

Dawn lights the windows. The singing subsides to a murmuring incantation. WARREN *comes in, wearing gloves and a windbreaker, wearily carrying a carton of used cleaning supplies. He puts it down, blows out a breath, and as the light grows brighter, peels off the tattered gloves, looking about and up at the loft.* MORRIS *comes in* DOWNSTAGE RIGHT.)

WARREN

Oh. Did you get any sleep?

MORRIS

Who can sleep with him davening?

(*He heads for the kitchen.* WARREN *drops the gloves in the carton.*)

WARREN

You should've gone back to *your* place.

MORRIS

More tea?

WARREN

I'll get it.

MORRIS

Sit. I got my second wind.

WARREN

(*Sits, unzips the windbreaker, sighs.*)
It's clean . . .

MORRIS

Good.

WARREN

Now the rest of it looks dirty.

(MORRIS *brings two mugs to the table.*)

WARREN

Thanks.

MORRIS

Maybe cereal? A sandwich?

WARREN

No. Thanks.

(MORRIS *sits.* WARREN *lifts his mug, sips.*)

WARREN

Ow.

MORRIS

I should'a left the spoon in.

(WARREN *lowers the mug, sighs. The low singing continues.* MORRIS *points distastefully* DOWNSTAGE RIGHT.)

MORRIS

What did they need with all the mirrors in there?

(WARREN *shrugs.* MORRIS *worries.*)

MORRIS

Lesley took *baths* there?

WARREN
　　(*Smiles.*)
That she did, that she did . . .

(*The smile fades.* MORRIS, *sorry he asked, shakes his head.*)

MORRIS

I hate to go in. I got so *old* . . .

(WARREN *glances at him, gives his arm a pat, sips.* MORRIS *sips, and nods bitterly at him.*)

MORRIS

Fliers on lampposts, nuch . . .

WARREN

You know what they say. It pays to advertise.

MORRIS

(*Gives him a look.*)
Jokes you're making?

WARREN

(*Shrugs.*)
I'm Jewish.

MORRIS

(*Waves him away and turns. After a moment.*)
Why did ya *t'ink* we shut down?

WARREN

(*Thinks, shrugs.*)
Dwindling membership.

MORRIS

(*Sighs, nods.*)
It's true, yes, we was dwindling . . . But also the windows was breaking. One upstairs they couldn't get at; the rest—solid plywood.

WARREN

Couldn't you have put up wire mesh outside?

MORRIS

With what? Who had money?
(*The singing asserts itself. He calls upward.*)
Enough already! Gay shluffen!

WARREN

(*Looks upward as the singing, lower, continues.*)
The building's the only body he's got now.

MORRIS

(*Glances at him, looks away.*)
He's a pest, like Teirstein said. Take down the fliers, put back
the furniture. It looks nice, the railing. She'll like it.
(*Sighs.*)
I gotta go open. Stay.

(*They rise.* WARREN *gets* MORRIS*'s coat from the vestibule.*)

WARREN

Take it easy. Close early today.

MORRIS

I'm gonna. It's Friday.

WARREN

(*Holds the coat for him.*)
I forgot.

MORRIS
(*Thinks, getting into it.*)
You wanna come to shul?

WARREN
(*Thinks about it.*)
On Pitt Street?

MORRIS
No, Fift' Avenue, Temple Emanuel. Yeh, on Pitt Street.

WARREN
(*Thinks.*)
No.

(MORRIS *shrugs.*)

WARREN
Thanks for asking.

MORRIS
You goin' to Shearson?

WARREN
I'd better. Yeh.

MORRIS
(*Pats on* WARREN*'s arm.*)
Some t'ings no one can restore, Warren. The world changes.
Shalom.
(*Pats his cheek and turns to go.*)

WARREN

Would you like to go for a ride Sunday? In the country?

(MORRIS *turns.* WARREN *takes his windbreaker off, his energy returning.*)

WARREN

The forecast is fine, there are still a few leaves on the trees . . .
      (*Moving to the platform.*)
The *posts,* with the candelabras . . . they're in Stockbridge, Mass.
I'm leaving at seven. In a car with a U Haul.

(MORRIS *stares at him as he leans against the railing.*)

WARREN

An antique dealer bought 'em. I was gonna surprise you . . .
What do you say, Morris?

MORRIS

      (*Stares at him with confused wonderment.*)
Du bist meshugeh . . . !

(*The lights fade to darkness.*

The chahzin sings the extension of "B'NAY BASE-CHOH," happy and confident again. As he repeats it, the lights come up. After-noon. Outside the windows a few snowflakes fall. A candelabra, glass flowers unlighted, tops a mahogany post on a corner of the rail-ing. Another post, candelabra sockets empty, lies on supports by the platform's other corner. A few pews stand about, one painted for a child's room. The table and chairs are farther UPSTAGE; *all other downstairs furniture is gone except the desk* LEFT *and the rocking chair* DOWNSTAGE RIGHT. *As the singing ends,* WARREN *comes up from the basement and enters* LEFT, *humming the melody, wearing a sweater and a wool watch cap. He closes the door, goes to the supported post, and inspects a raw section near its top. He goes onto the platform and rummages on the workbench.* LESLEY *looks in at right and knocks at the door.*)

LESLEY

Hi.

WARREN

(*Turns, stares.*)

Hi . . . !

(*She comes in, in a winter coat and shoulderbag.* WARREN *comes down off the platform.*)

WARREN

How are you?

(*They look, move closer—and are in each other's arms kissing.*)

WARREN

Oh God, I've missed you . . .

(*A longer kiss—and* LESLEY *frees herself and moves away, looks about.* WARREN *watches her.*)

WARREN

The furniture's downstairs . . .

(*She looks at the pews, the candelabra. He smiles uncertainly.*)

WARREN

The railing didn't complete it.

LESLEY

(*Gazing at the candelabra.*)
That's beautiful, Warren . . .

WARREN

Take it, it's yours.

LESLEY

(*Faces him, keeps her distance.*)
I called you at work the day before yesterday. You've taken three months' leave?

(*He nods.*)

LESLEY

The phone's been busy all day.

WARREN

I'm on the trail of a stained-glass window. There was one that wasn't broken; they took it out intact.

(*They look at each other.*)

WARREN	LESLEY
What's up? Is—	I felt that—

WARREN

Go ahead.

LESLEY

I felt that someone else should know what's going on . . .
I called your father.

WARREN

(*Sighs.*)
Damn . . . I've been meaning to write to him . . .

LESLEY

He wants to talk to you.

WARREN

(*Nods.*)
I'm sure. I hope he's running for something. Maybe he'll figure
he'll pick up some Jewish votes.

LESLEY

He's here.

(WARREN *stares at her.*)

LESLEY

He didn't know when he could get away till the last minute. I
tried to call . . .
(*Looks sad apology at him, turns toward the door.*)
Mr. Ives?

(WILLIAM IVES, *early 60s, comes to the door, in a hat, his hands in
the pockets of an open overcoat.* WARREN *goes to him.*)

WARREN

Hi, Dad.

IVES

Hi.

(*He looks closely at* WARREN *as they shake hands.*)

WARREN

Good to see you.

IVES

Same here . . .
          (*Walks in, looking about.*)

WARREN

          (*Follows.*)
You look great.

IVES

We were in St. Croix . . .

WARREN

How's Gretchen?

IVES

          (*Still looking.*)
Fine . . .
          (*Turns, takes his hat off.*)

LESLEY

I'm going to say hello to Morris. The grocer . . .

(IVES *nods.* LESLEY *gives* WARREN *another regretful look and goes*
RIGHT.)

IVES

Don't be too long if you want a lift.

LESLEY

All right.
        (*To* WARREN.)
Can I bring back anything?

(*He shakes his head. She goes out. The front door opens and closes.*)

IVES

Lovely girl. What does she do?

WARREN

Publicity. At Harper and Row. I've been meaning to write you.

IVES

I had some doubts about her sanity . . . when she said a ghost
told you you were Jewish . . .
        (*Looking up and around.*)
. . . and you were building a synagogue . . .

WARREN

*Re*building.

IVES

Excuse me, *re*building.
        (*Faces him.*)
Which is it, Warren? Coke? Heroin? LSD? Crack?

WARREN

None of the above.

IVES

Is there a new one?

WARREN

I'm not on drugs. Word of honor.

(IVES *studies him, and turns and moves away, toying thoughtfully
with his hat.*)

WARREN

The ghost is real. Lesley's heard him, her parents and sister and
brother-in-law have, and Morris.

IVES

And he told you you're Jewish.

WARREN

Indirectly. He doesn't sing when non-Jews are here.
                    (*Indicates the silence.*)

IVES

You've tested that conclusively?

WARREN

No need to. I know. The lawyer who got me for you was one
of your less reliable colleagues. My natural mother was Jewish.
So I am too.

IVES

If you were Jewish, Warren . . . *you wouldn't quit a high-paying
job to play with a synagogue.*

WARREN

I'm on leave, and I'm not playing.
(*Moves closer.*)
Look, I can understand this is unsettling for you. But now that I know who my *real people* are, and were . . . I guess I'm making up for lost time. That doesn't mean I'm not aware and appreciative of everything I owe *you*. And Mom, alav—may she rest in peace.

IVES

(*Looks at him a moment.*)
Mom, *Olive?*

WARREN

I—

IVES

Her name was Jean.

WARREN

I know, I—

IVES

And you tell me you're not on drugs?

WARREN

Dad . . . I started to use a Jewish expression "alav 'asholem." It means may the person rest in peace. My friend Morris says it all the time, it's catching. But I felt funny using Yiddish with you, or Hebrew, whichever it is, so I switched. It came out "Mom, alav."

IVES

(*Weighs it.*)
That's just bizarre enough to be true . . .

WARREN

Her middle name was Louise. Her maiden name was Atcheson.

(IVES *turns away and thinks.*)

WARREN

So please try to see this from my viewpoint and don't feel in-
jured about it, okay?

IVES

(*Faces him.*)

There are some facts you should know before you sign the papers
or take the Bar Mitzvah, whatever they do.

WARREN

Facts about what?

IVES

Your natural mother.
    (WARREN *looks at him.* IVES *hesitates.*)
Do we have to call her that? It sounds like health food.
    (WARREN *waits.* IVES *girds himself for confession.*)
Mom wasn't an ideal partner, with her heart condition. She
blamed it on an orgasm she once had . . . As a consequence . . .
I had a few extra-marital affairs . . . One of them was with a girl
at the firm, a secretary. She got pregnant and . . . stalled around
awhile, trying to get me to leave Mom and marry *her*. Which
I'd made clear at the outset I wasn't about to do.
    (WARREN *sits on one of the pews.* IVES *moves closer.*)
We'd been turned down by adoption agencies, because of
Mom's health. So I had a lawyer she didn't know come shuf-
fle some papers. After Carol gave birth—Carol Fletcher was

her name—the lawyer brought you back from Chicago. She went there when she began to show. Mom never knew. I think she suspected later on, but that may have been my conscience . . .

WARREN

What happened to her?

IVES

(*Behind the pew now.*)
Carol? She stayed in Chicago. I—gave her some money. I doubt she'd still be there. She talked about moving to California. She had a sister there.

WARREN

(*Looking back up at him.*)
You're my—

IVES

Don't say natural, please.
(WARREN *says nothing, looks front.* IVES *hesitates, and puts a hand on* WARREN's *shoulder.*)
I couldn't tell you while Mom was alive, you might have let her know. Inadvertently. And afterwards, what was the point? You didn't seem concerned, you were doing well . . . Then they had to start all this *roots* business . . .

(*He moves away, lets out a breath, plays with his hat.* WARREN, *sitting on the pew, looks smaller.*)

WARREN

She must have been Jewish.

IVES

She wasn't.

WARREN

Did you know her well enough to know?

IVES

We didn't hire Jews in those days.

WARREN

Maybe she lied to get the job.

IVES

Her father . . . was a fireman.

WARREN

(*Rises, draws a breath.*)
While you're here would you give me a hand with this? It's hard
to do alone and Morris is pretty old.

(*He goes to the post on supports and straightens wires at its base.*
IVES *watches, puzzled.*)

IVES

Warren. She wasn't Jewish.

WARREN

*I don't care WHAT she was! I'm doing a job and I want to finish
it! I need a hand here!*

IVES

I didn't come here to participate in this!

WARREN

I'm not asking for a major contribution! Help me lift the post!
I promise you, you won't sprout horns!

(*With a sigh,* IVES *puts his hat on and goes to the post.*)

WARREN

Get it there. We'll lift, and then you have to hold it at an angle
on there while I get the wires through.

(*They lift the post and lean it on the corner of the railing.*)

WARREN

Okay, hold it. So.

(WARREN *goes grimly onto the platform and works with the wires.*
IVES, *holding the post with both hands, studies the raw section.*)

IVES

Did *you* put this piece in?

WARREN

Someone sideswiped the U Haul when we were bringing them
back. It'll look good when it's stained.

IVES

It looks good now. Where'd you learn to do this?

WARREN

Books. I rewired these things . . .

(LESLEY *taps at the door.*)

WARREN

Come on in!

LESLEY

Morris would like to meet your father . . .

WARREN

Morris? Come on in!
> (LESLEY *and* MORRIS *come in,* MORRIS *in a hat and
> coat.* LESLEY *is taken aback seeing* IVES *holding the post.*
> WARREN *keeps working.*)

Hey, Morris! Post number two! We're gettin' there. This is
my—father. William Ives, Esquire. Morris Lipkind, gourmet
caterer.

MORRIS

How d'ya do? It's a pleasure.

IVES

(The campaign smile.)
How are you! You'll forgive me if I don't shake hands.

MORRIS

Certainly, certainly. It's nice you're helping.

> (IVES'*s smile thins.* LESLEY *watches* WARREN *from offside.*)

WARREN

Two seconds more . . .

MORRIS

It's called a mitzvah, when you do something like that.

IVES

A mitzvah . . .

MORRIS

Yeh.

IVES

I'll remember that.

(WARREN *signs to him and they set the post upright and lodge it.*)

WARREN

Thanks.

(*He works at the base of the post.* IVES *moves away, brushing his hand.*)

IVES

Well . . . I'm on a six o'clock flight.

MORRIS

So quick you come and go?

IVES

I'm speaking at a dinner tonight.

LESLEY

Could you wait one minute for me?

(*She indicates that she wants to talk to* WARREN. IVES *nods, and fastening his coat, moves closer to him.*)

WARREN

Running again?

IVES

Trying to get nominated. For a council seat. You know me,
never say die.

WARREN
      (*Looks at him.*)
Yeh.
            (*He reaches over the railing and they shake hands.*)
Give my love to Gretchen.

IVES

She sent hers. Keep in touch.

(WARREN *nods.* IVES *looks unhappily at him, and leans closer. Softly.*)

IVES

For God's sake, Warren . . . *Think!*

(*He looks at him a moment, and turns and goes.* MORRIS, *picking
up a cue from* LESLEY, *goes out after him.* WARREN *gets a small
carton from the workbench. As* LESLEY *approaches the platform,
he begins putting bulbs into the candelabra sockets.*)

WARREN

Did he tell you?

LESLEY
      (*Hesitates.*)
That he knew your natural mother, she wasn't Jewish . . .

WARREN
(*Working quickly.*)
He knew her all right . . . I'm an office romance. Or maybe just a few nooners. It could have been worse; I was almost an abortion.

LESLEY
He's—your natural father?

WARREN
Yep. Doesn't like the term. Can't say I blame him.

(LESLEY *watches helplessly as he begins putting flower cups over the bulbs, tightening set screws—too quickly.*)

WARREN
Found an apartment?

LESLEY
No. Nothing's right . . .

(*A car horn honks offstage* RIGHT.)

LESLEY
You're still going to go ahead?

WARREN
Nope. I want to get it symmetrical before I tear it down.
(*He draws a deep breath. The car horn honks.*)
Your ride's waiting. He's a busy man . . .

(*He takes another breath and works less quickly.* LESLEY *withdraws toward* RIGHT, *getting a key ring from her bag.*)

LESLEY

I'll give you the key . . .

WARREN

Keep it. Maybe you'll want to surprise me again. With
Kadaffi.

> (LESLEY *wrestles with the key ring, near tears.* WARREN
> *holds the railing, leans toward her.*)

Les . . . I'm sorry.

> (*She looks at him.*)

He'd have told me anyway, once I got around to writing him.
I was going to do it tonight. Keep it.

(*The car horn blasts.* LESLEY *despairs.*)

LESLEY

I—can't get it open anyway . . .

(*She turns and runs out.* WARREN *looks sorrowfully after her, draws
a breath, and resumes working at the candelabra, at a normal
tempo now, his face set.* MORRIS *comes in, ambles to the platform,
watches a moment.*)

MORRIS

She said *he* said he—

WARREN

> (*Interrupting.*)

Do you know an upholsterer, a good one?

(MORRIS *looks at him.*)

WARREN

(*Repeats.*)
An *upholsterer?*

MORRIS

Yeh, I know one . . .

WARREN

Living?

MORRIS

Last Shabbas he was.

WARREN

The seats of the pews are sixteen inches by forty-eight. Describe the cushions to him. See what he wants, to make them up. Tell him it's for the restoration of Ahavat Zedek; if he charges more than cost God'll kill him.
    (*The glass flowers are all in place, he returns the carton to the workbench and stands by the switch* UPSTAGE.)
Are you ready?
    (*He presses the switch. The lights of both candelabras come on.*)
Not bad, eh?

(MORRIS *shakes his head. The candelabra lights brighten and dim as* WARREN *plays with the switch.*)

WARREN

A dimmer is kosher, isn't it?

MORRIS

(*Thinks, nods.*)
A switch is a switch.

WARREN

That's what I figured.
(*Leaving the candelabra lights at medium, he turns to the
workbench and busies himself.*)
If you're gonna stay take your coat off.

MORRIS

(*Weighs going, but.*)
She said *he* knew your—

WARREN

(*Interrupting.*)
Look, I really don't want to discuss my parentage. It's irrelevant
at this point. I started a job, and I'm gonna do it right, and I'm
gonna finish it. I've got a zillion things to do by September and
worrying about what *she* said *he* said is very low on the list. See
you later, okay? Rye bread and a large apple juice. Eggs.

MORRIS

(*Stays, watching him.*)
September?

WARREN

The Holy Days. That's when we start.

MORRIS

Start what?

WARREN

(*Looks at him.*)

What do you mean, start what? Services.

MORRIS

(*Stares at him.*)

Services . . . ?

WARREN

(*At the railing.*)

Morris, what do you think I'm doing here, making a museum piece? Lean over the rope and look in? The Restoration of Ahavat Zedek means all of it, the woodwork, the windows, the cushions, the services. Everything the way it was.

MORRIS

Seven years ago we couldn't keep it going!

WARREN

Maybe you didn't try hard enough.

MORRIS

How d'ya like him? Listen, mister, you ain't just meshugeh, you're cockeyed crazy! You and him both! Services, nuch!

WARREN

A functioning synagogue. By the Holy Days.

MORRIS

(*Moving to the platform, grasping the railing.*)

You *can't*, Warren! Stop already!

WARREN

Why? 'Cause maybe my mother wasn't Jewish? What kind of reason is that?

MORRIS

You can't because it ain't possible, *that's* the reason! Will ya listen to *me* for a change instead a' him? What does *he* know from the world today? He's dead since 1943!

WARREN

Speak to the upholsterer.

MORRIS

For *Pete's sake*, Warren—!

WARREN

Just speak to the upholsterer, okay?

MORRIS

No! I ain't speakin' to nobody! Count me out! I'm through!
  (*Starts for the door.*)
I ain't going to be a partner to it!

WARREN

(*Coming off the platform.*)
Morris, you'll *see!*

MORRIS

From now on, strictly business between us! In the store you're welcome as a customer but I ain't settin' foot in—

WARREN
(*Grabs him and turns him around.*)
Morris, *who d'ya think's gonna be the rabbi?*

(MORRIS *stares at him.*)

WARREN
Not *me*, buddy! Not some kid fresh out of—wherever the hell they come from! *You*, Morris. *You're gonna be the rabbi of Ahavat Zedek!*

MORRIS
(*Stares more.*)
There's the proof you're crazy . . .

WARREN
Why? You're wise. You read Hebrew. You live within walking distance . . .

MORRIS
Will ya listen to him? *You can't just pick a rabbi!*

WARREN
Why not? I own a synagogue!

MORRIS
(*Pushing him away.*)
No! You don't! It ain't a synagogue! It ain't a synagogue until there's a Torah in the Ark, and the light burning over it, and ten men sayin' the prayers! *Then* it's a synagogue! A house with an Ark in it, that's what you got! A house with an Ark and a crazy dead chahzin! I wish to God he never—Ooy. Ooy.

(*Clutches his chest.*)

Ooy.

WARREN

(*Stares at him, holds him.*)

Are you all right?

MORRIS

(*Waits motionless. Takes a shallow breath.*)

I don't know. He could throw me a heart attack?

WARREN

No. No. Sit. Don't worry. Sit. Catch your breath.

(*He helps him to a pew.* MORRIS *sits, draws a breath, holding his chest.* WARREN *unbuttons* MORRIS*'s shirt collar, takes his hand, rubs it.*)

WARREN

Okay?

MORRIS

I t'ink . . .

(WARREN *rubs, watching him, then hurries into the kitchen, to the sink.* MORRIS *manages a deeper breath.* WARREN *hurries back with a glass of water, crouches, holds it while* MORRIS *drinks.* MORRIS *takes another breath.*)

MORRIS

He missed.

(*He takes the glass, another sip, a good breath.* WARREN *watches.*)

WARREN

You shouldn't get so excited . . .

MORRIS

You shouldn't talk so crazy.

WARREN

Sit for a minute.

MORRIS

I'm sitting.

(WARREN *takes the glass, puts it aside. Both take deep breaths.*)

WARREN

Whew!

MORRIS

Rabbi! Me! Tchhh . . .

(*Shaking his head, he laughs sadly to himself.* WARREN *stays crouching by him, watching him. After a moment.*)

WARREN

The eternal light . . . belongs to some people named Lefkowitz . . . In King's Point, on Long Island. They're giving it back to us, no charge. I'm picking it up Sunday.

(MORRIS *looks at him.*)

WARREN

You know Burns and Wachtel on Canal Street?

(MORRIS *nods.*)

WARREN

They've got a forty-five-year-old Torah in fairly good condition. Grade-A parchment, the seams neatly mended. They wanted nine thousand, they're down to eight-five, I think they'll go lower. I'll be able to swing it. I still have some IBM . . . As for the minyan . . . I figure if you're the rabbi, your friends over on Pitt Street, between the space invaders and the pipe cutters . . . I figure they'll come along too. A quiet shul, comfortable seats, you speaking, the chahzin singing . . .

MORRIS

(*Staring at him.*)
It ain't possible . . .

WARREN

(*Pats his hand.*)
Speak to the upholsterer.

(*They look at each other.* MORRIS *draws a breath and gets to his feet.* WARREN *takes his elbow.*)

WARREN

I'll walk you to the store.

MORRIS

(*Draws his arm free.*)
I can walk by myself, thank you.

(WARREN *watches uneasily as* MORRIS *goes slowly to the door. He
stops and turns.*)

MORRIS

If I *see* him I'll speak to him; out a' my way I ain't goin'!

WARREN

(*Smiles.*)

Sixteen by forty-eight. Give him details.

MORRIS

(*Looks at him.*)

Fongool.

(*He goes.*)

WARREN

(*Laughs.*)

He's hooked, Izzy! He's hooked!

(*Smiling, he admires the glowing candelabras. The windows are growing dark. He takes a closer critical look up
at the raw section of the post and goes onto the platform
to the workbench.*)

How about a little "Aitz Chiam He"? Or if you're sick of that,
"Atoh Chonane."

(*With a piece of sandpaper he comes off the platform,
takes a stepladder from* UPSTAGE, *and brings it to the
post. He opens the ladder, mounts it, touches the wood,
sands lightly, blows.*)

Sunset, Izzy! You're on!

(*He sands, blows—and goes cold. Looks up. Holds onto
the post.*)

Hey, Iz . . . ?

> (*He looks around. And comes down off the ladder, looks
> up, around.*)

Her *mother* could've been . . .

> (*He looks at the sandpaper, lets it fall, looks around, rubs
> his brow, sits on the edge of the platform. He stares ahead,
> then bows his head, pulls the watch cap off, buries his face
> in it. He sits huddled there . . .*)

(LESLEY *comes to the door. She watches him. He lifts his head,
turns.*)

LESLEY

I made it as far as Houston Street.

> (*Comes a step in.*)

I could kill myself for bringing him.

WARREN

> (*Rising.*)

No, no! I *told* you, I was going to write him tonight! Honestly.
I've got a note on the desk.

LESLEY

> (*Comes farther in.*)

I just saw Morris. I mean Rabbi Lipkind. He thinks you're
crazy . . . But he—*announced* it, rabbinically . . . !

(WARREN *watches as she comes closer.*)

LESLEY

With the right publicity, in the right places . . . I'll bet you
could pick up some funding . . . And a fair-size congregation
too, even without mentioning *him*. It's a natural for features.

"Young Couple Restoring Lower East Side Synagogue. He May Be Jewish . . . She May Be a Feminist . . ." You still *could* be, you know. Her mother could have been.

WARREN

He's not singing any more.

(*They look at each other.*)

WARREN

He's not here. He's gone.

LESLEY

(*Thinks a moment.*)

Maybe . . . because he knew he accomplished what he hung around for. He heard you tell Morris you were going to do it, didn't he? He knew you meant it . . .

WARREN

May *be* . . .

LESLEY

I'll bet I'm right. It must have been an effort, really.
(*Shrugs.*)
We'll find a live cantor.

WARREN

(*Gazes at her, takes her hands.*)

I adore you . . .

LESLEY

You damn well better.

(Smiling, they kiss—and gaze at each other as she takes her coat off and he pulls the cap down onto his head. He sings to her.)

WARREN

B'nay base-choh, k'vot chee-loh . . .

(He picks up the sandpaper and backs to the stepladder as she puts her coat on the painted pew.)

V'chonane migdoshe-choh-oh, ol-may choh-oh-noy . . .

(She picks up a can of paint remover, glances at it as he mounts the stepladder, singing the Chahzin's song at her.)

V'ha-ray-nu, v'veen-yoh-noh!

(She looks at him with awed wonder as he sings confidently.)

V'sah-om-chay-nu, b'see-ee ku-u-noh!

(Radiant in the glow of the candelabra lights, he joyously repeats the song—)

B'nay base-choh, k'vot chee-loh . . . !

(As—)

THE CURTAIN FALLS

THE END